GOOD & PLENTY

GOOD & PLENTY

AMERICA'S NEW HOME COOKING

VICTORIA WISE and
SUSANNA HOFFMAN

Illustrated by Philippe Weisbecker

1817

HARPER & ROW, PUBLISHERS, NEW YORK
CAMBRIDGE, PHILADELPHIA, SAN FRANCISCO
LONDON, MEXICO CITY, SÃO PAULO, SINGAPORE, SYDNEY

GOOD & PLENTY: AMERICA'S NEW HOME COOKING. Copyright © 1988 by Victoria Wise and Susanna Hoffman. All rights reserved. Printed in the United States of America. No part of this book may be used or reproduced in any manner whatsoever without written permission except in the case of brief quotations embodied in critical articles and reviews. For information address Harper & Row, Publishers, Inc., 10 East 53rd Street, New York, N.Y. 10022. Published simultaneously in Canada by Fitzhenry & Whiteside Limited, Toronto.

FIRST EDITION

DESIGNED BY JOEL AVIROM

LIBRARY OF CONGRESS CATALOG CARD NUMBER: 88-45071

ISBN 0-06-181928-X

88 89 90 91 92 **MPC** 10 9 8 7 6 5 4 3 2 1

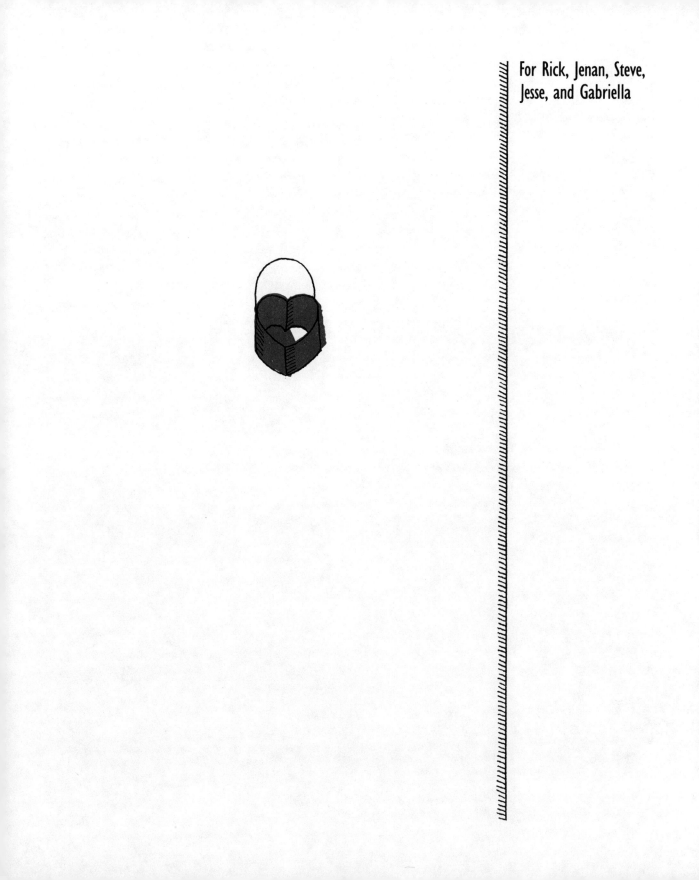

For Rick, Jenan, Steve,
Jesse, and Gabriella

Acknowledgments

They aided us. They abetted us. They supported us. They cheered us on. They gave us recipes, served as guinea pigs, and more importantly, they often fed us!

For our first food experiences and countless luscious meals ever since, we never can thank enough our parents, Hank and Ruth Jenanyan and Abe and Florence Hoffman.

For the support and recipe sharing only siblings, affines, and aunts can give, our thanks to Arayah and Paul Rude, Deborah and Jerry Budrick, Beverly Jenanyan, Deborah and Levi Bendele, and Elaine Fahlstrom.

Almost as close as kin and always there were: Bill Chambers, Richard Cowan, Karen Frerichs, Robbie Greenberg, Curtis Hardyck, Barbara Haugeland, John Haugeland, Gale Hayman, Marida Hollos, Ken Hom, D. Michael Hughes, Karin Knowles, Tim Knowles, Stuart Lake, Jesse Miller, Susan Mitchell, Nancy Podbielniak, Lisa Rich, Tim Savinar, Nancy Scheper-Hughes, Charles Shere, Lindsey Shere, Gail Stempler, and Milton Stern, with special thanks to Bobby Weinstein, who probably has forgotten why, Patty Unterman, and Alice Waters.

To Robert Mandel, on whose culinary creativity we have poached throughout the years, and who wittingly or not donated several dishes to this book, we give our heartfelt gratitude. Our grateful appreciation also goes to Martha Casselman, our tireless agent and dear friend, and Patricia Brown, our editor, whose knowledge of food and cooking is so sound, she could ask if we really meant to press the garlic or not.

Gary Frisvold who owns Lenny's Meats (Butcher to the Gods and Hams That Just Won't Quit), The Cheese Board Collective, Ron Fujii of the Berkeley Produce Center, and Paul and Joan Johnson and Connie Lenoir of Monterey Fish answered a thousand questions and provided products that make home cooking a joy. Larry Strand of the University of California, Davis, kindly researched our agricultural concerns. David Ramirez and Craig Brock kept our houses running, entertained our children, fed dogs and cats, and tended our gardens. Charles Bonkofsky helped in countless ways and at every turn during Pig-by-the-Tail's twelve years. A million thanks to each of them. Our appreciation is boundless.

For their caring support, we also wish to acknowledge the people of other countries, especially Greece, where we've lived, marketed, and cooked; all the people who come to our dining rooms, and usually end up standing in our kitchens; the pediatricians, schoolteachers, and other parents who shore up the other part of our lives while we write books; and especially Dale Ketten and her staff, who keep the larder stocked and the customers happy at the Good & Plenty Café.

Finally, our abundant love and endless gratitude to Rick and Jenan Wise, Jesse and Gabriella Aratow, and Stephen Hettenback, who put up with women who cook as work, and work only to come home and cook. ■

Contents

GOOD & PLENTY

A calico cat named Cato was the unwitting cause of our meeting. That afternoon a sun brightened the usually foggy northern California summer sky. Susanna was taking a breather from knocking down walls and installing plumbing in the old house that was to become Chez Panisse restaurant. She took a litter of kittens, the progeny of diffident Cato, down to the sidewalk in hope of donating the rascally brood to cat-loving passersby. A man strolled up and stopped to chat. Not interested in a kitten, he was rather more interested in Susanna. When she politely declined his overtures, he recovered with, "Well, if you aren't interested in me, would you be interested in a good cook?" Definitely, answered Susanna, and a few hours later down the hill and up to the door came Victoria.

Our kinship was settled on first sight. We laughed the instant we saw each other, began talking as if we'd always been friends, and immediately thought of all the things we'd have to do together. Those things have included shopping, eating, traveling, healing, feeding, nagging, lending, minding, sighing, sunning, and, above all, cooking.

Victoria became the first chef at Chez Panisse, turning out dinners galore, going from cooking for four to 140 overnight. Susanna, after seeing the restaurant to its opening, returned to her professorship at the University of San Francisco. From the lore and habits of wondrous isolated cultures by day, she returned to hostess and occasionally help in the restaurant kitchen by night. In the hectic years that followed, Victoria left Chez Panisse to open Pig-by-the-Tail Charcuterie, the first classic French delicatessen in the United States. Susanna started a family—two children in 18 months—began to make anthropology films, and turned her skills to popular books, all the while cooking up a storm. Victoria helped Susanna work on her manuscripts. Susanna helped Victoria cook and cater, and bestowed on the Pig many of its most popular dishes. Victoria married, began supplying major stores and other restaurants with her sublime edibles, and brought her delicatessen to national recognition. She wrote her first cookbook, contributed to others, and added a son to our collection of children.

We've been part and parcel of all each other's occasions since we met. Victoria dared to decorate Susanna's wedding cake with nasturtium flowers, then a little-known dainty. The guests, thinking the flowers might be poisonous, wouldn't eat the cake until checking with her, the bride, the groom, and the reference librarian. Once Susanna invited four people—Victoria was one—for duck and cherry sauce to celebrate a book sale. Sixteen showed up. While Susanna ran out to quadruple the ducks, Victoria stretched the sauce—like the fish and the loaves—to feed the multitude.

As much as we cherish each other, we both cherish our homes and families. They are the center of our lives. Despite our connections to professional cooking, we are home cooks and always have been.

Like almost everyone else across the country, we come from a background of classic American fare, and we love traditional home cooking. But what we cook is different from what homemakers cooked thirty years ago. Our menus have been affected by our busy lives and by what has happened to American food in the last three decades. We know more about health and nutrition and our menus reflect that knowledge. The immigrant cuisines that have entered American fare have influenced our home meals.

We have embraced the fresh foods, the herbs and other seasonings, the variety of vegetables, and scrumptious, light salads that have trickled down to us from modern inventive American restaurant chefs.

We cook the old and the new. Sometimes we make spaghetti topped with a long-cooked red sauce, but sometimes we make pasta with shrimp, carrots, and lima beans. We still love hamburgers off the barbecue, but other nights we grill turkey breast or make vegetable tacos filled with fried potatoes and sprinkled with fresh tomato salsa. We roast a leg of lamb and bake potatoes, but we also make a quick pizza.

Good & Plenty is for people like us. In it we cover the entire range of America's new home cooking. From tacos and pizzas to grills and stovetop dishes, treats and nibbles to dinner salads and delightful do-able desserts, we include the classics and the new, the beloved and the innovative, the things Americans now like and eat.

Good & Plenty is primarily a dinner cookbook. What we cook and how we eat together nowadays has pretty much "boiled down" to one main meal at the end of the day. Dashing forth on our daily missions, we often have breakfast on the run, lunch from a brown bag or in a café, but we gather together for supper. We like the ritual and the comfort of our nightly meal. We rarely have time to see family and friends except over dinner, and preparing food is relaxing.

We include easy-to-assemble nibbles and treats to serve as appetizers, offer company, or munch on at that five-o'clock hour when everyone is ravenous for a tidbit. We also present a banquet of desserts. But in general we shy away from heavy sweets or elaborate baking. We prefer quick, light, fruit-based delicacies that cook while you eat or that whip together in a jiffy after dinner.

We strongly believe in fresh foods. Fresh fruits, vegetables, dairy products, meats, and fish are more healthful. They taste better, and fortunately for us all, they are now available in abundance due to modern shipping and customer demand.

The ingredients we use can be found most anytime and anywhere. Supermarkets have fresh pasta, fish, good grains, French bread, tortillas, bean sprouts, chili peppers, fresh herbs, and good ice creams.

Like most modern home cooks, we rely on foods that are steadily available. Most of our dishes can be made year round. When the ingredients are affected by season, we list choices and substitutes and tell you which is best to use when.

We tout the cutting of corners. Food preparation can take hours of exacting technical effort. But you can also make delicious meals with quick steps and timesaving devices.

Beside each recipe is a line stating the "ball park" time it takes to prepare and cook the dish. Many are very quick to make, designated with the phrase "20 minutes or less." Other timings are "20 to 40 minutes" and "40 to 60 minutes." For the few recipes that take more than 60 minutes, we give the specific amount of time required. For the long-cooked dishes, especially red sauces, we recommend you make plenty and stock the freezer with them.

We energetically endorse stocking. In the front of this book you will find an inventory for a basic larder, including cupboard, refrigerator, and freezer items. The larder we outline, with some weekly extra shopping, will get you through all the recipes in this book, to say nothing of lunches, breakfasts, and dinners of your own creation. Ranging from capers to condiments, the larder even contains enough to provide complete meals in those numerous moments when "what to have for dinner?" is the pitiful cry of the beleaguered cook who doesn't want to go to the store. Following the larder section, we give you storage hints and a list of basic equipment. We tell you how to cure ducks and rabbits overnight to make them more tender.

We use considerable wine and sometimes spirits in our cooking. Wine and spirits give a flavor essence you can't get from any other source. Except for one or two dessert sauces in this book, all the alcohol called for in our recipes is burned off, leaving behind only the special taste we seek.

We don't cook with a microwave oven. We find microwaved food is not as good as when it is grilled, sautéed, steamed, or baked in a conventional oven. We also find that microwave ovens don't particularly save time. The recipes that can be made successfully in a microwave oven are marked with a ≈. In our own kitchens we sometimes use a pressure cooker. If you own a pressure cooker, the recipes that can be done well with one are marked with ≡.

A good meal, the time and coin we spend on it, turns effort into the purest of value. Cooking is gift giving. Something we have made and offered is consumed, not saved. It is enjoyed, not squandered. When we make a meal and serve it to our loved ones, it is given and gone. We get nothing back save the joy of offering. The gift of food need not be costly. A dish can come from a trip to the store and a special purchase, but it can also result from rummaging through the larder and putting together found objects.

Many of the recipes in this book are compositions of small bits of meats, vegetables, a handful of nuts, a few olives, or some such. With them we mean to demonstrate the pleasure of putting together diverse morsels of food and coming up with dinner. We hope to encourage an approach to cooking that is adventurous and lighthearted. If you scavenge the netherlands of your cupboards and refrigerator and keep your sense of humor, you will bring forth many a serendipitous dish.

This compendium of America's new home cooking is a celebration of our cooking lives together. From our home and professional experience, there's one definite thing we can tell you. Nothing mysterious reigns over good cooking. Turning out a delectable meal is mostly a matter of good sense and a sense of fun. There are some tricks, and we pass on as many as we could think of as we wrote this book. There are some guidelines about what goes together and what does not. We hope we've given those as well.

The world is peopled with lots of really good cooks, and it's easy to become one of them. But if that's not your inclination, it's still easy to cook Good & Plenty. ■

A well-stocked larder is a must for the busy cook. With the right basics and peripherals in your pantry you can turn out a meal day after night without laboring over extensive shopping lists or daily marketing. The following is a list of items we recommend you keep in your cupboard, refrigerator, and freezer. With them on hand you will always have the elements to create a whole meal, either from what is in the larder, or with only a quick stop for meat, fish, poultry, or perhaps a special type of produce.

Every week or two, run an eye over your supplies, make a list, and restock on shopping day.

THE CUPBOARD

ANCHOVIES: for everything from pizza to salad. Keep several small tins of flat fillets in oil. Better yet, stock a large tin of the far superior salt-packed anchovies available in specialty food stores and Italian markets. After opening, add a few drops of water to the tin to create a preserving brine, cover the tin with a saucer that fits inside, and refrigerate for up to several months.

ARROWROOT: for the rare occasions you need to thicken a sauce or dessert, arrowroot is our thickening agent of choice. It is preferable to cornstarch or flour because it works in smaller quantities and keeps sauces clear.

BAKING POWDER: for the occasional shortcake or pizza crust.

BAKING SODA: for putting out grease fires, soothing bee stings, and deodorizing refrigerators, if not for baking.

BREAD CRUMBS: homemade are best, not too finely crumbled (see page 136). If you aren't going to use them within a month, freeze them.

CAPERS: the best are those packaged in a saltwater brine rather than vinegar, such as Roland and Peloponnese brands. Vinegar-brined capers are less versatile for cooking. Italian markets often carry salt-packed capers in bulk. These are good, but need soaking in several changes of water before you add them to a dish. If submerged in saltwater brine, capers can be stored in the cupboard, but once the salt brine or pack is rinsed off, keep them in the refrigerator.

CHILIES: the new home kitchen is not complete without some dried chilies in the larder. They go into many of the sauces, breadings, and marinades in this book. You need:

Chili Flakes—often called Crushed Red Pepper Flakes.

Chili Peppers—small whole red ones that come in jars or packages. For other kinds to use in taco sauces, see the introduction to the taco chapter.

CORNMEAL: any one of the three types generally available—yellow, white, or polenta—will do for your cooking needs. Cornmeal has many uses, from a side dish of polenta, to an ingredient in pizza crust or shortcake, to a breading for fish or meats.

CRACKERS: a selection, always including water crackers, for treats, nibbles, and dessert cheese plates.

DRIED FRUITS:

Apricots—preferably sun-dried

Currants—you can occasionally find currants in boxes in the grocery store; otherwise, they are usually sold in bulk in produce markets and health food stores. Store them in the cupboard in sealed containers. For long-term storage freeze to prevent hardening and graininess.

Golden Raisins—sometimes called Sultanas. Golden raisins add a pleasingly sweet and tart fruit taste to a dish. Black raisins are fine for children's snacks, but they are too sweet for cooking.

Prunes—pitted ones are easier to deal with, but any boxed prunes are fine.

FLOUR: recipes in this book use unbleached all-purpose flour. Unless you do a lot of baking, a 5-pound sack will last quite some time.

HERBS: We always have on hand a stock of dried herbs for those times when fresh herbs are not available or we haven't been to the market. The basics are:

Basil

Bay Leaves

Dill

Marjoram

Mint—a relatively fresh jar because dried mint loses its aroma when kept too long.

Oregano—preferably Greek.

Rosemary

Sage

Tarragon

Thyme

HONEY: a small jar of good perfumed honey is a trump to have for an occasional glaze or inspiration. Honey keeps for months. If it crystallizes, heat in a small pan of water until smooth again.

HORSERADISH: preservative-free bottled or fresh to grate yourself.

Both our larders always include one inedible item that we consider no kitchen should be without —an aloe vera plant. The gooey sap within its leaves is a burn remedy without compare. It makes a light burn disappear in minutes and keeps a bad burn from blistering. For light burns, cut off a piece of one of the leaves and rub the sap over the burn, repeating every few minutes until you feel no more sting. For a deeper burn, cut a piece of a leaf the size of the whole burned area, slit the leaf open to expose the center, and bandage the gooey side down over the burn. Leave the aloe bandage in place for several hours. If the burn begins to blister, leave the bandage on at least overnight. Aloe's magic also works to relieve sunburn and itching from insect bites. Any light, temperate spot will do for a small pot of aloe; the plant doesn't need to be very large to have an adequate supply of leaves. Victoria keeps hers on the back porch outside the kitchen door. Susanna keeps hers on the kitchen counter.

MUSTARD: a well-stocked larder needs two kinds:

Coleman's dry mustard in a tin.

Dijon prepared mustard in a jar.

NUTS: They add tremendous flavor and versatility to everything from treats and nibbles to desserts. Store air-tight to preserve freshness. We occasionally use cashews, pistachios, and macadamias. For regular use, we always have on hand:

Almonds—both slivered and sliced.

Peanuts

Pecans

Pine Nuts

Walnuts

OILS: a creative key to good and varied cooking. We think five kinds are essential:

Olive Oil—our major cooking oil; we recommend keeping plenty. Have on hand at least one bottle or can of extra-virgin, one of light. It helps to keep another unopened in stock because running out of olive oil is debilitating.

Peanut Oil—our second most-used oil. We use it when we want a change from olive oil, and especially for mayonnaise. It is the best oil to use for deep frying, Oriental-style dishes, and many dishes that include nuts.

Sesame Oil—a must for certain marinades, Oriental-style sauces, and dishes including sesame seeds.

Vegetable Oil—corn and safflower are both good. Both are all-purpose, unsaturated cooking oils, and are useful for deep frying and sautéing when the oil is not a major flavoring.

Walnut Oil—a special occasion oil, particularly good for salads and duck dishes, but not for cooking.

OLIVES: used in countless ways, on treats, on pizza, on pasta, on meats, in sauces. Keep in the cupboard or refrigerator:

Greek—or other Kalamata-type black olives.

Niçoise—tiny black French olives.

Oil Cured—also good and can be substituted for Kalamatas.

PASTA NOODLES: a must. We use a pack or two a week and pick up replacements every time we shop. You might keep several types, including:

Spaghetti, Vermicelli, or *Linguine*

Lasagne Noodles

PEPPERCORNS: whole black, to grind fresh. You will need a good supply. For a good pepper grinder, see pages 31–32.

PRODUCE: see also the list under "Refrigerator."

Fruit—we always keep apples, oranges, papayas, pears, and grapes, except when they are strictly out of season, plus a selection of what's in season. Fruit is a major component in many of today's healthful, light desserts.

Garlic—keep 3 or 4 heads as running stock. A garlic paste alone takes at least one full head; four salads take another, to say nothing of Desperation Chicken.

Lemons—Keep plenty. Lemon juice is a cooking constant.

Onions—always have 4 or more yellows, plus whites and reds when they are good.

Potatoes—a selection of russet, white, and red, plus, if we can find them, Finnish yellows. Potatoes should be stored in a special way; see the margin note on page 20.

Shallots—for the handful of dishes that can't do without their special flavor.

Tomatoes—preferably saladette, also called Roma or Italian plum tomatoes, except in late summer and early fall when other kinds are ripe and flavorful. Tomatoes also should be stored in a special way; see Storing Hints, page 20.

RICE: preferably American long grain, or the Italian rice called Arborio, available in specialty food shops and better supermarkets.

SALT: You need two kinds:

Gros Sel—for pan frying and curing. *Gros sel* is like rock salt, but with smaller crystals. It is a sea salt with a clean, nonsodium taste, and we prefer it to rock salt for cooking. You can find it in cylindrical boxes at specialty food stores and better supermarkets. Rock salt will do if *gros sel* is not available. Kosher salt is not coarse enough for pan frying or curing.

Table Salt—preferably sea salt, available in bulk in health food stores or packaged in cylindrical boxes in specialty food stores and better grocery stores.

SEEDS: the increased use of seeds is one of the delightful additions to our new home cooking. They add both crunch and protein to many entrees.

Pumpkin—also called *pepitas*.
Sesame
Sunflower

SOY SAUCE: We prefer "light" or "mild" soy sauce rather than the dark. The best, most flavorful, and least salty are available in health food stores. Organic soy sauces are superior tasting, but have a higher sodium content.

SPECIALTY ITEMS:

Arrowhead Blue Cornmeal Pancake Mix—a wonderful product for hors d'oeuvres, cakes, and Sunday morning breakfast. Arrowhead products are

---

To store potatoes, keep them at room temperature out of the light, not in the refrigerator, the sun, or near the oven.

Tomatoes will ripen quicker and develop more flavor if they are kept in a dark place at room temperature. Don't refrigerate until they are so ripe there is danger of rotting.

available in many supermarkets, produce markets, and most health food stores. Or, you can mail order from Arrowhead Mills, Inc., Box 2059, Hereford, Texas 79045.

Artichoke Hearts—bottled in marinade. Always useful for pizza, spaghetti sauce, and Desperation Chicken.

Boboli Packaged Pizza Crust—when we don't have time to make our own pizza crust, this is what we use. Available nationwide; look for it in the specialty foods section or the freezer section in supermarkets. Freeze if storing longer than 1 week.

Peloponnese Olive Spread—for anytime you need a sauce and don't have the time or inclination to make one. Also delicious spread on crackers.

Roasted Red Peppers—a corner cutter for many of the dishes calling for red peppers. Mezzetta and Progresso brands are particularly good, packed in water rather than a brine so they taste like roasted peppers, not pickled peppers.

SPICES: The emphasis in our recipes is on herbs, but we always have the following spices:

Allspice—whole berries.

Cardamom Seed

Cayenne—ground.

Cinnamon—sticks and ground.

Cloves—whole.

Cumin—ground.

Curry Powder

Fennel Seed—for turning ground pork into Quick Sweet Sausage (page 62).

Herbes de Provence

Juniper Berries—especially for curing duck and rabbit, see page 28.

Nutmeg—whole.

Paprika—preferably Hungarian.

Saffron Threads

Turmeric

White Pepper—whole corns or ground, for peppering white foods, such as noodles and cream sauces, without leaving black specks.

SPIRITS: we occasionally use spirits for cooking. When the alcohol is burned off, the flavor base of spirits remains to enliven and accent the food. We keep four main spirits on hand; others we pick up in small bottles for special recipes.

Bourbon

Brandy

Rum

Tequila

SUGAR: we find we need the same three kinds our mothers needed. Store in tightly covered jars or plastic bags sealed with a tie to keep the bugs out.

Brown

Granulated

Powdered (confectioners')

TOMATOES: in spite of the availability of excellent fresh saladette tomatoes most of the year, canned tomatoes are still a necessity for many red sauces. We recommend crushed tomatoes in puree, preferably Progresso brand, for the richest tomato taste.

TOMATO PASTE: an irreplaceable ingredient for thickening and enriching sauces and stews. Keep a stock of 3 or 4 small cans—unless you are making a large amount of sauce, you only need a tablespoon or so at a time —in the cupboard. For how to store tomato paste after opening the cans, see the margin note on page 20.

TUNA: the chunk style packed in water, preferably Bumblebee or Geisha brand. Imported Italian tuna packed in olive oil is also excellent.

VANILLA EXTRACT: pure, for flavoring cookies, cakes, and other desserts.

VINEGARS: not only for salad, but also as a seasoning for stews, sauces, and vegetables. The flavors of vinegars vary as widely as their colors, and you need one of each color.

Balsamic—woody, aged in oak, with a flavor that matches its ruddy color.

Red Wine—sharper than balsamic, it provides a good punch to any dish. Experiment with the many domestic and imported kinds available and also those from small producers.

Sherry—use it sparingly to add a clean, sharp accent to salad dressings.

White Wine or *Champagne*—for a snappy, crisp flavor in salad dressings and pickles.

WINES: essential for cooking. We use it throughout this book to flavor pan sauces, stews, marinades, fillings, and desserts. Leftover or jug is fine. You need both:

Red Wine

White Wine

In addition, we keep two other classic cooking wines in stock:

Port—ruby or tawny.

Sherry—amontillado (dry) or oloroso (sweet).

YEAST: active dry, especially for pizza crust.

A coat of oil works wonders to preserve those extra tablespoons of tomato paste leftover from a can. Transfer the tomato paste to a glass or plastic container, smooth it flat with the back of a spoon, cover with oil, and refrigerate. To use, scoop aside the oil, including any unharmful mold that has formed on top of the oil, and spoon out as much tomato paste as you need. Pat down any remaining paste and cover with oil again to restore.

THE REFRIGERATOR

BACON: in the refrigerator, or frozen if you are storing it longer than 2 weeks, means you can always make a pizza, fast pasta *Amatriciana,* or perk up vegetables.

BUTTER: although we prefer olive oil for most cooking, we use butter every now and then. We recommend salted butter for cooking because it keeps in the refrigerator longer. If you prefer sweet butter, store it in the freezer if keeping longer than a week.

CHEESE: keep a supply of several basic types:
   Blue—preferably Roquefort or Gorgonzola.
   Cheddar—or other firm white or yellow cheese.
   Feta—preferably Bulgarian or Corsican.
   Grating cheese—aged Asiago, Parmesan, or Romano.
   Jack—or other soft white cheese, mainly for tacos.
In addition, we like to try new ones all the time because cheese stands alone as a nibble or dessert.

CHICKEN STOCK: It's easier than you think to keep at least a pint of homemade chicken stock on hand in the refrigerator; see page 134. Will keep well for up to 5 days; freeze for longer storage.

COLD CUTS: Have on hand a little capocollo, ham, and salami.

CREAM: have:
   Heavy Cream—Keep a small carton on hand to make pasta and pan sauces, taco toppings, and desserts. Unopened or tightly closed after opening, it will keep for at least 2 weeks. Brands with no stabilizers added, even if ultra-pasteurized, are superior.
   Sour Cream—especially essential for tacos, great as an herbed sauce base, or as a salmon pizza topping.

EGGS: Fertile eggs have more flavor. Many grocery stores carry them alongside the regular eggs.

FRESH HERBS: They add immeasurably to your cooking. We use them in almost every dish we make. Many can be used interchangeably with the specific herbs called for in the recipes. We keep on hand according to availability:
   Basil
   Chives
   Cilantro—also called fresh coriander and Chinese parsley. Cilantro must be fresh. It doesn't dry, freeze, or cook well. Also, coriander seed is not a substitute for fresh cilantro even though it is from the same plant.
   Dill
   Mint

Oregano

Parsley—preferably Italian. Parsley must be fresh. It doesn't dry or freeze well.

Rosemary

Sage

Tarragon

Thyme

MAYONNAISE: Keep a good commercial mayonnaise, such as Best Foods, Hellman's, or a good deli variety.

PRODUCE: aside from daily and seasonal specials, always have on hand:

Bell Peppers—a selection of green, red, and yellow.

Chili Peppers—Anaheim, Poblano, Fresno, jalapeño, serrano, yellow wax, or a selection of whatever is available.

Carrots

Celery

Ginger Root

Green Onions or scallions

Lettuces—a selection.

SALSA: keep a large jar of at least one homemade salsa in the refrigerator. Salsas go with practically any grilled or sautéed meat. They are wonderful on chips and toast for snacks, and, of course, are the spice of tacos. Salsas keep from 1 to 2 weeks, depending on the type.

TORTILLAS: wrapped well, will keep in the refrigerator for up to 2 weeks. For longer storage, freeze them. We always have a package of both:

Corn

Flour

YOGURT: a tub of plain keeps for weeks in the refrigerator.

THE FREEZER

BERRIES: many berries freeze surprisingly well, and they are a boon for a desperation dessert. We keep:

Cranberries—to have before and after their short growing season.

Other Berries—especially raspberries and blackberries, for fruit sauces, shortcake, and topping ice cream.

BREAD: preferably French bread, and preferably a baguette. Bread freezes well and can be refreshed with success (see page 230). Don't store bread in the refrigerator; it will dry out and lose its flavor.

ICE CREAM: have a selection of flavors, including some sherbet, for quick desserts.

PASTA DOUGH: when mixing a batch, make extra and keep on hand in the freezer.

PASTRY CRUST: wrap well and store disks of pastry crust in the freezer. Thaw for several hours before rolling out.

PIZZA DOUGH: like pastry crust and pasta dough, make large batches and freeze in single-portion quantities.

SAUCES: double or triple batches of freezable sauces and have them on hand for quick dinners. Some that freeze well are:
   Basic Meat Sauce Bolognese, page 118.
   Corsican Lasagne Sauce, page 256.
   Red Pepper Pesto, page 43, or any other pesto.
   Red Pizza Sauce, page 61.
   Basic Red Zucchini Tomato Sauce, page 116.

SMOKED FISH: especially smoked salmon. The texture changes with freezing, but it works fine for cooking.

SPONGE CAKE: keep some on hand in the freezer for unexpected company; see page 310.

TACO FILLINGS: especially Turkey (page 96), and Beef, Currant, and Pine Nuts (page 89).

Storing Hints

UNCOOKED MEATS, POULTRY, AND FISH

In the best possible world, we would all purchase our meat and fish fresh every day. But the way most of us live now requires that we stockpile, refrigerate, and freeze items to save ourselves a million trips to the store. You can refrigerate meat, poultry, or fish as it comes from the grocery store or specialty market. When freezing meats or poultry—but never fish —some special attention should be given to the wrapping. Meats and poultry should be tightly wrapped in butcher paper, freezer paper, or meat storage wrap with the wax-coated side against the meat or poultry and sealed with tape to help maintain freshness. Unlike plastic wrap, butcher paper or the like allows evaporation of internal moisture which helps prevent freezer burn. Also, the wax coating keeps the meat or poultry from sticking to the paper.

LEFTOVERS

APPETIZERS: Many of our appetizers will keep well for several days or even weeks in the refrigerator. The ones that are already oil saturated, such as Mom's Marinated Roasted Red and Green Bell Peppers, Eggplant Salad Peasant Style, Marinated Feta Cheese, and Chick Pea Paste, need only be well wrapped. Jalapeño Chili Peppers Stuffed with Feta Cheese or filleted anchovies can be immersed in oil and then kept for several days. Those appetizers with fish other than anchovies deteriorate and should be used within a few days.

PIZZA: Wrap leftover pizza in plastic and store in the refrigerator for a day or two. Reheat in the oven if desired, but don't freeze or microwave it. Both treatments toughen the dough and cheese.

TACOS: Taco fillings can be kept in the refrigerator for several days. Some, such as Turkey and Beef, Currant, and Pine Nuts, can be frozen. Taco toppings, with the exception of guacamole, can be put in containers and refrigerated for several days. Potatoes will need refrying. Uncooked tortillas should be wrapped in plastic and refrigerated. If you have leftover cooked tortillas, make them into chips by crisping them in the oven or frying in oil.

PASTA: Wrap leftover pasta dishes in plastic wrap and store in the refrigerator. Learn to enjoy the leftovers cold, as most, except for tomato sauce dishes, don't reheat well. None freeze well.

GRILLS: Wrap leftover meats and vegetables in plastic wrap and store in the refrigerator. Think of a way to have them cold, such as in a salad, as they don't reheat or freeze well.

STOVETOP DISHES: Wrap in plastic and store in the refrigerator. In general, stovetop dishes do not reheat or freeze well.

SALADS: Once salad has been dressed, it should be eaten right away. The exception is Farmer's Salad, which can be kept in the refrigerator for 2 or 3 days before it is too stale to enjoy.

OVEN DISHES: Wrap in plastic and store in the refrigerator. Many, such as lasagne, stuffed eggplant, and oven stews, reheat well. These even can be frozen for a brief time.

DESSERTS: Cakes, cookies, and poached fruit keep well, but other desserts such as pies, crisps, and cut fresh fruit should be eaten right away.

SAUCES, SALSAS, AND SALAD DRESSINGS

SAUCES: Cooked fruit sauces and wine sauces keep several weeks in the refrigerator, or you can freeze them. Butter sauces and cream sauces should be used the day they are made because they do not reheat well. Fresh fruit chutneys ferment after a day or so.

COOKED TOMATO SAUCES: If the sauce is dense enough to allow a layer of oil to float on top, meatless cooked tomato sauces, such as Red Pizza Sauce, Basic Red Zucchini Tomato Sauce, and Corsican Lasagne Sauce (without meat), can be stored in the refrigerator for several weeks, up to a few months. Pat down the top of the sauce and pour up to ¼ inch of olive oil over the top to seal out air. Any mold that forms is harmless, and can be easily removed from the top of the oil when you wish to use the sauce. If the sauce is too watery for an oil coating to float on top, freeze the sauce to preserve it.

Tomato sauces that include meat as an ingredient must be frozen if you are storing them longer than a few days.

DESSERT SAUCES: Ice cream toppings, with the exception of caramel and strawberry, and sauces for poached fruit keep for months in the refrigerator. Cover them well to block out refrigerator odors.

SALSA: Salsas are uncooked sauces and they do not freeze well. They keep in the refrigerator from several days to several weeks, depending on the kind (see the individual recipes). If you have Tomato Salsa, Corn and Red Bell Pepper Salsa, or Tomatillo Sauce that won't be used before it "turns" or becomes too stale to enjoy, you can extend its shelf life by cooking it for a few minutes. This changes it into a chili sauce which you can refrigerate for a few more days or freeze. Cilantro, which is part of so many salsas, will not come through the cooking or freezing with any aplomb. Add some fresh just before using to perk up the sauce.

SALAD DRESSINGS: Although we prefer making a vinaigrette as we toss the salad, to save time you can mix a vinaigrette base and store it out of the refrigerator up to 3 days. To remain fresh, it should have no seasonings added except salt, pepper, mustard, and perhaps dry herbs. Add other seasonings such as garlic, lemon, or fresh herbs just before serving.

Curing Duck and Rabbit

For 2 ducks or rabbits

Overnight in the refrigerator

Duck and rabbit can be moist and tender or they can be dry, tough, and bland. We have a magic solution to ensure that all of your ducks are tender and all of your rabbits tasty. We cure them with rock salt and herbs and let them sit overnight. It is simple and virtually effortless, and we strongly suggest that you adopt it as part of your cooking technique.

2 ducks or rabbits, cut in quarters or pieces
1 tablespoon juniper berries
2 large or 4 small bay leaves
2 tablespoons *gros sel* or rock salt
2 teaspoons freshly ground black pepper
2 teaspoons dried or several sprigs fresh thyme

Place the duck or rabbit pieces skin side up in a nonreactive dish. Use 2 containers if necessary so that the pieces are in a single layer.

Smash the juniper berries with a wooden mallet or hammer. Crumble the bay leaves.

Sprinkle the salt, juniper, bay, black pepper, and thyme over the duck or rabbit pieces, distributing as evenly as possible. Loosely cover the dish with plastic wrap. Pat down the plastic wrap all over, pressing the spices into the duck or rabbit pieces. Refrigerate overnight, up to 2 days.

Just before cooking, brush the spices off the duck or rabbit pieces with paper toweling and proceed with the recipe.

TO CUT UP A DUCK, first remove the wings at the shoulder joints. Next, grasp the neck and shoulder with one hand and with the other hand, run the knife down each side of the backbone as close to the bone as possible, severing the hip joint. Now, open out the duck. Place it skin side down on a cutting surface. Cut the duck in half, severing the wishbone and breastbone. This is the only difficult part because the duck's wishbone is quite hard. Center the knife along the breastbone and middle of the wishbone. Cover the top of the knife with a folded towel to protect your hand, and pound down on the knife to cut. Finally, cut each half in half again along the diagonal line between the bottom of the breasts and top of the thighs to wind up with 4 quarters.

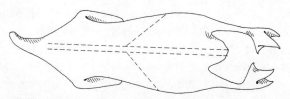

TO CUT UP A RABBIT, first cut it crosswise under the front legs to make 2 sections. Cut the front leg section in half the long way, along the backbone. Next, cut the bottom section of the rabbit crosswise where the back joins the hind legs. Cut the hind leg section in half lengthwise, along the back-bone. Cut the remaining piece, called the saddle, in half crosswise. You will wind up with 6 pieces.

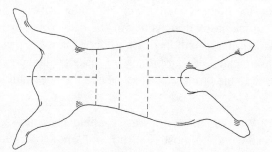

NOTES AND AFTERTHOUGHTS

1. Use only *gros sel* or rock salt for curing duck and rabbit. Kosher salt crystals are too small and will make the meat salty.

2. If you prefer, you can skin the duck after curing and before cooking it. The meat will still be more tender because of the curing. Don't remove the skin before curing, though, or the meat will be too salty.

3. If it turns out you are not going to cook the duck or rabbit within two days after curing it, wash the spices off the pieces, pat them dry, and refrigerate until ready to cook. Curing longer than two days will result in salty meat.

Equipment

E very kitchen needs a few basic tools, no matter how or what you like to cook. To cook well, with the least amount of bother, we believe in using a minimal amount of equipment—but what you use should be top quality. The essentials:

COLANDERS: We like to have at least 2 colanders, one medium and one larger. They are useful for all kinds of cooking needs from draining noodles to rinsing vegetables and washing fruit.

CUTTING BOARD: We prefer wood cutting boards to plastic. While plastic is easy to clean, its surface dulls knives, is slippery, and makes an unpleasant sound when being chopped upon. A butcher block is best (and a joy to have if you have room in the kitchen for one), and can be adjusted to suit your height and avoid back strain. A countertop wood board will do as long as it is at least 12 by 15 inches, or large enough to accommodate a whole chicken or a reasonable amount of vegetables at a time. It should be at least 1½ inches thick so that it is heavy enough not to scoot around while chopping or crack when pounding. Also, a wood board with a trough to catch juices is useful for carving meat. Cutting boards should be cleaned with soap and water after cutting poultry.

FOOD PROCESSOR: A food processor is an indispensable time- and effort-saving device for home cooking. For chopping, mixing, pureeing, salsa making, and quick pastry doughs, it can't be beat. You may not use it every day, but having it handy will lead you to cook many recipes you might not otherwise have tackled. If your processing tasks are limited mainly to chopping onions and nuts or making salsa, one of the new mini processors will serve in place of a larger model.

GARLIC PRESS: We recommend a basic simple hand press, the type you squeeze. These work the most efficiently and are the least expensive. The Zyliss "Susi" is one of the best models. Some purists think you should never press raw garlic because it inadvertently affects the taste. We think this is extreme. Garlic gets bruised or mashed in chopping anyway, and for some foods, such as vinaigrette salad dressing, the taste and texture of pressed garlic is superior to that of chopped.

GRATERS: Every kitchen needs one or two grating devices. A hand grater is versatile and fills most grating needs from shredding cheese to mincing citrus peel and juicing onions. Even for pizzas and tacos, we find shredding the cheese on a hand grater as quick as using the food processor unless there is a large crowd to feed. Some people like to have a special grater for cheese, and these are fine tools. In addition, we suggest a nutmeg grater so that you can grate fresh nutmeg into pastas and desserts and enjoy the full benefit of this aromatic spice.

KITCHEN SCALE: We find a kitchen scale useful in following recipes and recommend having one in the well-equipped kitchen. Soehnle and Braun make inexpensive models with a bowl on top to hold ingredients while you are weighing. It is not absolutely necessary to have one, though, and we have tried to measure ingredients in our recipes so that you can follow them with or without a scale.

KNIFE SHARPENER: What good are your knives if they aren't sharp? You don't need to go to the extreme of having a whetstone and oil, but to keep the blades keen on a daily basis, you should have a sharpening steel or simple sharpening roller. To hone knife blades properly, take them to a knife sharpener once a year.

KNIVES: Skip the inexpensive, "all purpose" sets and invest in sturdy, well-balanced blades. Good knives are truly mandatory. You need at least one 8- or 9-inch chef's knife and one 3½- to 4½-inch paring knife made of high-quality stainless steel. Poor quality stainless steel does not stay sharp. Carbon steel, though it sharpens well, is difficult to keep clean and turns black on contact with any acidic surface. It is, in fact, useful to have 2 chef's knives and 2 paring knives, especially if you like help in the kitchen. Also, a boning knife is useful for occasional boning tasks, although you can make do with your other knives.

LEMON JUICER: Since lemon juice is part of so many dishes, we find a lemon juicer more than handy—it's in the stack of dirty dishes every day. The best kind has the squeezer/strainer set over a bowl so that the seeds are strained out and the juice is caught in the bowl.

MEAT THERMOMETER: An instant-reading meat thermometer is a security blanket and a liberator to boot. Admittedly, one of us got along for years without one until halfway through this book, but it meant that she was always returning to poke and prod the food, guess, or keep careful track of time. With an instant-reading meat thermometer, you can readily tell when your roasted or grilled meats are properly cooked, whether they are rare, medium or well done, when they have required less time than the directions state, or for whatever reason, say the whims of your oven, need still more time to cook. An instant-reading meat thermometer also frees you to walk away from roasting meats and more or less "forget" the clock while you do other things. You can judge when your food is done by temperature rather than by countdown.

PEPPERMILL: For kitchen use, it is important to have a peppermill that will easily grind large amounts of pepper so you aren't tempted to buy pre-ground pepper. This presents a problem because most peppermills turn out only a few grains at a time. There are two solutions. One is to use an old-fashioned coffee grinder, reserving it exclusively for pepper and other spices. The other is to purchase the Peppermate Peppermill. You can pour ½ cup of peppercorns at a time into its wide-mouthed bin and, with a few cranks of the easy-to-grasp handle, grind out plenty of pepper for any recipe. The Peppermate Peppermill is available in the New York Musuem of Modern Art Gift Shop, or by mail order from East Hampton Industries, Inc., East Hampton, New York 11927, 800-645-1188, for around $30.

POTS AND PANS: There's no denying that a good set of pots and pans makes a major difference in the quality of your cooking, to say nothing of the pleasure you get from using them. There are many excellent cooking vessels available, and you should choose your pots and pans to fit your cooking style and personal aesthetic. Select pots and pans that are heavy enough to conduct heat well and are made of material that doesn't react with acidic foods so that you never have to worry about adding a dash of wine or dollop of tomato sauce. In general, you need one or two large, heavy skillets, a medium size skillet, a large stovetop-to-oven casserole, 1 or 2 saucepans, and whatever else is required for your particular cooking preferences. What we *don't* recommend are stainless steel pots and pans, even copper clad, because they always manage to develop hot spots and cook unevenly. We also don't like lightweight aluminum for the same reason.

ROLLING PIN: Anachronism that they seem to be, rolling pins are still necessary to roll out an occasional pizza or pie crust, crush cookies, or make bread crumbs. If the one you get is too big to fit in a drawer, tie a piece of string around one end and hang it on the wall or on the pantry door. If you really don't care to keep one, you can use an empty wine bottle filled with water to give it weight, or cut a foot-long piece off an old broom or rake like Greek and Italian cooks do. It's easy to store and works just fine.

SPATULAS: To remove cooked food from a pan or grill, a metal spatula is the best tool. It should be medium in size, big enough to lift large pieces, but small enough to fit in your pans, and slightly flexible so you can push it under the food. Stainless steel is the easiest to keep clean. In addition to a metal spatula, a rubber, not plastic, spatula with a 2-inch-wide head is requisite. Nothing else works as well to scrape down the sides of bowls and the bottoms of saucepans.

WHISKS: Spoons and forks can do a lot of your mixing, but there are times when to beat a sauce properly, you need a wire whisk. Whisking makes sauces smooth and takes the lumps out of sour cream or yogurt. You can also whip cream easily with one and save yourself the trouble of hooking up your electric mixer.

WOODEN MALLET: In the process of cooking, occasionally ingredients, such as turkey cutlets, must be pounded or, like allspice or juniper berries, must be crushed. You can search for a substitute, but bottle and can bottoms are often concave, saucers not heavy enough, and a hammer too small-headed. A wooden mallet does the job deftly in a few pleasing thwacks. Like a rolling pin, if it is too large for your drawer, tie a string around it and hang it.

WOODEN SPOONS: Long ones, shorts ones, thin ones, broad ones, you simply have to have wooden spoons to cook, and plenty of them. If you buy sets, you might throw away the forks and tenderizer that are included, but keep all of the spoons. Wooden spoons do not heat up when you are stirring food over the stovetop or on the grill. Where metal spoons and forks damage pots and pans, sometimes taking whole chunks out of the surface, wooden spoons are kind to your equipment. You need them for mixing, blending, testing—everything. They do wear out in time, get char marks from being left on hot pans, or crack if you put them in the dishwasher. But when they wear out, burn or crack, buy more. They cost only pennies.

Handy to have but not vital are a pair of kitchen scissors, lightweight string, a long-tined meat fork, and stereo speakers.

In addition to the utensils mentioned here, the introduction to each chapter in this book covers any special equipment you might need for the recipes in that section. These include such items as pizza pans, casseroles, and barbecue tongs.

TREATS
AND
NIBBLES

Quick Snack Crackers
　　Little Toasts
　　Homemade Tortilla Chips

Melted Cheese with Gherkin Pickles
　　Variations

Cream Cheese with Deviled Pine Nuts and Pumpkin Seeds

Boats of Belgian Endive Filled with Brie or Roquefort Cheese
　　Brie Cheese Filling
　　Roquefort Cheese Filling

Marinated Feta Cheese

Jalapeño Chili Peppers Stuffed with Feta Cheese

Red Pepper Pesto

Potted Mushrooms with Sherry and Butter

Chick Pea Paste

Broccoli and Cauliflower with Yogurt and Feta Cheese Dip
　　Yogurt and Feta Cheese Dip

Mom's Marinated Roasted Red and Green Bell Peppers

Eggplant Salad Peasant Style

Tuna Bits with Capers and Onion

Marinated Shrimp

Homemade Pickled Salmon

Crab Cakes with Sage Butter Sauce

Blue Cornmeal Pancakes with Caviar

Burmese-Style Chicken Curry Soup

Mushroom Essence Soup

Dishes from Other Chapters That Make Good Treats and Nibbles

Sometimes tired to the bone, sometimes excited by events, at the end of the day we come together. Often it's the first moment we've had to take a breather. We're hungry, but before we can go on to prepare the dinner, we need to feed ourselves before we eat, funny as that sounds.

Or, maybe company is coming. We give some elegant dinners, but we give many more casual ones with pals, acquaintances, and associates. We sit down for appetizers, or everybody hangs around the kitchen talking, helping, or just watching us prepare the rest of the meal.

We need something that is quick and lively, appetite whetting, but not filling. We need quick treats and nibbles.

From cream cheese topped with deviled nuts to Crab Cakes with Sage Butter Sauce, the following pages unfurl an array of appetizers that you can serve for a formal first course, spread informally across the butcher block, or nibble to sustain yourself until dinner. In addition, we have added two extraordinary soups, both refreshing and memorable, for those special occasions when you would like a hot first course.

Excellent packaged products—the huge variety of cheeses available, good pancake mixes, tiny marinated vegetables and pickles, rosy-hued smoked salmon, crunchy nuts and seeds, roasted peppers in jars, white tuna, salt-packed anchovies, tangy Greek olives—provide a good start. A food processor often lends a helping hand. With a little doctoring and a dash of imagination, we can turn out treats and nibbles in the blink of an eye.

And if you like the grazing style of eating, a little of this and a little of that without any one main dish, you can make a whole meal out of these delectables. ■

Quick Snack Crackers

Most treats and nibbles need a scooper or edible plate for serving. Both Little Toasts and Tortilla Chips go with almost anything. They are quite easy to make and are far tastier than most boxed crackers.

Little Toasts

1 baguette French bread or ½ loaf full-sized French or Italian bread
½ cup olive oil

Heat the oven to 375°F. Cut the baguette into ¼-inch-thick slices (if using the regular-shaped French or Italian bread, cut each slice into 4 rectangles).

Using a pastry brush, brush a little olive oil on both sides of each slice of bread. Place the bread slices on a baking sheet.

Bake 6 minutes. Turn and bake 6 minutes more, or until just turning golden.

Serve right away, or store airtight until ready to use

NOTES AND AFTERTHOUGHTS

You can also make Little Toasts without the olive oil. Just place the bread slices on a baking sheet and cook the same way. Unoiled Little Toasts are best for appetizers that are moist, such as Eggplant Salad Peasant Style (page 48) or already oily, such as Mom's Marinated Roasted Red and Green Bell Peppers (page 47).

Homemade Tortilla Chips

6 corn tortillas

Heat the oven to 500°F.

Cut the corn tortillas in half, then cut each half into 3 triangles. Place the tortilla triangles on a baking sheet.

Bake 5 minutes. Turn and bake 5 minutes more.

Serve right away or store airtight until ready to use.

Plenty for 6
Makes 36 little toasts

20 minutes or less

Little Toasts can become the treat and nibble by themselves: Press a clove of garlic into the olive oil before spreading it on the bread slices. Or sprinkle the bread slices with Parmesan or some other grated cheese on the top side after turning them over in the oven. You can also top Little Toasts with a thin slice of fresh tomato, a small piece of bacon, or an anchovy fillet.

Plenty for 6
Makes 36 tortilla chips

20 minutes or less

Homemade Tortilla Chips crisped in the oven aren't oily or salty. And they turn out flat, which makes them handier to use for scooping or dipping.

Melted Cheese with Gherkin Pickles

1 ¾-pound piece semisoft sharp cheese, such as Gruyère, Emmentaler,
    Appenzeller, Jarlsberg, Gouda, Edam, or Raclette
1 jar (12 ounces) tiny gherkin pickles or *cornichons*

Homemade Tortilla Chips (page 38)

Heat the oven to 500°F. Set the cheese on a heatproof plate. Place in the oven for 15 minutes or so, until the cheese is completely melted.

Drain the gherkins and place them in a small bowl.

When the cheese is melted, serve it right away with the bowl of gherkins and the tortilla chips. Dip a gherkin or a chip into the cheese and pop it into your mouth.

VARIATIONS

You can diversify your melted cheese portfolio with the following options:

BREADS AND CRACKERS
    Slices of French or Italian bread, toasted or untoasted
    Rye bread wafers

VEGETABLES
    Brussels sprouts, grilled, blanched, or pickled
    Green onions
    Potatoes, tiny red or white potatoes, boiled in their jackets until just done
    Mushrooms, whole small ones
    Radishes
    Pickled onions, from a jar

NUTS
    Walnut or Pecan halves

SALSA
    Tomato or Chive Salsa or Tomatillo Sauce (pages 82, 83, 85). Serve in a bowl. Dip a Little Toast or tortilla chip in the cheese and then in the salsa.

Plenty for 6

20 minutes or less

This is the French version of nachos or the American version of Swiss fondue. Traditionally, the French and Swiss use Raclette cheese for their nachos, which they serve with gherkins and boiled tiny potatoes. The Swiss also use Gruyère cheese, which they serve with forks.

Any good semisoft sharp melting cheese will do, and the tortilla chips give the dish a resolutely American accent.

Once upon a time cheesecloth was a common part of the well-stocked kitchen. That was when home cheesemaking was a regular part of kitchen activities. Cream cheese is one of the easiest cheeses to make at home. If you are so inclined, heat some cream, stir in rennet to curdle the cream, then wrap the curdled cream in a length of cheesecloth to hang and drain. In 24 hours you will have your own fresh, sweet cream cheese.

Of course, now it's easier to buy the cheese and cheesecloth has become almost a curio. When you are buying cream cheese, look for it in bulk at your butcher or cheese store. The silver-wrapped commercial brands contain gum stabilizers that interfere with the true creamy texture of fresh cream cheese.

Cream Cheese with Deviled Pine Nuts and Pumpkin Seeds

1 tablespoon walnut oil
½ cup pine nuts (about 2½ ounces)
½ cup pumpkin seeds (about 2½ ounces)
⅛ teaspoon cayenne pepper
¼ teaspoon salt
6 ounces cream cheese, at room temperature
2½ tablespoons milk

Little Toasts or Homemade Tortilla Chips (page 38) or water crackers

Heat the walnut oil in a medium skillet until the oil begins to smoke. Add the pine nuts, pumpkin seeds, cayenne, and salt. Stir over medium-high heat until the nuts and seeds are well toasted, about 2 minutes. Remove to a bowl.

Place the cream cheese in a medium bowl or a food processor. Add the milk and mix until the cream cheese is smooth. Spread the cream cheese on a salad plate. Smooth the top. Arrange half of the toasted nuts and seeds over the cream cheese. Place the remaining nuts and seeds in a small bowl.

Serve with Little Toasts, Homemade Tortilla Chips, or water crackers, with the remaining nuts on the side.

Boats of Belgian Endive Filled with Brie or Roquefort Cheese

½ pound Belgian endive (enough to yield 24 medium spears or half-spears)
1 cup Brie Cheese or Roquefort Cheese Filling (see below)

Cut off the ends of the Belgian endive about ¾ inch from the stem end. Separate the spears down to the core, reserving the core for a salad. Leave the smaller spears whole. Cut the larger leaves, more than 2 inches wide, lengthwise in half.

Fill the spears with ½ tablespoon Brie or Roquefort Cheese Filling.

Arrange on a platter and serve chilled or at room temperature.

Brie Cheese Filling

9 ounces Brie cheese, at room temperature
1 medium green onion
2 ½ tablespoons white wine

Makes 1 cup

Remove the rind from the Brie with a paring knife.

Place the cheese in the food processor along with the onion. Add the wine and process until smooth.

Trim off the root end and limp top of the green onion. Mince the onion in a food processor or with a chef's knife.

Place the minced onion in a medium bowl. Add the cheese and wine and mix until smooth.

Roquefort Cheese Filling

¼ pound Roquefort cheese
½ teaspoon walnut or peanut oil
⅓ cup walnut pieces (about 1 ounce)
½ tablespoon white wine

Makes 1 cup

Place the Roquefort in a small bowl and let soften while toasting the walnuts.

Heat the oil in a small frying pan until the oil begins to smoke. Add the walnut pieces and stir over medium-high heat until the walnuts are browned, about 1 minute.

Remove the walnuts to a cutting board and allow to cool, then chop fine. Add the nuts and wine to the Roquefort. Mix with a fork until well blended.

NOTES AND AFTERTHOUGHTS

Camembert, Caprella, or Mascarpone will do in place of the Brie; and any creamy blue cheese, such as Bavarian Blue, Cambozola, or Gorgonzola will do in place of the Roquefort.

Marinated Feta Cheese

¾ pound Feta Cheese, preferably Bulgarian or Corsican
3 garlic cloves
¼ cup tiny black *Niçoise* or oil-cured black olives
¼ cup mixed fresh herb leaves, such as sage, thyme, rosemary, oregano, or chives
1 cup olive oil

Little Toasts (page 38) or crackers

Cut the Feta into ¾-inch-thick slabs and lay them down in a deep casserole or flat-bottomed bowl. Peel the garlic and cut into slivers. Arrange the garlic slivers, olives, and herbs over and around the Feta cheese. Pour the oil into the casserole. Cover the cheese with plastic wrap, refrigerate, and let marinate several hours, up to several weeks.

To serve, cut off a bite-size piece of cheese and place on top of a Little Toast or cracker, along with a sliver of garlic if desired. Eat the olives separately.

NOTES AND AFTERTHOUGHTS
Lacking fresh herbs for the marinade, you can use a mixture of dried oregano, marjoram, rosemary, or thyme with 2 crumbled bay leaves.

Plenty for 6

20 minutes or less

We use a considerable amount of Feta cheese. We stuff it in hot peppers, crumble it on eggplant pizza, blend it with yogurt for a vegetable dip, spread it with sour cream over salmon tacos. Everywhere, it soothes the overly piquant or perks up the overly bland. We prefer Bulgarian or Corsican Feta because they are the least salty and most creamy. Here, marinated in olive oil with herbs, the Feta stands by itself.

Jalapeño Chili Peppers Stuffed with Feta Cheese

18 pickled jalapeño peppers (about one 12-ounce can)
½ pound Feta cheese, preferably Bulgarian or Corsican
⅛ cup olive oil
1 teaspoon chopped fresh oregano or ¼ teaspoon dried

Drain the jalapeño peppers and rinse well. Wearing rubber gloves to protect your hands from burning, remove the stems and cores. Cut the peppers in half lengthwise. Place them in a large bowl of cold water to soak while preparing the stuffing. Change the water once.

Crumble the Feta into a medium bowl. Add the oil and oregano. Mash together with a fork, blending well, but not until completely smooth.

Drain the jalapeños and rinse them again. Fill each half with about 1 teaspoon of the Feta stuffing.

Arrange the stuffed jalapeños on a platter and serve chilled or at room temperature.

NOTES AND AFTERTHOUGHTS
Whole pickled jalapeños in brine are available in Latin markets or in the Mexican or international food section of supermarkets.

Plenty for 6

20 minutes or less

For those who think something hot and fiery whets—or quenches—the appetite, this is it. The Feta stuffing tones down the heat, but on a scale of one to ten, pickled jalapeños still rate a solid 9.

Red Pepper Pesto

4 large or 6 medium red bell peppers (about two pounds)
½ teaspoon walnut or peanut oil
¼ cup pine nuts
4 to 6 medium garlic cloves
¼ cup grated Parmesan, Romano or aged Asiago cheese
¼ cup olive oil
¼ teaspoon salt

Little Toasts or Homemade Tortilla Chips (page 38), or water crackers

Roast and peel the red peppers according to the instructions on page 47.

While the peppers roast, heat the walnut or peanut oil in a small frying pan until the oil begins to smoke. Add the pine nuts and stir over medium-high heat about 2 minutes, or until the nuts are browned. Remove the nuts to a food processor and allow to cool.

When the peppers are roasted and peeled, cut them into quarters. Peel the garlic. Add the peppers, garlic, cheese, oil, and salt to the food processor. Process until smooth. Remove to a serving dish.

Serve with Homemade Tortilla Chips or Little Toasts or water crackers.

NOTES AND AFTERTHOUGHTS
It's a wonderful, offbeat combination to serve Red Pepper Pesto with tortilla chips. For a more traditional use, mix it with pasta for a first course or main dish.

Plenty for 6

20 to 40 minutes

Basil isn't the only good base for a "battered" sauce. Roasted red peppers also make a marvelous vehicle for the classical pine nuts, grated cheese, and garlic with olive oil that make up a pesto sauce.

Potted Mushrooms with Sherry and Butter

Plenty for 6
Makes 1¾ cups

20 to 40 minutes

A version of potted mushrooms baked in a tart was Victoria's most demanded hors d'oeuvre when she catered parties. We find this simpler rendition sublime, but if you care to take the trouble, bake the potted mushrooms in a covered pie. Make enough pastry dough for a 2-crust 9-inch pie. Brown the bottom crust for 10 minutes in a 350°F oven. Spread the mushroom mixture evenly over the crust and cover with a top crust. Bake 30 minutes, or until the top is golden.

While food processors are indeed a miracle of modern kitchen technology and make short shrift of almost all chopping chores, they do have their drawbacks. One is that you cannot chop mushrooms with anything else in the bowl at the same time. The mushrooms will absorb any moisture released from other ingredients and wind up a soggy mass. Also, to cut mushrooms evenly, you must do them in small batches. Otherwise, the pieces on the bottom totally disintegrate.

1 small or ½ medium onion (about 4 ounces)
1 pound mushrooms
2 tablespoons butter
1½ teaspoons paprika
½ teaspoon salt
1 tablespoon lemon juice
1 tablespoon dry sherry

Little Toasts (page 38) or crackers

Peel the onion. If using a food processor, medium chop the onion without mincing. Remove from the food processor and set aside.

Clean the mushrooms and trim off the stem ends. Place half the mushrooms in the food processor and chop fine without mincing. Remove and chop the remaining mushrooms the same way. Or, fine chop the onion with a chef's knife and set aside, then fine chop the mushrooms.

Melt the butter in a large skillet over medium heat. Add the onion and cook 2 minutes until wilted. Add the mushrooms. Increase the heat to medium-high and cook for 2 minutes. Add the paprika, salt, lemon juice, and sherry. Cook 4 to 5 minutes, or until the liquid evaporates. Remove the mixture to a small serving bowl or crock.

Serve the potted mushrooms chilled or at room temperature, spreading about ½ tablespoon on each Little Toast or cracker.

NOTES AND AFTERTHOUGHTS

This recipe actually makes more than plenty for 6, unless your crowd likes more than 6 crackers each. Luckily, though, the potted mushroom mixture freezes like a dream. Just put it in a tightly sealed plastic container or self lock bag. Or you might have it for your next day's sandwich.

Chick Pea Paste

2 cups canned chick peas
3 large or 4 medium garlic cloves
½ cup olive oil
¼ cup sesame oil
2 tablespoons lemon juice
¼ teaspoon salt

Little Toasts (page 38), Armenian cracker bread (Lavosh), or water crackers

Drain the chick peas and place them in a food processor. Peel the garlic cloves. Cut them into 3 or 4 pieces and add them to the processor. Process a few seconds to mash the chick peas. Add the olive oil, sesame oil, lemon juice, and salt. Process until pureed and smooth. Remove the Chick Pea Paste to a bowl.

Serve chilled or at room temperature with Little Toasts or crackers.

NOTES AND AFTERTHOUGHTS

Chick Pea Paste keeps practically forever refrigerated in a glass or plastic jar, patted down on top, and coated with a little olive oil.

Plenty for 6
Makes 2¼ cups

20 minutes or less

Chick peas—the famous peas of "pease porridge hot, pease porridge cold" —were a staple of Europe and the Near East long before upstart potatoes arrived from the New World.

Chick Pea Paste is one of the fastest and most pleasing treats to make. People sometimes hesitate to whip it up because most Chick Pea Paste recipes call for tahini, a thick sesame seed paste used in Near Eastern cooking. Tahini may be difficult to find, so in its place we use sesame oil to duplicate the taste. If you have tahini handy, you can use it instead of the sesame oil called for in this recipe.

Broccoli and Cauliflower with Yogurt and Feta Cheese Dip

Blanching broccoli and cauliflower in boiling water makes them taste sweeter, removes the acrid, "old cabbage" smell, and turns their colors bright.

2 cups Yogurt and Feta Cheese Dip (see below)
1 pound broccoli
1 small head cauliflower (about 1½ pounds)

Make the Yogurt and Feta Cheese Dip.

Bring a large pot of water to boil. Cut the florets off the broccoli stems. Remove the core from the cauliflower and separate the head into florets the same size as the broccoli.

When the water boils, add the broccoli and cauliflower, cover the pot, and cook 2 minutes. Drain the vegetables and rinse with cold water until cooled all the way through. Set aside to drip dry. Just before serving, pat the vegetables completely dry with paper towels.

To serve, place the Yogurt and Feta Cheese Dip in a small bowl. Set the bowl in the middle of a serving platter and arrange the broccoli and cauliflower florets all around.

Yogurt and Feta Cheese Dip

Makes 2 cups

6 ounces Feta cheese, preferably Bulgarian or Corsican
1½ cups plain yogurt
3 tablespoons chopped fresh dill or 1 tablespoon dried

Place the Feta cheese in a small bowl and crumble it with a fork. Add the yogurt and dill. Mix until the yogurt is creamy and the Feta is blended in.

Mom's Marinated Roasted Red and Green Bell Peppers

2 large or 3 medium red bell peppers (about 1 pound)
3 medium green bell peppers (about 1 pound)
6 large garlic cloves
4 tablespoons balsamic or red wine vinegar
1 cup olive oil
½ teaspoon salt

Little Toasts (page 38) or French bread slices

To roast the peppers: heat the oven to 500°F. Place the peppers on the oven rack and roast, turning, until the skins are charred all over, 20 to 25 minutes. Remove the peppers to a paper bag, close the bag, and let the peppers steam for 10 minutes. With your fingers and a paring knife, remove the charred skins and the seeds and cores from the peppers.

Cut the peppers lengthwise into ¼-inch-wide strips. Place the strips in a large bowl. Peel the garlic cloves and slice them into thin slivers. Add the garlic to the peppers.

In a small bowl, mix together the vinegar, oil, and salt. Pour over the peppers. Set aside to marinate for 1 hour or so before serving.

Serve at room temperature with Little Toasts or slices of French bread.

NOTES AND AFTERTHOUGHTS

There are excellent jarred roasted red peppers available, and they are suitable for making a quick version of this dish. You will sacrifice some of the smoky flavor you get from roasting your own, though.

Plenty for 6

40 to 60 minutes

The "mom" in this recipe title is Victoria's. One day she decided that "all these marinated pepper recipes needed a little kick." She roasted and peeled some peppers, put in plenty of garlic and a little balsamic vinegar, and now it's our favorite.

Roasting peppers, whether in the oven or on the grill, imparts a nutty, smoky flavor that is indescribably good. Just stick the peppers in a hot oven until the skins char. Peeling the roasted peppers is also easy if you know the "bag trick." Once roasted, the trick to peeling them easily is to place them in a brown bag, seal it, and let them steam a few minutes. Their charred skins loosen and lift right off.

You can also char pepper skins by placing the peppers directly on a gas burner with the flame on medium high or by broiling them. But, it's difficult to remove all the charred bits of skin. Also, the pepper doesn't get thoroughly cooked so this method is good only if you are going to cook them further.

Eggplant Salad Peasant Style always reminds us of the hot, sunny Fourth of July when Victoria got married and Susanna made gallons of the dish. Bowls of it were placed at strategic points up and down the terraces where a Latin band played and lambs roasted on their spits. Everywhere there was laughter, clusters of merry celebrants, and the salad. So much remained after the music finally died down that we favored the departing guests with eggplant salad in lieu of sugared almonds. Eggplant salad is like an Adriatic "salsa." You can serve it on lettuce leaves, to accompany grilled fish or softshell crabs, or slather it over lamb.

Eggplant Salad Peasant Style

1 large eggplant (about 1½ pounds)
½ medium onion (about 4 ounces)
2 to 4 large garlic cloves
1 medium tomato (about 4 ounces)
¼ cup chopped fresh parsley leaves
½ teaspoon chopped fresh mint leaves
1 teaspoon chopped fresh oregano leaves or ¼ teaspoon dried
¼ teaspoon dry mustard
3 teaspoons red wine vinegar
½ tablespoon lemon juice
½ cup olive oil
¼ teaspoon salt
⅛ teaspoon freshly ground black pepper

thin slices French bread, pieces of Armenian cracker bread, or water crackers

Heat oven to 450°F. Place the eggplant on a baking sheet. Roast in the oven about 50 minutes, or until the skin is wrinkled and the eggplant collapses. Remove from the oven, and let cool 10 minutes.

While the eggplant roasts, peel the onion and garlic. With a chef's knife, medium chop the onion, garlic, and tomato. Remove to a bowl and add the parsley, mint, oregano, mustard, vinegar, lemon juice, oil, salt, and pepper. If using a food processor, cut the onion, garlic, and tomato into quarters. Place in the food processor bowl and add the parsley, mint, oregano, mustard, vinegar, lemon juice, oil, salt, and pepper. Process just until coarsely chopped.

Slit the cooled eggplant open. Holding the stem, scrape the pulp off the skin.

With a chef's knife coarsely chop the eggplant pulp. Add it to the other ingredients and mix to blend well. Or, add the eggplant pulp to the processor and process until the vegetables are just barely medium chopped. Remove to a bowl, and chill.

Serve with thin slices of French bread, pieces of Armenian cracker bread, or water crackers.

NOTES AND AFTERTHOUGHTS

1. If you are chopping the eggplant pulp by hand, use a stainless steel knife. Carbon steel will discolor the eggplant, and the eggplant will discolor your knife.

2. If using a food processor, be careful not to overchop this salad. It should be peasant style, medium chopped with bits of vegetables, like a salsa, not a puree.

Tuna Bits with Capers and Onions

2 6½-ounce cans chunk white tuna in water
3 tablespoons capers
3 tablespoons chopped green onion tops
3 tablespoons olive oil
1 tablespoon lemon juice
¼ teaspoon freshly ground black pepper

Little Toasts (page 38) or crackers

Drain the tuna and capers. Place the tuna, capers, green onion, oil, lemon juice, and black pepper in a bowl. Mix with a fork, breaking up the tuna without mashing it and blending the ingredients together.

Spoon about ½ tablespoon of the tuna mixture on a Little Toast or cracker.

Plenty for 6
Makes 2 cups

20 minutes or less

Tuna used to come packed in olive oil. Only occasionally could you find it packed in water. Eventually, manufacturers switched to less expensive, less tasty oils to save costs. Then, at about the same time people began to demand tuna packed in water for health reasons, manufacturers found that packing it in water saved still more cost. Some imported brands are still packed in olive oil. It is delicious. If you use it for this spread, reduce the amount of olive oil in the recipe by half.

Marinated Shrimp

2 pounds small or medium shrimp
5 medium garlic cloves
¼ cup olive oil
6 tablespoons lemon juice
1½ tablespoons chopped fresh tarragon leaves or 1½ teaspoons dried
6 tablespoons chopped fresh parsley leaves, preferably Italian

If the shrimp have a black line, called a sand vein, running from head to tail, remove it by cutting along the line through the shell and skin with a sharp paring knife. Rinse the shrimp and pat them dry.

Peel the garlic cloves and cut them into thin slivers.

Heat the olive oil in a large skillet until the oil begins to smoke. Add the shrimp and garlic slivers and stir for 3 minutes over medium-high heat. Remove the shrimp to a large bowl. Add the lemon juice, tarragon, and parsley and toss.

Serve chilled or at room temperature.

Plenty for 6

20 to 40 minutes

Homemade Pickled Salmon

1¾ to 2 pounds salmon, in one piece, not filleted
1 small onion (about 4 ounces)
1 bay leaf
⅔ cup olive oil
⅔ cup dry white wine
3 tablespoons white wine vinegar
½ teaspoon salt

Little Toasts (page 38) or water crackers

Bring a large pot of water to a boil. Cut two lengths of string and tie them crosswise around the salmon in two places, like a roast. When the water boils, add the salmon and reduce the heat to a simmer. Cook 15 minutes. Drain the salmon in a colander; let cool 20 minutes.

Quarter the onion lengthwise. Cut the quarters crosswise into ¼-inch-thick slices. Separate the layers and place them in a deep casserole large enough to hold the salmon.

Cut the bay leaf crosswise into ¼-inch-wide slices. Add to the onions, along with the oil, white wine, vinegar, and salt. Mix to blend.

When the salmon is cool, untie it. With your fingers, remove the skin and bones. Break the salmon meat into large, 2- to 3-inch chunks. Place the salmon chunks in the casserole. Gently turn the salmon to coat with the marinade. Cover and marinate in the refrigerator for several hours or up to 3 days.

To serve, place a tidbit of salmon on a Little Toast or cracker. Garnish with a slice of onion if desired.

NOTES AND AFTERTHOUGHTS

1. The large King salmon is the preferable variety to use for pickling. The smaller Silver salmon are too bland to stand up to the marinade.

2. This recipe makes enough to serve 12 or so for a before dinner snack. Even if you are serving fewer people, it is not a good idea to pickle a smaller piece of salmon because it will not poach properly. Instead plan on leftovers. They will keep several days in the refrigerator.

Crab Cakes with Sage Butter Sauce

1 pound crabmeat (about 3 cups)
2 eggs
2 tablespoons minced green onions
3 tablespoons chopped fresh parsley leaves, preferably Italian
2 tablespoons cornmeal
2 teaspoons lemon juice
2 pinches cayenne pepper
4 to 6 tablespoons butter for frying

FOR THE SAGE BUTTER:

3 teaspoons thinly shredded fresh sage leaves or 1 teaspoon dried rubbed sage
4 tablespoons butter

1 lemon

Plenty for 6
Makes 24 small crab cakes

20 minutes or less

Drain the crabmeat in a colander, pressing out excess liquid.

Break the eggs into a small bowl and lightly beat with a fork. Add the crabmeat, green onions, parsley, cornmeal, lemon juice, and cayenne. Mix together.

To make the sage butter, combine the sage and 4 tablespoons butter in a small saucepan. Heat until the butter melts without letting it boil. Set aside in a warm place.

Divide the crabmeat mixture into 24 small 2-inch patties using about 1½ tablespoons for each. In a large skillet, heat 4 tablespoons butter until it foams. Place as many patties as will fit in the pan in a single uncrowded layer and fry 1 minute over medium-high heat. Turn and and fry 1 minute on the other side. Remove the cooked crab cakes to a platter. Place another tablespoon of butter in the skillet and continue until all the crab cakes are cooked.

Cut the lemon in half lengthwise, then cut each half into 3 wedges.

To serve, spoon the sage butter over the crab cakes on the platter and arrange the lemon wedges all around.

NOTES AND AFTERTHOUGHTS

The crabmeat should be very fresh to make a succulent, savory crab cake. The best way to tell if the crab is fresh is by the amount of liquid it is sitting in. The more liquid, the longer it has been sitting around.

While good caviar has not yet descended into the realm of everyday cooking, it has at least come within reach with the harvesting and marketing of some excellent American products. Both the golden caviar from Michigan freshwater whitefish and the black caviar from Oregon sturgeon are delicious and affordable for an occasional splurge.

Blue Cornmeal Pancakes with Caviar

1½ cups blue cornmeal pancake mix
3 tablespoons butter
4½ to 5 ounces caviar
1½ cups sour cream

Make the pancake batter according to the instructions on the package.

Melt 1 tablespoon of the butter in a large skillet until the butter foams. Make sure the butter coats the entire bottom of the pan. Spoon in 1½ tablespoons of batter at a time to make as many small pancakes as will fit in a single uncrowded layer. Cook 1 minute over medium-high heat. Turn and cook 1 minute more. Remove the pancakes to a platter. Add 1 tablespoon more butter to the pan and continue with another batch until all the batter is cooked.

To serve, spoon a dollop of sour cream onto each pancake, then place a teaspoon of caviar on top of the sour cream.

NOTES AND AFTERTHOUGHTS

1. Buckwheat pancakes also make an utterly delicious accompaniment to caviar and sour cream. You can find both blue cornmeal and buckwheat pancake mixes in upscale grocery or health food stores, and they are worth having in your larder. Arrowhead Mills is one of the best brands for both. See also page 21.

2. If you don't care to make your own pancakes, whole wheat tortillas are an excellent, quick substitute. Heat them in a small skillet with a little melted butter, turning once to coat both sides with the butter. Cut the warmed tortillas into quarters and top with caviar and sour cream as above.

Burmese-Style Chicken Curry Soup

¼ **pound spaghetti or vermicelli (about 2 cups when cooked)**
6 **cups chicken stock, preferably homemade**
2 **cans (14 ounces each) coconut milk (about 3 cups)**
4 **teaspoons curry powder**
1 **teaspoon salt**
¾ **cup dried coconut strips**
½ **cup shredded chicken (optional)**
¾ **cup cilantro leaves**

Bring a medium pot of water to boil. When the water boils, drop in the spaghetti or vermicelli and cook until just tender. Drain and set aside.

Place the chicken stock and coconut milk in a medium saucepan and bring to a boil. Stir in the curry powder and salt. Simmer 2 minutes.

Place the coconut strips in an ungreased frying pan and stir over medium heat 3 to 4 minutes, until the coconut is browned.

To assemble the soup, stir the drained spaghetti or vermicelli into the stock and coconut milk mixture. Add the shredded chicken if using.

Ladle the soup into individual bowls and garnish each bowl with coconut strips and cilantro leaves.

NOTES AND AFTERTHOUGHTS

1. Canned coconut milk is available in the international food section of most supermarkets. Dried coconut strips are available in produce markets.

2. To serve the soup as a meal, use the shredded chicken and double the amount of noodles.

Plenty for 6

20 minutes or less

We came upon Burmese-Style Chicken Curry Soup separately at a tiny Burmese restaurant and each instantly fell madly, unforgettably in love with it. This was especially unusual for Susanna, who doesn't much care for any soup. We couldn't rest until we had unraveled the puzzle of its compelling, creamy taste. Finally, we summoned the courage to ask the chef what was in it and found out the mystery ingredient. Not a complex white sauce, nor even cream, but coconut milk! How simple, how easy. In a trice, you too can have an unforgettable soup.

It is best not to cook noodles, rice, or matzoh balls in your soup. Simmer them separately in a pot of their own and add them later. Such elements boiled in the soup muddy the broth and make it starchy-tasting.

Mushroom Essence Soup

6 ounces fresh shiitake mushrooms or 2 ounces dried
2 pounds cultivated mushrooms
16 cups water
1½ teaspoons salt
½ cup white wine

If using fresh shiitake mushrooms, cut off the stems and set the caps aside. If using dried shiitakes, place in a bowl and add water to cover. Set aside to rehydrate 15 minutes or so. Cut off the stems. Save the soaking water to add to the soup.

Wash the mushrooms and rough chop them in a food processor or with a chef's knife.

Place the chopped mushrooms and shiitake stems in a large pot. Add the water and salt. Bring to a boil over high heat. If you have reserved soaking water, add it. Reduce the heat to low and partially cover the pot. Simmer 2 hours.

While the mushrooms simmer, cut the shiitake mushroom caps into thin slices.

When the soup has simmered 2 hours, strain it into a clean pot. Let the mushroom pieces cool in the strainer a few minutes if necessary. Then place them in a cloth or square of cheesecloth. Wring all of their juices into the soup liquid. Discard the mushroom pieces. Add the sliced shiitakes and wine to the soup. Bring to a boil and simmer 15 minutes.

To serve, ladle the soup into individual bowls, making sure each bowl has several slices of mushroom floating in it.

NOTES AND AFTERTHOUGHTS

If you can't find fresh or dried shiitake mushrooms, you can still make a rich Mushroom Essence Soup. You will need an extra ½ pound of cultivated mushrooms to slice and cook in the soup in place of the shiitake caps. In addition, add 1 cup hearty beef stock or canned beef bouillon while cooking the mushroom pieces. If you use canned beef bouillon, omit the salt.

≡ You can considerably reduce the time it takes to make Mushroom Essence Soup with a pressure cooker. Follow the recipe and cook the mushroom pieces 40 minutes. Reduce the pressure, remove the lid, and boil another 20 minutes. Strain. Add the mushroom slices and wine and cook under pressure 5 minutes more.

≈ You can also save time by making this soup in a microwave oven. The timing is the same as for pressure cooking.

DISHES FROM OTHER CHAPTERS THAT MAKE GOOD TREATS AND NIBBLES

Just as many treats and nibbles make savory, satisfying dinners, many dinner dishes make tempting appetizers. Pizzas, grills, stovetop sautés, and light tacos—in bite-size portions, of course—pique the palate and spark the appetite. For instance, try:

Beef Fajita, page 91
Chicken Fajita, page 95
Fresh or Grilled Vegetables, hot or cold, page 176. Try with:
  Brie Cheese Filling, page 41
  Chick Pea Paste, page 45
  Curry Yogurt Sauce, page 162
  Greek Sour Cream or Yogurt Sauce, page 70
  Yogurt and Feta Cheese Dip, page 46
  Vietnamese-Style Dipping Sauce, page 107
Garlic Horseradish Sauce, especially for sliced leftover meats, page 149
Garlic Pine Nut Paste, with hot, soft bread, vegetables, or cold leftover meats, page 247
Grilled Oysters, page 175
Guacamole, with Homemade Tortilla Chips, page 86
Quail with Pepper and Sage, hot or cold, page 203
Pizzas, any of them, see the pizza chapter. You can make tiny individual pizzas or cut larger pizzas into small appetizer slices, page 57
Pork Carnitas, page 92
Quesadillas, page 104
Salsa, any of them except the Melon Salsa, with Homemade Tortilla Chips, page 82
Shrimp and Mussels Sautéed with Celery and Tarragon, page 207
Spicy Pecan Sauce, with cold meats, or soft French bread, page 159
Vietnamese-Style Taco, with or without the tortilla, page 106

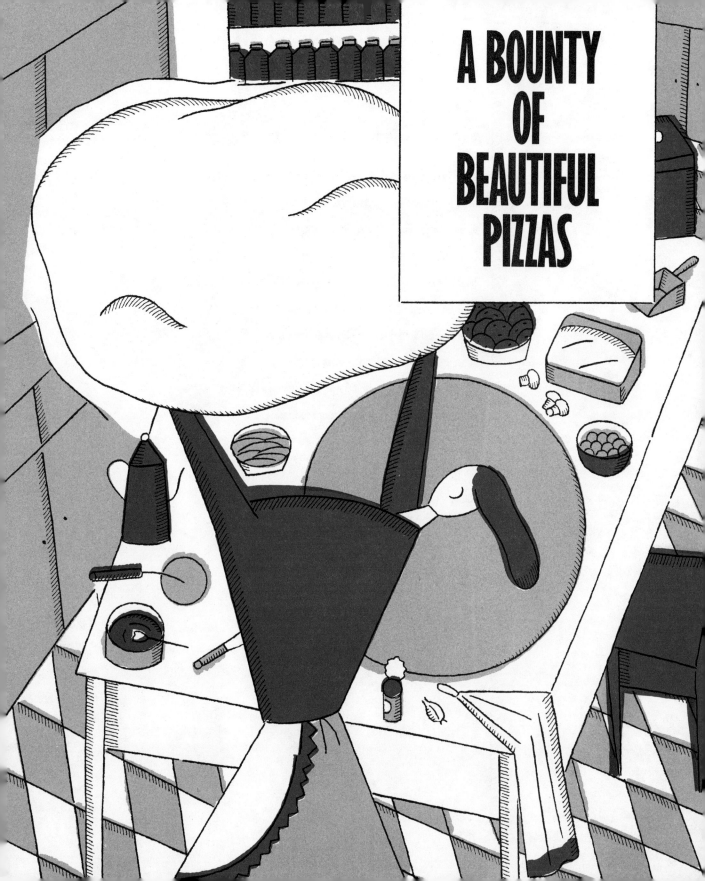

A BOUNTY
OF
BEAUTIFUL
PIZZAS

Basic Pizza Dough
French Bread Pizza Crust

Red Pizza Sauce

Green Bell Pepper, Caper, and Quick Sweet Sausage Pizza
Quick Sweet Sausage

Quick Sweet Sausage, Mushroom, and Black Olive Pizza

Ham, Artichoke Heart, and Fontina Cheese Pizza

Bacon, Tomato, Zucchini, and Garlic Pizza

Eggplant and Feta Cheese Pizza with Red Pizza Sauce

Tex-Mex Pizza with Green Chilies, Cheese, and Tomatoes

Fried Onion and Garlic Pizza with Mushrooms and Basil

Fried Onion, Bacon, Fontina Cheese, and Pecan Pizza

Parsnip, Parmesan, and Parsley Pizza

Red Chard, Smoked Ham, and Gorgonzola Cheese Pizza

Greek-Style Pizza with Lamb, Tomato, and Greek Sour Cream or Yogurt Sauce
Greek Sour Cream or Yogurt Sauce

Salmon, Caper, and Onion Pizza with Sour Cream Sauce
Sour Cream Sauce

Scallop Pizza with Red Pizza Sauce

Mussel or Oyster Pizza with Shallot, Celery, Carrot, and Thyme

izza! Along with hamburgers, hot dogs, and ice cream cones, it's America's favorite food. And while we all think of going to pizza parlors or having one delivered, the only way to get the choice ones, the ones with fresh food, with your favorite ingredients, is to make them yourself. That's why more and more people are making pizza at home. Tomato-and- cheese-maybe-a-little-sausage-or-green-pepper-pizza has given way to innovative toppings your Italian grandmother probably never dreamed of.

Pizza is quick, easy, and inexpensive to make. Very small amounts of topping make enough to feed six people in a most satisfying manner. Often leftover bits and pieces from your refrigerator, along with a jar of something from the cupboard are all you need. It takes only an hour or so to make your own dough, which suffers not at all from being made ahead of time or frozen. In a pinch, halves of French or Italian bread, soft centers removed, can also serve as pizza crust. Assembling the pizza takes a mere 20 minutes, or less.

There's no need to be put off by talk of paddles, peels, and lining your oven with bricks to obtain just the right texture. The new pizza pans with holes all over the bottom surface (about $8) ensure a crisp and evenly cooked crust in a matter of minutes. Then again, you can make pizza with no special equipment. As long as you have an oven that heats to a good hot 500°F, a cookie sheet will turn out a fine pizza.

Since pizza is really an open-faced edible platter, keep in mind that you can put two or more combinations on the same pie and please your guests' differing prejudices. If you have a young curmudgeon who insists on salami only, you can put oysters on the other side. And while pizza makes a wonderful hot meal, cold pizza is a leftover-lover's delight. Some are even good for breakfast. Try the Fried Onion, Bacon, Fontina Cheese, and Pecan Pizza with your morning coffee.

Most home-size round pizza pans are 14 inches in diameter; cookie sheets average about 11 by 14 inches. These pizza recipes are written for these pans, yielding enough to feed three people. Pizzas are done when the crust is golden and the toppings are bubbling. We give a baking time for all our pizza recipes. But remember, depending on the thickness and moisture of the ingredients, the temperature of your oven, and the altitude, you may have to cook the pizza a minute or two more. A microwave oven won't work for baking pizza. The crust remains soggy. ■

Makes two 14-inch
pizzas

20 minutes or less
plus 1 to 1½ hours
rising time

"Hard" flour, such as that made from durum wheat, is often so hard and coarse it can only be milled into semolina for dried pasta noodles. Slightly less coarse, but still hard, flour serves to make bread dough. "Soft" flour, on the other hand, is so crumbly and high in starch, it works only for cakes. Full-time cooks and homemakers who used to make all of their own baked products from honey buns to macaroni had to keep a selection of two or three types of flour. For most of us today, flour has sifted down to the "all-purpose" variety. All-purpose flour is a blend of hard and soft flours and is meant to serve a wide range of uses. With it you can make bread, though not as tasty as with the harder bread flour, and you can make cakes, though not as fine as you can with delicate cake flour. All-purpose flour, like other flours, is naturally a mottled light yellow color. What makes flour evenly white is bleaching. Bleaching adds no nutrients, and since it destroys the small amount of vitamin E that flour contains, we recommend the unbleached.

Pizza dough is often made with hard flour so that the crust will have a little crunch and crackle and not be too bready. Adding a small amount of cornmeal to all-purpose flour achieves the same end.

Basic Pizza Dough

½ cup lukewarm water
Active dry yeast (about 1½ packages)
½ teaspooon sugar
3 cups unbleached all-purpose flour
¼ cup cornmeal
1 teaspoon salt
2 tablespoons olive oil
1 cup tepid water
Extra flour for rolling out dough
Oil to coat bowl and dough

Pour the lukewarm water into a small bowl. Sprinkle in the yeast and sugar. Set aside in a warm place while measuring out the remaining ingredients.

In a large mixing bowl, blend the flour, cornmeal, and salt with a fork. Add the oil, yeast mixture, and tepid water. Mix with a wooden spoon until the dough comes together. If the dough sticks to the sides of the bowl, sprinkle on a little more flour until it is dry enough to pull away. If the dough is too dry to cohere, add a little more water. The dough should be moist and soft, and still a little sticky.

Place the dough on a lightly floured surface and knead for 1 or 2 minutes.

Wipe out the mixing bowl with a dry cloth or paper towel. Lightly oil the inside of the bowl. Place the dough in the bowl and turn it over once or twice to coat with the oil. Set aside, uncovered, in a warm place until the dough doubles in size, 1 to 1½ hours.

Punch down the dough and divide into 2 balls.

To make one 14-inch round or one 11- by 14-inch rectangular pizza crust, use 1 ball of dough. On a lightly floured surface, roll out the dough into a circle or rectangle ⅛ inch thick. Press the dough into the baking pan.

NOTES AND AFTERTHOUGHTS

You can use the pizza dough right away or wrap the balls in plastic wrap and refrigerate. To keep longer, freeze. Use within 2 days after defrosting.

French Bread Pizza Crust

French bread makes a fast pizza crust. A 1-pound loaf takes the same amount of topping ingredients as one 14-inch pizza.

Cut the bread in half lengthwise and open it out like a long sandwich. Remove the soft centers.

Build the pizza as described in the recipe instructions. You will have a thicker crust than when you are using the Basic Pizza Dough.

NOTES AND AFTERTHOUGHTS

If you are using French bread for a pizza crust, cover the pizza with foil for the first half of baking to prevent the edges of the bread from burning.

For fast pizza, you can also buy packaged pizza crust. See the margin note for suggestions.

We have sampled most packaged and frozen pizza crusts. Boboli brand, available in the freezer section of many supermarkets, is an outstanding product, and while not as good as our own homemade crust, it serves as a worthy backup in times of need. We prefer it over French bread for a quick crust. Boboli comes in two sizes. Two of the large or 4 of the small provide enough crust for the amount of topping in any of our pizza recipes.

Red Pizza Sauce

Red pizza sauce isn't a horse of one color. It can be used for spaghetti, as an accompaniment for fish, or as a basting sauce for barbecued chicken or ribs.

Makes 5 cups
Plenty for six 14-inch pizzas

40 to 60 minutes

1 medium onion (about 7 ounces)
5 medium garlic cloves
⅓ cup olive oil
5 cups canned crushed tomatoes in puree (about 1½ 28-ounce cans)
1 tablespoon chopped fresh oregano leaves or 1 teaspoon dried
½ teaspoon dried basil
1 bay leaf
2 tablespoons chopped fresh parsley leaves
¼ teaspoon grated nutmeg
⅛ teaspoon cayenne pepper
1 cup dry, hearty red wine

Peel the onion and garlic. Fine chop the onion and garlic in a food processor or with a chef's knife.

Heat the oil in a nonreactive medium saucepan. Add the onions and garlic and cook over medium-low heat until wilted, about 10 minutes.

Add the tomatoes, oregano, basil, bay leaf, parsley, nutmeg, cayenne, and red wine. Stir and simmer, uncovered, for 30 minutes. If the sauce is watery, increase the heat and cook a few minutes more, until thickened.

NOTES AND AFTERTHOUGHTS

1. Our red sauce for pizza is good right away, but like many cooked tomato sauces, it is even better if the flavors have time to blend at least overnight. Try to make it ahead, if you have a chance. It will last for a week in the refrigerator or up to 6 months in the freezer. For storing hints see the larder section, page 22.

2. We use dried basil for this recipe because fresh basil does not stand up to long simmering.

(continued)

3. This sauce is remarkably quick and easy to make. However, if you are really pressed for time, you can use one of the better brands of ready-made pizza sauces zipped up with herbs of your choice. Contadina and Progresso brands are both good and widely available.

Green Bell Pepper, Caper, and Quick Sweet Sausage Pizza

Makes one 14-inch pizza
Plenty for 3

20 to 40 minutes

Using ground pork, it takes only a few minutes to make fresh sausage, with *no nitrates*. All you need is the pork and herbs. Mix up a batch to have on hand and you will find you can use it for many dishes besides pizza—breakfast patties, baked potato fillings, meatballs, or pasta sauce.

Dough or bread for pizza crust (page 60)
½ pound Quick Sweet Sausage (see below)
1 medium green bell pepper (about 6 ounces)
¾ cup Red Pizza Sauce (page 61)
1 tablespoon capers
⅓ cup grated Parmesan, Romano, aged Asiago, or other hard cheese

Heat the oven to 500 ° F. Prepare the pizza crust.

Make the Quick Sweet Sausage.

Quarter the bell pepper lengthwise and remove the seeds and core. Cut each quarter crosswise into ⅛-inch-thick slices.

To assemble the pizza, spread the Red Pizza Sauce over the crust. Crumble the sausage evenly over the sauce. Arrange the bell pepper slices over the sausage. Sprinkle the capers and cheese over the sausage.

Bake 15 to 18 minutes, until the crust is golden.

Quick Sweet Sausage

Makes ½ pound
Plenty for one 14-inch pizza

20 minutes or less

This sausage will keep in the refrigerator 5 or 6 days without freezing. There is a special trick to storing it. To prevent its breaking down and becoming sticky, keep it in a glass, stainless steel, or ceramic—*not plastic*—bowl. Cover loosely to allow air circulation. Or you can wrap it first in waxed paper, then in plastic wrap.

½ pound ground pork
1 small garlic clove
½ tablespoon minced fresh chives or green onion tops
1 teaspoon chopped fresh sage leaves or ¼ teaspoon rubbed dried sage
1 teaspoon chopped fresh oregano or ¼ teaspoon dried
⅛ teaspoon fennel seed
½ teaspoon salt
⅛ teaspoon freshly ground black pepper

Place the ground pork in a bowl. Peel the garlic and chop it fine. Add the garlic, chives, sage, oregano, fennel seed, salt, and pepper to the pork. With your hands, mix to blend well without mashing the meat. If not using right away, cover with plastic wrap and refrigerate.

NOTES AND AFTERTHOUGHTS

1. If your store has good sausage already prepared and you are pressed for time, you can use store-bought sausage.

2. For quick homemade pork and chicken sausage, see Sausage Burgers, page 155.

Quick Sweet Sausage, Mushroom, and Black Olive Pizza

Dough or bread for pizza crust (page 60)
Oil to coat crust

½ pound Quick Sweet Sausage (page 62)
½ pound fresh mushrooms
1 cup Kalamata or other good black olives
½ medium red bell pepper (about 3 ounces), or ½ pound cherry tomatoes, or ¾ cup
   Red Pizza Sauce (page 61)
3 tablespoons olive oil
⅓ cup grated Parmesan, Romano, aged Asiago or other hard cheese

Heat the oven to 500°F. Prepare the pizza crust and coat it with oil.

Make the Quick Sweet Sausage.

Clean the mushrooms and trim off the stem ends. Slice the mushrooms ¼ inch thick. Pit the olives and cut them in half.

If using red bell pepper, quarter it lengthwise; remove seeds and core. Cut the quarters into very thin strips. If using tomatoes, halve them.

To assemble the pizza, coat the crust with Red Pizza Sauce if you are using it. Otherwise, crumble the sausage evenly over the crust. Arrange the mushrooms, olives, and bell pepper or tomatoes over the sausage. Drizzle on the olive oil. Sprinkle the grated cheese on top. Bake 15 minutes, until the crust is golden.

Makes one 14-inch pizza
Plenty for 3

20 to 40 minutes

With this pizza you have a number of choices. You can make it like a traditional pizza with a red pizza sauce. You can use fresh tomatoes. Or you can make a lighter version using fresh red peppers instead. It all depends on what you like and what you have handy. Usually, we prefer red peppers. Then again, sometimes we prefer tomatoes. But our kids always like red sauce.

If you don't have Kalamata or other good olives, you can spruce up American canned olives by tossing them with I teaspoon red wine or sherry vinegar and I minced garlic clove.

Ham, Artichoke Heart, and Fontina Cheese Pizza

Dough or bread for pizza crust (page 60)
Oil to coat crust

2 medium garlic cloves
½ pound thin-sliced mild ham
1 jar (6 ounces) marinated artichoke hearts
¼ teaspoon fresh rosemary or ⅛ teaspoon dried
1½ cups shredded Fontina cheese (about 10 ounces)
⅓ cup grated Parmesan or Romano cheese

Preheat the oven to 500°F. Prepare the pizza crust and coat it with oil.

Peel the garlic. Cut the ham into ¼-inch-wide strips. Drain the artichoke hearts, and cut them into quarters.

To assemble the pizza, press the garlic, and rub it over the crust. Sprinkle on the rosemary, and then the Fontina cheese. Layer the strips of ham over the cheese. Arrange the artichoke hearts over the ham. Sprinkle the grated cheese over all.

Bake 15 minutes, until the crust is golden.

Makes one 14-inch pizza
Plenty for 3

20 minutes or less

Nothing in the refrigerator? Not so. You have a few slices of ham, a hunk of Fontina, and there's a jar of artichoke hearts in the pantry. You don't have to go to the store. You can make a pizza.

(continued)

The garlic and oil base of this pizza make it spectacularly good on halved French bread, but remember to cover with foil for the first 7 minutes.

Bacon, Tomato, Zucchini, and Garlic Pizza

Dough or bread for pizza crust (page 60)
Oil to coat crust

2 medium tomatoes (about ½ pound)
3 small zucchini (about 5 ounces)
6 slices bacon (about 6 ounces)
1 large garlic clove
2 teaspoons fresh or ¾ teaspoon dried tarragon leaves
½ cup shredded mozzarella cheese
¼ cup shredded Provolone cheese

Heat the oven to 500°F. Prepare the pizza crust and coat it with oil.

Slice the tomatoes and zucchini into ¼-inch-thick rounds. Cut the bacon strips into 1-inch squares.

To assemble the pizza, peel the garlic. Press the garlic, and rub it over the crust. Arrange the tomato and zucchini slices over the garlic. Sprinkle on the tarragon. Spread the shredded cheeses over the tomatoes and zucchini. Arrange the bacon over the cheese. Bake 15 minutes, until the crust is golden.

NOTES AND AFTERTHOUGHTS
There's a wealth of cold cuts you can substitute for the bacon on this pizza. Try ham, pancetta, capocollo, or salami.

Eggplant and Feta Cheese Pizza with Red Pizza Sauce

Dough or bread for pizza crust (page 60)
Oil to coat crust

2 Japanese or ½ medium eggplant (about ½ pound)
6 tablespoons olive oil
1½ teaspoons chopped fresh oregano leaves or ½ teaspoon dried
Salt
¾ cup Red Pizza Sauce (page 61)
⅓ cup Feta cheese (about 2 ounces)
2 tablespoons very thin-sliced fresh basil leaves or chopped fresh chives

Heat the oven to 500° F. Prepare the pizza crust and coat it with oil.

Trim off the stem end and cut the eggplant into ¼-inch-thick slices.

Makes one 14-inch pizza
Plenty for 3

20 minutes or less

Michele, the pizza maker at Chez Panisse restaurant, loves children. When twirling his pies above his head, he can be quite diffident toward the crowds of patrons, but when besieged by a gaggle of children, he changes. He sits the children on the counter by the trays of ingredients. He pulls chairs over by the oven and lets them help hold the paddle as he slides the pies onto the hot bricks. He twirls pizzas for them, and, when a hiatus in the orders comes, he lets them create their own pies from whatever ingredients he has. The children may not think of bacon, zucchini, and garlic as the best pizza combo, but they happily devour it once they've made it themselves.

Makes one 14-inch pizza
Plenty for 3

20 to 40 minutes

Heat the 6 tablespoons of oil in a skillet large enough to hold the eggplant in a single layer. Add the eggplant slices. Sprinkle on the oregano and season lightly with salt. Fry over medium heat 5 or 6 minutes. Turn and fry 5 or 6 minutes more, until soft and browned. Add a little more oil if the pieces are sticking.

To assemble the pizza, spread the Red Pizza Sauce over the crust. Arrange the eggplant slices over the sauce. Crumble the Feta over the eggplant. Bake 15 to 18 minutes, until the crust is golden.

When the pizza is done, sprinkle the basil over the top and serve.

Tex-Mex Pizza with Green Chilies, Cheese, and Tomatoes

Dough or bread for pizza crust (page 60)
Oil to coat crust

4 fresh Anaheim chilies, or 1 cup canned roasted green chilies
⅔ cup shredded Jack cheese
⅔ cup shredded sharp cheddar cheese
2 medium or 4 small fresh tomatoes (about ½ pound)
1 tablespoon chopped fresh oregano leaves or 1 teaspoon dried
¼ teaspoon cayenne pepper, or to taste
⅓ cup grated Parmesan or Romano, or crumbled Feta or Cotija cheese

Heat the oven to 500°F. Prepare the pizza crust and coat it with oil.

If using fresh chilies, roast and peel them (page 47). Remove the seeds and core. Cut the chilies into ¼- by 1-inch strips. If using canned chilies, cut them the same way.

To assemble the pizza, spread the chilies over the crust. Top with the shredded cheeses.

Slice the tomatoes into ¼-inch-wide rounds. Arrange over the cheese in circles or an overlapping spiral. Sprinkle on the oregano and cayenne. Top with the grated cheese.

Bake 15 minutes, until the crust is golden.

NOTES AND AFTERTHOUGHTS
Large, mild Anaheim chilies are available fresh just about everywhere now, and they are perfect for this pizza. But you also can used canned roasted chilies. We suggest Ortega brand.

Makes one 14-inch pizza
Plenty for 3

20 minutes or less

This pizza was invented for Susanna's brother-in-law, a six-foot-six, Texas-born outdoorsman who has been known to eat three pizzas at one sitting without gaining an ounce. It's a Tex-Mex twist on an Italian theme—a cheese lover's pizza, Southwest style, with roasted green chilies.

Fried Onion and Garlic Pizza with Mushrooms and Basil

*Makes one 14-inch
pizza
Plenty for 3*

20 to 40 minutes

Precooking the onions
makes a quite different
pizza than when they are
used raw. Precooked,
they come out sweet,
swimming in their own
gravy, with a jamlike
texture. This onion jam
makes a rich-tasting base
for pizza, eliminating the
need for tomato or red
sauce, somewhat like the
French *pissaladière*.

Dough or bread for pizza crust (page 60)
Oil to coat crust

4 medium onions (about 1¾ pounds)
2 tablespoons olive oil
6 garlic cloves
½ pound fresh mushrooms
3 tablespoons thinly sliced fresh basil leaves
⅓ cup grated Parmesan, Romano, aged Asiago, or other hard cheese

Heat the oven to 500° F. Prepare the pizza crust and coat it with oil.

Peel the onions. Cut them in half, then cut the halves crosswise into ⅛-inch-thick slices. Heat the 2 tablespoons oil in a large skillet. Add the onions and fry on medium-high heat. Peel and rough chop the garlic, then add to the onions. Cook, stirring, about 10 minutes, or until quite brown. Reduce the heat to low and continue cooking 5 minutes more.

Clean the mushrooms and trim the stem ends. Cut into ¼-inch-thick slices.

To assemble the pizza, spread the onions and garlic over the crust. Arrange the mushrooms on top. Sprinkle on the basil. Top with the grated cheese. Bake 15 minutes, until the crust is golden.

NOTES AND AFTERTHOUGHTS
For a spicier version of fried onions to use on this pizza, see the next recipe, page 67.

Fried Onion, Bacon, Fontina Cheese, and Pecan Pizza

Dough or bread for pizza crust (page 60)
Oil to coat crust

4 medium onions (about 1¾ pounds)
2 tablespoons olive oil
2 teaspoons chopped fresh sage leaves or ½ teaspoon dried rubbed sage
1 teaspoon paprika, preferably Hungarian
⅛ teaspoon cayenne pepper
½ teaspoon salt
1 teaspoon sherry or red wine vinegar
¾ cup shredded Fontina cheese
6 slices bacon (about 6 ounces)
¼ cup minced pecans
1½ teaspoons chopped fresh sage leaves or ¼ teaspoon dried rubbed sage

Heat the oven to 500°F. Prepare the pizza crust and coat it with oil.

Peel the onions. Cut them in half, then cut the halves crosswise into ¼-inch-thick slices.

Heat the oil in a large skillet. Add the onions, 2 teaspoons sage, the paprika, cayenne, and salt. Cook over medium-high heat about 10 minutes, until the onions are soft and browned. Stir in the vinegar and cook 1 or 2 minutes more.

To assemble the pizza, spread the cooked onions over the crust. Sprinkle the Fontina over the onions.

Slice the bacon strips crosswise at ½-inch intervals. Arrange the bacon over the cheese and onion. Sprinkle on 1½ teaspoons sage. Top with the pecans.

Bake 15 to 18 minutes, until the crust is golden.

NOTES AND AFTERTHOUGHTS
Be sure to use regular bacon, not thick sliced, on this pizza. While regular slices cook through in 15 to 18 minutes, thick slices do not.

Makes one 14-inch pizza
Plenty for 3

20 to 40 minutes

The combination of cayenne fried onions with bacon and pecans gives this pizza a Louisiana flair. It calls to mind the old town square in New Orleans and the aroma of chicory coffee, which is why we like it for breakfast.

Parsnip, Parmesan, and Parsley Pizza

Dough or bread for pizza crust (page 60)
Oil to coat pizza crust

1½ to 2 pounds parsnips, if possible frozen for several hours then thawed
2 large garlic cloves
½ cup olive oil
⅔ cup coarsely shredded Parmesan cheese
2 tablespoons minced walnuts
1½ cups fresh parsley leaves, preferably Italian
¾ teaspoon sherry or red wine vinegar
1 tablespoon olive oil
Salt
Freshly ground black pepper

Heat the oven to 500°F. Prepare the pizza crust and coat it with oil.

Peel the parsnips with a potato peeler and trim off the ends. Halve the parsnips lengthwise. Slice the halves into half rounds about ⅛ inch thick. Peel and rough chop the garlic.

Heat the ½ cup oil in a medium skillet. Add the parsnips and garlic and fry until soft and browned, about 12 minutes. If pieces stick to the bottom, use a spatula to loosen and add a little more oil.

To assemble the pizza, arrange the parsnips over the prepared crust. Shred the Parmesan cheese through the large holes of a hand grater or food processor. Scatter the cheese and walnuts over the parsnips. Bake 18 minutes, or until the crust is golden.

While the pizza bakes, wash and dry the parsley leaves. In a small bowl, toss them with the vinegar, the 1 tablespoon oil, and salt and pepper to taste.

When the pizza is done, sprinkle the parsley over the top and serve.

Makes one 14-inch pizza
Plenty for 3

20 to 40 minutes

What? Freeze your parsnips? Yes, yes, yes.

Lying dormant in the core of this much maligned root is a delicious sweet and nutty flavor that only cold releases. That's why in parts of Europe parsnips aren't harvested until after the first frost. You can get the same effect city-style. Just toss them in your freezer for a few hours.

Red Chard, Smoked Ham, and Gorgonzola Cheese Pizza

Dough or bread for pizza crust (page 60)
Olive oil to coat crust

1½ pounds fresh red chard
2 medium garlic cloves
3 tablespoons olive oil
½ teaspoon sherry or red wine vinegar
6 ounces thin-sliced mild smoked ham
⅓ cup Gorgonzola cheese (about 6 ounces)

Heat the oven to 500°F. Prepare the pizza crust and coat it with oil.

Cut the chard crosswise into ½-inch strips including the tender part of the stems. Wash in plenty of cold water and transfer to a colander to drain.

Heat the oil in a large frying pan. Add as much of the moist chard as will fit into the pan and stir over medium heat until wilted. As you stir, add the remaining chard. Peel and crush the garlic. Add to the chard. Stir in the vinegar and reduce the heat to low. Continue cooking until most of the moisture has evaporated, about 10 minutes. Remove the chard to a colander and set aside.

Cut the ham into ½-inch squares.

To assemble the pizza, spread the chard over the crust. Scatter the ham squares over the chard and crumble the Gorgonzola over the top.

Bake 18 minutes, until the crust is golden and the cheese just starts to melt.

NOTES AND AFTERTHOUGHTS

1. This pizza takes a little longer to cook because of the moist chard.

2. If you can't find Gorgonzola cheese, substitute any creamy blue cheese, such as Danish or Bavarian Blue.

3. The chard can be prepared several hours or overnight in advance.

Makes one 14-inch pizza
Plenty for 3

20 to 40 minutes

Unfamiliar to many cooks, chard is a member of the beet family bred for its leaves rather than its root. It comes in two colors, red and green. The red chard is a bit more tender, but both are delectable and, amazingly, work well on a pizza.

For another version of sautéed chard that would be good on a pizza, see page 211.

Greek-Style Pizza with Lamb, Tomato, and Greek Sour Cream or Yogurt Sauce

*Makes one 14-inch
pizza
Plenty for 3*

20 to 40 minutes

When Susanna returned from her anthropology field work in Greece, she sorely missed the *souvlaki* of spiced meat with garlic, cucumber, and yogurt *tzatziki* sauce she used to get from the little stands in the towns and cities. This truly wonderful pizza is a recreation of that enchanting flavor combination.

1½ cups Greek Sour Cream or Yogurt Sauce (see below)

Dough or bread for pizza crust (page 60)
Oil to coat crust
¾ pound ground lamb
2 medium garlic cloves
½ teaspoon chopped fresh oregano or ¼ teaspoon dried
½ teaspoon chopped fresh thyme or ¼ teaspoon dried
1 tablespoon olive oil
¼ teaspoon salt
¼ teaspoon freshly ground black pepper
2 or 3 medium tomatoes (about ½ pound)
½ cup grated Kasseri, Parmesan, Romano, aged Asiago, or other hard cheese
½ medium onion (about 4 ounces)

Make Greek Sour Cream or Yogurt Sauce so flavors have time to blend.

Heat the oven to 500°F. Prepare the pizza crust and coat it with oil.

Place the lamb in a mixing bowl. Peel the garlic, fine chop it, and add the garlic, oregano, thyme, oil, salt, and pepper to the lamb. Knead together. Set aside.

Slice the tomatoes into ⅛-inch-thick rounds.

To assemble the pizza, spread the tomatoes over the crust. Crumble the meat mixture over the tomatoes. Sprinkle on the grated cheese.

Bake 15 minutes, until the crust is golden.

While the pizza bakes, peel and cut the onion into very thin half rounds.

When the pizza is done, top with the onion. Cut the pizza. Spoon a generous amount of sauce on each slice and serve.

Greek Sour Cream or Yogurt Sauce

Makes 1½ cups

Chopping garlic in salt tones down the ammonia flavor while it sharpens the bite. It's a nice touch and really makes this sauce special.

½ teaspoon salt
2 garlic cloves
1 cup sour cream or plain yogurt
1 tablespoon red wine vinegar
¼ teaspoon freshly ground black pepper
½ medium cucumber

Place the salt on a chopping board. Peel the garlic, then chop it in the salt. In a bowl, stir the sour cream or yogurt until creamy. Add the garlic and salt, vinegar, and pepper.

Peel cucumber. Shred in a grater. Stir into sauce. Chill before serving.

NOTES AND AFTERTHOUGHTS
The sauce gets even better if it sits several hours or overnight. If you have a chance, make it ahead of time.

Salmon, Caper, and Onion Pizza with Sour Cream Sauce

Dough or bread for pizza crust (page 60)
Oil to coat pizza crust

1 medium onion (about 6 ounces)
3 tablespoons capers
1 tablespoon lemon juice
¼ pound smoked salmon
¾ cup Sour Cream Sauce (see below)

Heat the oven to 500°F. Prepare the pizza crust and coat it with oil.

Peel the onion. Cut in half and slice into ⅛-inch-thick half rounds. Place the onion in a medium bowl. Add the capers and lemon juice and toss. Spread the onions and capers over the crust.

Bake 15 minutes, until the crust is golden.

While the pizza bakes, cut the salmon into ½-inch-wide strips. Set aside.

When the crust is done, arrange the salmon over the onions and capers. Top with the Sour Cream Sauce.

NOTES AND AFTERTHOUGHTS

You don't have to use expensive sliced salmon for this pizza. You can use the inexpensive ends and pieces as well. They taste just as good and with the sour cream sauce, they can be arranged to look pretty. Try drizzling the sauce over the pizza in an artistic pattern: zigzags, latticework, or just plain Jackson Pollock.

Sour Cream Sauce

½ cup sour cream
4 tablespoons heavy cream
3 teaspoons chopped fresh tarragon or dill or ¾ teaspoon dried

In a small bowl, mix together the sour cream, heavy cream, and tarragon or dill.

Makes one 14-inch pizza
Plenty for 3

20 minutes or less

The word "supper" conjures thoughts of candlelight. Often it's a late meal, well after the normal dinner hour, when you want to eat lightly and elegantly. We think of this pizza as a supper one. With a fresh green salad it makes perfect late-evening fare.

Makes 1½ cups

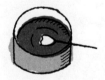

Scallop Pizza with Red Pizza Sauce

Makes one 14-inch pizza
Plenty for 3

20 minutes or less

Being both seafood and pizza lovers, we rack our brains over how to put the two together. Seafood often doesn't work as a pizza topping. It dries out well before the crust is cooked. One day Victoria had scallops in the fridge so we tried them on a pizza. Eureka, along with smoked salmon and mussels, another fabulous exception! Sliced thick enough, scallops remain moist and succulent and make a very special, simple and elegant pizza.

Dough or bread for pizza crust (page 60)

½ pound large sea scallops
1 tablespoon lemon juice
1 medium onion (about 6 ounces)
1 tablespoon olive oil
Pinch of salt
¾ cup Red Pizza Sauce (page 61)
16 whole fresh tarragon leaves or tiny sprigs or ½ teaspoon dried

Heat the oven to 500°F. Prepare the pizza crust.

Slice the scallops into ½-inch-thick rounds and toss with the lemon juice.

Peel the onion and quarter lengthwise. Cut each quarter into ¼-inch-thick slices. Toss the onions with the oil and salt.

To assemble the pizza, spread the Red Pizza Sauce over the crust. Arrange the whole tarragon leaves over the sauce or sprinkle on the dried tarragon. Scatter the onion slices over the surface. Top with the scallops.

Bake 15 minutes, until the crust just starts to turn golden.

NOTES AND AFTERTHOUGHTS

This recipe works best with large, plump sea scallops. They don't overcook while the pizza bakes.

Mussel or Oyster Pizza with Shallot, Celery, Carrot, and Thyme

Dough or bread for pizza crust (page 60)
Olive oil to coat crust

2 pounds mussels, or 24 fresh medium-size oysters, shucked
2 tablespoons olive oil
2 large shallots
2 celery ribs
1 teaspoon fresh thyme leaves or ¼ teaspoon dried
3 tablespoons chopped fresh parsley or chives
1 large carrot
⅓ cup grated Romano, Parmesan, aged Asiago, or other hard cheese

Heat the oven to 500°F. Prepare the pizza crust and coat it with oil.

If using mussels, pull off the beards. Place the mussels in a colander, rinse under cold water, and set aside to drain.

Heat the 2 tablespoons oil in a large skillet or pot over medium heat. Add the mussels, cover (the lid doesn't have to fit tightly), and cook, stirring once or twice, for about 6 minutes, or just until the shells open. Set aside to cool. When cooled, remove mussels from the shells. Discard any that do not open.

If using oysters out of a jar, drain them.

Chop the shallots and celery. Place in a small bowl and stir in the thyme and parsley or chives. Peel the carrot and cut it into thin strips.

To assemble the pizza, spread the shallot and celery mixture over the crust. Arrange the mussels or oysters over the vegetables. Scatter the carrot strips over the shellfish. Sprinkle the grated cheese over all.

Bake for 13 to 15 minutes, until the crust is barely golden, to avoid overcooking the shellfish.

NOTES AND AFTERTHOUGHTS

You can use a microwave oven to steam mussels. Arrange them in one layer and cover with microwave wrap. The timing is the same as for stovetop cooking.

Makes one 14-inch pizza
Plenty for 3

20 to 40 minutes

The farm-raised mussels available in markets today are so clean you usually don't have to scrub them or pull off any beards. Just rinse them and pop them into a hot pan. In 5 or 6 minutes they open for the plucking. If you are storing mussels overnight in the refrigerator, be sure to have them in an open container so air can circulate around them. Odd as it seems, they will suffocate if they are stored airtight in a plastic bag.

As for oysters, you don't have to shuck them at all if you have a market that sells fresh shucked oysters in jars. They are a wonderful answer to having oysters any way but on the half shell. No gloves, hammer, or chisel required.

New Spice in Our Lives:
A TABLE FULL OF TACOS

Salsas and Sauces for Tacos
Tomato Salsa
Chive Salsa
Corn and Red Bell Pepper Salsa
Melon and Jalapeño Salsa
Tomatillo Sauce
Ancho Chili Sauce

Taco Toppings
Guacamole
   Victoria's Guacamole
   Susanna's Guacamole
Fried Potatoes
Diced Tomatoes
Shredded Cheese
Shredded Lettuce
Sour Cream

Beef Tacos with Currants and Pine Nuts

Tacos of Grilled Beef Fajita Marinated in Lime and Onion Juice with Grilled Green Onions

Steak, Roasted Red Pepper, Pepperoncini, and Olive Paste Tacos

Pork Carnitas Tacos

Pork Tenderloin, Chili, and Watercress Tacos with Pumpkin Seed Topping

Stewed Chicken Tacos with Tomatillo-Dipped Tortillas

Tacos of Chicken Fajita Rolled in Chili Flakes and Marjoram

Turkey Tacos with Salsa and White Wine

Fried Fish and Roasted Red Bell Pepper Tacos

Salmon with Lime, Cheese, and Sour Cream Tacos

Lobster or Crab Tacos with Pan-Grilled Green Onions

Fried Potato Tacos
  Fried Potatoes and Eggs Northern Style
  Fried Potatoes, Chili Strips, and Canadian Bacon
  Fried Potatoes and Bananas

Vegetables Stewed with White Wine Tacos

Quesadillas or Cheese Tacos
  Basic Quesadillas
  Variations

Mu Shu-Style Tacos with Mock Hoisin Sauce
  Mock Hoisin Sauce

Vietnamese-Style Tacos with Shrimp, Noodles, Lettuce, and Dipping Sauce
  Vietnamese-Style Dipping Sauce

Cool Salads to Go with Hot Tacos
  Orange and Curly Endive Salad
  Wilted Cucumber Salad
  Grated Carrot, Lemon, and Cumin Salad
  Lima Bean and Chick Pea Salad

First you could only get them in New Mexico, Arizona, and Colorado, then in Texas and California. Wherever there were people of Mexican and Central American descent, their cuisine slipped into ours. Now they're in New York, Maine, Georgia, anywhere you go in the U.S.A., and we love their fresh and lively flavor.

More than just ground beef, a red sauce, some sprinkles of cheddar cheese and a brick-hard shell, where tacos come from, they have anything and everything in them. They are a way of eating that's fun, fast, and relaxed. Most of the fillings take less time than a hat dance to make. The toppings and salsas can be whipped out by the time you say "olé." Since the fillings and salsas by and large keep well, you can have the makings on hand in the refrigerator for anytime you want tacos in two minutes. An added boon for modern life is that tacos are the perfect "build your own" food. With tacos, every person at the table or running past the stove on the way to the next meeting or basketball game can add what he or she likes, mix those flavors and toppings preferred, dollop on a favorite sauce or salsa, roll it up, and eat it on the run. Each time you can put together a different combination, spice it as you please, and never get tired of them.

Tacos also serve as a noble way to revitalize leftovers. You can recycle the remains of meats and fish in them. You can pop in lettuce left over from a salad, tomato slices that didn't fit in a sandwich, a deserted chunk of cheese, grated now, or one sorry egg left from a dozen.

Tacos take practically no special ingredients. The only unusual elements are the chili peppers and tortillas, and these are turning up in supermarkets everywhere.

CHILI PEPPERS

A taco is hardly a taco without some form of chili pepper. Some taco fillings have chili peppers right in them, but mostly chilies are used in the salsas and sauces that are the crowning glory of tacos. Some chili peppers are mild and musky, some hot. They come two ways, fresh and dried.

FRESH CHILI PEPPERS

Chili peppers fresh off the plant range from mild to fiery hot. They are the least hot in the spring, and the most hot in summer and fall.

ANAHEIMS —6 to 7 inches long, about 1½ inches wide at the top, tapering at the end. Light green ripening to red. Not at all hot to mildly warm.

FRESNOS —2 to 3 inches long, pointed tips. Green ripening to red. Mildly hot to hot.

JALAPEÑOS —1½ to 2½ inches long, stubby, rounded tip. Green ripening to mottled green and orange. Mildly hot to very hot.

POBLANOS —3 to 5 inches long, rounded, 2 to 3 inches wide at the stem. Dark green ripening to red-brown. Mild to fairly hot.

SANTA FE GRANDES —3 to 4 inches long, 1 inch wide at the stem, curving to a tapered end. Pale green ripening through orange to deep red. Fairly hot to very hot.

SERRANOS —around 1½ inches long, thin, ¼ to ½ inch wide. Green ripening through orange to red. Hot to very hot.

YELLOW WAX —called *Gueros* in Spanish, 1½ to 2½ inches long, 1 inch wide at the top, tapering to a rounded end. Pale yellow to pale green. Fairly hot to hot.

DRIED CHILI PEPPERS

Dried chili peppers range in flavor from sweet through mildly hot to fiery. The only dried chili peppers we use in our recipes are anchos because we like their flavor best and because you don't have to scrape the pulp off the skin once they are moistened and before you puree them, as you do with other dried chilis. If you can't find anchos, you can use pasilla, California, or New Mexico dried chilies. They provide a similarly musky flavor, but they are slightly sweeter, and you must scrape the pulp off the skins before pureeing.

ANCHOS —3½ to 5 inches long, about 3 inches wide. Dark red-brown. Mild to slightly hot. Ancho chilies are the dried form of fresh poblano chilies.

CALIFORNIAS OR NEW MEXICOS —6 to 8 inches long, 1 to 1½ inches wide, tapering to a point. Bright red. Mild. California chilies are the dried form of fresh Anaheim chilies. The dried form is also known as Colorado chilies.

PASILLAS —5 to 7 inches long, about 1 inch wide. Very dark brown to almost black. Mild to warm. Pasilla chilies are also a dried form of poblano chilies.

CHILI FLAKES —come from numerous sorts of dried chilies, including ancho, pasilla, California, Mexico, and New Mexico.

GROUND CHILI OR CHILI POWDER —also comes from many varieties, including the cayenne pepper. When buying ground chili, try to find a pure version and not the kind mixed with cumin.

PREPARING TORTILLAS FOR TACOS

Originally tortillas were made only from corn, and these are the most nutritious kind. Then flour tortillas became popular, even in Mexico. And it's true, flour ones go very well with certain foods. More recently, tortillas of whole wheat and the delicate blue cornmeal of the Southwest have also

We've never found the need to wear rubber gloves when cutting up fresh chili peppers. But do remember not to rub your eyes before washing your hands.

become available. For tacos we prefer corn and white flour tortillas. We suggest in each recipe which kind of tortilla we think goes best.

Standard-size flour tortillas are about 8 inches in diameter. Two well-filled flour tortillas are usually enough for the avid diner. Corn tortillas are about 6½ inches in diameter, slightly smaller than flour tortillas, so we recommend serving 3 corn tortilla tacos per person.

The tortillas for tacos are either slightly crisped or soft and warm. Both ways bring out the tortilla's flavor and make them malleable. Sometimes the tortillas for tacos are dipped into a dish of salsa or sauce before cooking. You can also spread the salsa or sauce over both sides of the tortilla before cooking it. Particularly good for dipping are Tomatillo or Ancho Chili Sauce and Chive or Tomato Salsa. Dipped tortillas add an extra pleasing tang to many tacos, especially those filled with grilled meat and chicken.

To crisp tortillas, you can use a frying pan or griddle, a grill, or place them directly on a stovetop burner:

In a frying pan or on a griddle: Pour 1 teaspoon vegetable or peanut oil into a 9-inch skillet or onto the griddle. When the oil begins to smoke, place the unfolded tortilla in the pan or on the griddle and cook about 1 minute. Turn and cook the other side 1 minute more. You will need to add a little more oil for each round.

To crisp more than one at a time, use a larger pan and 2 to 3 teaspoons of oil, but don't overlap them. You will need to add a little oil for each round.

On the grill: Crisp the tortillas on the grill right along with the meat, chicken, fish, or vegetables. The timing is the same as for pan crisping.

On the burner: Set the heat at medium. Place the tortillas directly on the electric ring or the guard over the gas flame. Leave the tortilla only a few seconds and flip it very fast or it will burn.

When serving a crowd, you can crisp the tortillas ahead, place them in a cloth-covered bowl or basket, and hold them in a warm oven. They stay warm and fairly crisp, but do soften a little.

To warm tortillas until soft, you can use the oven or a steamer:

In the oven: Heat the oven to 400°F. Place the tortillas on the oven rack and leave for 3 minutes.

In a steamer: Stack the tortillas and wrap the stack in a cloth towel or several cloth napkins to enclose completely. Place the wrapped stack in the basket of a vegetable steamer over an inch or so of boiling water. Cover the steamer and leave for 6 to 10 minutes, depending on how many tortillas are in the stack.

Dipped tortillas come out especially well when steamed. Coat them with the sauce or salsa, then stack and steam as described above.

When serving a crowd, you can soften the tortillas ahead, place them in a cloth covered bowl or basket, and hold them in a very low oven.

TO ASSEMBLE TACOS

The assemblage of your taco is a matter of personal taste. In general, the filling goes on the bottom of the tortilla. Then you add toppings and sauces according to your predilection. Some people like to put the cheese next, right on top of the warm filling, because that way it melts a bit. Others like to save the cheese for the coup de grace. Tomatoes and sour cream go wherever you want a little moisture. Salsas go wherever you want the heat. Lettuce goes in the middle or at the top, depending on whether you like it crunchy or wilted. We suggest a building order in each taco recipe, but this is arbitrary. We also suggest complementary relishes—salsas, sauces, and toppings—for each taco, but many tacos go with everything.

You can fold your taco in half, roll it, leave it open like a plate in *tostada* form, or tuck the ends in, envelope style. Envelope style, you can put it back in the skillet stuffing and all and lightly fry it to crisp all around. This is a wonderful way to heat the filling when you are using leftovers for your tacos. It works best with flour tortillas. In some places rolled or envelope tacos are called *burritos, chimichangas*, and other names. For simplicity we call them all tacos.

As when confronted with a smorgasbord, it is tempting to overdo the toppings and overrun the flavors as you assemble your taco. It is best to exercise some restraint in your building frenzy. If you use many toppings, add smaller amounts of each than we have allotted in the recipes. If you have fewer, feel free to lay on more.

EQUIPMENT

To make tacos, no special equipment is needed, although it helps to have a food processor for the salsas and sauces. Otherwise, a large skillet, large pot, or grill serve to make the fillings. The best pan for crisping tortillas is an old omelet pan, preferably the kind with curved sides. You can let it get blackened with oil. It doesn't matter, the tortillas will still love it. ∎

SALSAS AND SAUCES FOR TACOS

The verve, the spice, the punch of tacos comes from the taco sauce. Fresh ones, called salsas, are made from chopped raw vegetables and chili peppers. Cooked ones, called sauces, are made of ingredients that have been briefly simmered.

The ingredients for salsa, including our recipes here, have no hard and fast rules. You can put radish in or not, use regular onion for green onion, omit cilantro if you don't care for it, reduce or raise the chili factor as you like, and so on, as long as it turns out as a fresh and lively relish.

The vegetables in salsa should be in small tasty chunks, rather than minced. If you are using a food processor, take care not to over-chop them. It's better to have the pieces a little too large than too fine. Too fine a salsa disintegrates into a soggy mass.

If you have any Tomato, Chive, or Corn and Red Bell Pepper Salsa left after a week or 10 days and past its prime, transfer it to a saucepan and cook it for a few minutes. It turns into a cooked chili sauce that can be kept several weeks more in the refrigerator, or frozen.

Makes 2½ cups

Set out in cups on the tables of almost any Southwest or Mexican restaurant, tomato salsa has become the most familiar fresh salsa, and is one of the easiest to make. For this salsa, you can chop tomatoes in a food processor.

Tomato Salsa

2 medium tomatoes (about ½ pound)
2 jalapeño chili peppers
2 serrano chili peppers
2 yellow wax chili peppers
  Or 2 ounces mixed fresh chili peppers, whatever is available
3 garlic cloves
3 radishes
1 bunch green onions, or ½ medium onion
1 cup cilantro leaves
¼ teaspoon salt
½ cup water
1 tablespoon tomato paste

To make the salsa in a food processor, cut the tomatoes into 8 pieces. Trim the stems off the chili peppers and cut the peppers into 3 or 4 pieces each. Peel the garlic cloves and cut into 2 or 3 pieces each. Trim the tops off the radishes, and cut the radishes in half. Trim the root ends and dark green tops off the green onions and cut the onions into 6 pieces each. Or, peel the half onion and cut it into 6 pieces.

Place the tomatoes, chili peppers, garlic, radishes, onions and cilantro in a food processor and carefully rough chop to about ¼-inch dice. Remove the vegetables to a bowl. Add the salt, water, and tomato paste. Mix to blend well.

To make the salsa by hand, use a chef's knife to chop the tomatoes, chili peppers, garlic, radishes, onions, and cilantro into ¼-inch dice. Place in a bowl. Add the salt, water, and tomato paste. Mix to blend well.

NOTES AND AFTERTHOUGHTS
Tomato Salsa keeps in the refrigerator up to 10 days.

Chive Salsa

2 cups rough-chopped fresh chives (2–4 bunches, depending on the size)
3 jalapeño chili peppers
2 serrano chili peppers
3 yellow wax chili peppers
2 Fresno or Santa Fe Grande chili peppers
    Or 2 ounces mixed hot fresh chili peppers, whatever is available
3 large garlic cloves
4 radishes
⅓ cup fresh mint leaves
1 cup cilantro leaves
1 cup water
¾ teaspoon salt

To make the salsa in a food processor, trim the stems off the chili peppers and cut the peppers into 3 or 4 pieces each. Peel the garlic cloves and cut them into 2 or 3 pieces each. Trim the ends off the radishes, and cut the radishes in half.

Place the chives, chili peppers, garlic, radishes, mint, and ¾ cup of the cilantro in a food processor. Carefully rough-chop until the vegetables are ¼-inch dice. Remove the ingredients to a bowl. Add the water, salt, and remaining ¼ cup cilantro. Mix to blend well.

To make the salsa by hand, use a chef's knife to chop the chives, chili peppers, garlic, radishes, mint and ¾ cup of the cilantro leaves into ¼-inch dice. Place the ingredients in a bowl and add the water, salt, and remaining ¼ cup cilantro. Mix to blend well.

NOTES AND AFTERTHOUGHTS
Chive Salsa keeps refrigerated 1 week.

Makes 2 cups

This salsa is for those who like it hot. How hot depends on the kind of chilies, the time of year, and, of course, the number of chilies you use. Some people take the seeds out of the chilies, but we think more than half the fun of salsa is the heat, so we leave the seeds in. If you want the salsa less hot, 1) use fewer chilies, 2) stick to Anaheim chilies, or 3) only make your salsa in the spring.

The whole cilantro leaves vary the texture and look of this salsa. The same touch can be added to any of the other salsas.

Corn and Red Bell Pepper Salsa

Makes 2½ cups

Fresh corn is best for this unusual salsa, but in the dead of winter, frozen corn will do. It's one of the better frozen vegetables.

2 cups fresh corn kernels (about two ears) or 1 16-ounce package frozen petite corn
1 small or ½ large red bell pepper (about ¼ pound)
4 jalapeño chili peppers
¼ cup cilantro leaves
½ teaspoon ground cumin
¼ teaspoon salt
¾ cup water

If using fresh corn, cook in boiling water to cover for 3 to 5 minutes, until just done. Drain and let cool. With a paring knife, shave the kernels off the cob. If using frozen corn, simmer in ½ cup water for 3 minutes. Drain. Place the corn kernels in a bowl.

Remove the core and seeds from the bell peppers. Cut the stems off the jalapeños. In a food processor or with a chef's knife, rough-chop all the peppers into ¼-inch dice. Add the peppers, cilantro, cumin, salt, and water to the corn. Mix to blend well.

NOTES AND AFTERTHOUGHTS
Corn and Red Bell Pepper Salsa keeps up to 10 days in the refrigerator.

Melon and Jalapeño Salsa

Makes about 2¼ cups

Melon Salsa is for mid to late summer, when the melons are at their peak and fully sweet. It is especially good with chicken tacos. The melon must be chopped by hand, not in a food processor, or it will be too watery and thin tasting.

3 pounds canteloupe or honeydew melon, or a mixture of the two
1 yellow wax or jalapeño or 2 serrano chili peppers
⅓ pound tomatillos
1½ tablespoons lime juice

Halve the melon and remove the seeds. Scoop out the pulp with a spoon and chop fine with a chef's knife. Place the pulp in a bowl.

Cut off the stems from the chili peppers. Remove the papery husks from the tomatillos and cut the tomatillos into quarters. Mince the chili pepper and tomatillos in a food processor or with a chef's knife. Stir the chilies and tomatillos into the melon. Stir in the lime juice and blend.

NOTES AND AFTERTHOUGHTS
Depending on the firmness and ripeness of the melon, Melon and Jalapeño Salsa keeps 4 to 7 days in the refrigerator.

Tomatillo Sauce

1 pound tomatillos
Water to cover
2 yellow wax chili peppers
2 cups cilantro leaves (about 1 bunch)
¼ teaspoon salt

Remove the papery husks from the tomatillos. Place the tomatillos in a saucepan just large enough to hold them in a single layer and add water to cover. Bring the water to a boil. Reduce the heat and simmer 5 to 6 minutes, depending on their size, until tomatillos give when pressed with your finger.

To make the sauce in a food processor, immediately remove the tomatillos to a food processor, reserving the liquid from the saucepan. Trim the stems off the chilies and cut them into 2 or 3 pieces. Add to the food processor with the cilantro, salt, and ½ cup of the reserved cooking liquid. Blend until almost pureed.

To make the sauce by hand, place the cooked tomatillos in a bowl and mash them to release the juices. Fish out the skins. Mince with a knife and return the minced skins to the bowl. Mince the chili peppers and the cilantro. Add to the tomatillos. Add the salt and ½ cup of the reserved liquid from the saucepan. Stir to blend.

NOTES AND AFTERTHOUGHTS
Tomatillo Sauce keeps refrigerated up to 1 week.

Makes about 2½ cups

Tomatillos look like little green tomatoes, and, in fact, their name means "little tomatoes." In actuality, they aren't tomatoes at all; though like tomatoes, they belong to the nightshade family and are related to eggplants and potatoes.

Ancho Chili Sauce

8 dried ancho chilies
4 large garlic cloves
2 teaspoons pure chili powder
3 cups water
¾ teaspoon salt

Remove the stems and seeds from the ancho chilies. Peel the garlic cloves and cut them into quarters.

Combine the chilies, garlic, chili powder and water in a saucepan. Bring to a boil. Reduce the heat to a simmer, cover, and cook 15 minutes. Set aside to cool 10 minutes.

When cool, puree in a blender or food processor. Add salt and mix well.

Or strain the cooled liquid into a bowl. On a chopping board or in a mortar, puree the chilies and garlic with a mallet or pestle. Add the puree to the liquid in the bowl. Add the salt and stir to mix well.

NOTES AND AFTERTHOUGHTS
Ancho Chili Sauce keeps in the refrigerator several months.

Makes about 2½ cups

From Nogales to Nantucket, the first Mexican sauce most of us met was a dried chili sauce. And no wonder. It is the type of sauce common to New Mexico, Arizona, and the border towns. Its appealing feature is, while pungent and sweet, it is not at all hot.

TACO TOPPINGS

The joy of tacos is the toppings. From ever-popular guacamole and smooth sour cream to crisp fried potatoes and shredded cheese, here's how to make the classics.

Guacamole

The best guacamole is a simple guacamole, just lots of avocado with a little lemon and perhaps a touch of something hot.

Victoria's Guacamole

Makes about 2 cups

No, not the blender or food processor for guacamole! They make the texture gluey and take the heart out of the wonderful avocado flavor. Ripe avocados mash instantly with a fork, anyway, without cleaning up a machine or depriving yourself of those occasional melt-in-your-mouth chunks surrounded by the smooth avocado puree.

3 ripe avocados
½ medium onion (about ¼ pound)
1 large jalapeño or yellow wax chili pepper, or 2 serrano chili peppers
1½ tablespoons lemon juice
⅜ teaspoon salt

Cut the avocados in half and remove the seeds. Scoop out the pulp with a spoon and place in a medium bowl.

Peel the onion and grate it through the small holes of a hand grater, holding the grater over the bowl to catch the juices. Mince the chili pepper and add to the bowl. Add the salt and lemon juice. Mash the ingredients with a fork until the avocado is almost smooth but not pureed.

Use 2 tablespoons per taco.

Susanna's Guacamole

Makes about 2 cups

3 ripe avocados
1 tablespoon lemon juice
¼ cup Tomato Salsa (page 82), or 1 small tomato, ½ small onion, and 1 large clove garlic

Cut the avocados in half and remove the seeds. Scoop out the pulp with a spoon, and place in a medium bowl. Add the lemon juice and tomato salsa. Mash in ingredients with a fork until the avocado is almost smooth but not pureed.

Or peel and fine chop the onion. Add to the avocado. Cut the tomato into ⅛-inch dice and add to the bowl. Peel the garlic and press it into the bowl. Mash together with a fork until the avocado is almost smooth but not pureed.

Use 2 tablespoons per taco.

Fried Potatoes

2 pounds red or white potatoes
½ cup vegetable or peanut oil

Wash the potatoes and cut them into ¼-inch dice. Heat the oil in a large skillet until the oil begins to smoke. Add the potatoes and stir to coat with oil. Cook 15 to 20 minutes over medium-high heat, turning once.

Serve plain or, if the crowd can take it, sprinkle with dried chili flakes, chili powder, or the Mexican spice *achiote.*

Use ⅓ cup per taco.

NOTES AND AFTERTHOUGHTS

Achiote is the seed of the annatto tree. In seed or paste form it adds a mild, musky, nutty flavor to taco fillings, fish, and chicken in Mexican and Caribbean cooking. It is available in Mexican and Puerto Rican markets. Grind or smash the seeds before using.

Diced Tomatoes

4 medium tomatoes (about 1 pound)
1 tablespoon chopped fresh herb, such as oregano, basil, thyme, marjoram, parsley, chives, or cilantro
¼ teaspoon salt
1 teaspoon vinegar (optional)

Cut the tomatoes into quarters, then cut each quarter into 3 thin wedges. Cut the wedges crosswise at ¼-inch intervals. Place the tomatoes in a bowl. Add the herb, salt, and vinegar if using. Toss.

Use 2 tablespoons per taco.

Makes 4 cups

Russets or baking potatoes are okay to use if that's all you have, but they have a tendency to collapse into mush in the frying pan, usually just as they are done. Red and white potatoes stay crisper, which is what you want for a taco topping.

Makes 2 cups

Fresh ripe garden tomatoes with a touch of herb are wonderful by themselves on tacos. But, if the tomatoes aren't perfect, as so often is the case unless you grow them in your garden, a touch of almost any kind of vinegar will bring up their flavor and make them a spunkier addition to your tacos.

The trick to cutting through the tough outer skins of tomatoes, if you haven't got a really sharp chef's knife, is to use a serrated bread knife for the first cut through the skins. Then switch to a chef's knife for dicing the slices.

If you have a Mexicatessen—that's what they're called—to shop in, *quesa fresca* or *quesa cotija* make, as you would imagine, the most authentic tasting cheese topping for tacos. *Quesa fresca,* or Mexican fresh cheese, is similar to a sharp ricotta. *Quesa cotija,* a Mexican semi-hard white cheese, is similar to a dried, less salty Feta. In general Mexican cheeses are far sharper than ours, enough so to add a distinctive bite to a taco. They are crumbled rather than grated for topping tacos. You might use Parmesan or aged Asiago as well, particularly with Ancho Chili Sauce.

Makes 4 to 5 cups

Although it's the lettuce often used, we cannot in all good conscience recommend Iceberg lettuce for tacos, or anything else. Try your tacos with crunchy Romaine or sweet red leaf lettuce and taste the difference.

Makes 2 to 2¼ cups

You can tell where you are in Mexico by the type of cream and its use in the cuisine. In the very north, the cream is much like American sour cream. Further south, especially around the western sea coast, the

Shredded Cheese

1½ cups sharp hard yellow cheese, such as American or English cheddar or Holland Gouda (about 6 ounces)
1½ cups sharp hard or semi-hard white cheese, such as Jack, Feta, Mexican *quesa fresca,* or Cotija (about 6 ounces)

Grate the hard cheeses with a food processor or through the large holes of a hand grater.

Grate the semisoft cheese through the large holes of a hand grater. Mix the two cheeses together.

Use ⅓ cup per taco.

NOTES AND AFTERTHOUGHTS

Semisoft cheese when grated in a food processor becomes creamed, not shredded.

Shredded Lettuce

1 large head romaine, curly leaf, or escarole lettuce, or 2 heads red leaf lettuce

Remove the limp outer leaves from the lettuce. Starting at the top of the head, slice the lettuce into ¼-inch-thick shreds, cutting down to the core. Rinse the shredded lettuce thoroughly in cool water. Spin dry.

Use ⅓ cup per taco.

Sour Cream

2 cups sour cream
¼ cup light cream, or 2 tablespoons melted butter (optional)

Place the sour cream in a bowl and stir to smooth. Serve plain or blend in light cream or melted butter, according to the style of cream desired.

Use 1½ to 2 tablespoons per taco.

NOTES AND AFTERTHOUGHTS

Adding melted butter to sour cream makes the cream slightly lumpy, but this is in keeping with less processed farm-style creams.

Beef Tacos with Currants and Pine Nuts

2 medium onions (about 14 ounces)
2 tablespoons oil
2½ pounds ground beef chuck or round
½ cup currants
½ cup pine nuts
1 cup packed mint leaves
⅛ teaspoon ground cinnamon
½ cup red wine
¼ teaspoon salt

2 cups Chive Salsa (page 83) or Ancho Chili Sauce (page 85)

FOR THE TOPPINGS:
3 medium green bell peppers
1½ cups Sour Cream (page 88)
3 cups Shredded Lettuce (page 88)

12 flour tortillas

Peel and chop the onions into ¼-inch dice.

Heat the oil in a large skillet until the oil begins to smoke. Add the onions and cook over medium heat until translucent, about 5 minutes.

Add the ground beef and cook, stirring to break up any large chunks, until thoroughly browned, about 10 minutes.

Add the currants, pine nuts, mint, cinnamon, wine, and salt. Simmer until the liquid is almost evaporated but the beef is still moist, about 15 minutes.

While the taco filling cooks, remove the seeds and core from the bell pepper. Slice into ⅛-inch-thick strips.

(continued)

cream has an earthy flavor and, while still thick, it is somewhat more runny than our commercial sour cream. As you enter the highland beef areas, cream is hardly used. South of Mexico City toward Oaxaca, the cream is sweet like whipping cream, not sour cream at all. You can duplicate these flavors by using straight sour cream for the Northern version, adding a little melted butter to sour cream to make the cream's flavor earthier, or by adding light cream to the sour cream to sweeten it and make it runnier.

Plenty for 6

20 to 40 minutes

Not your regular ground beef one, this taco filling is based on a dish served in a nunnery-cum-restaurant outside Mexico City. The original sisters there must have been Spanish, for the filling is reminiscent of a forcemeat used to stuff chickens in Spanish cooking. Clearly, Mexican touches slipped in over time. In the Mexican nuns' version, the filling was used to stuff mildly spicy green bell peppers. The peppers were oven baked and then sour cream was poured over them. The whole shebang was topped with a candied cherry.

We've borrowed the filling for these tacos, kept the sour cream, and use the green pepper for garnish. But we've, ah . . . , skipped the candied cherry.

Just before serving, crisp the tortillas (page 80).

To assemble the tacos, spread about ⅓ cup of the beef filling on the bottom of a hot flour tortilla. Sprinkle lettuce over the filling. Spoon on 1½ tablespoons salsa. Top with 1½ tablespoons of Sour Cream and several slices of bell pepper. Fold and serve.

Steak, Roasted Red Pepper, Pepperoncini, and Olive Paste Tacos

2 pounds boneless steak (skirt, market, New York, sirloin), or leftover roast beef
2 jars (6 ounces) roasted red peppers
1 jar (7½ ounces) pepperoncini
1 jar (6 ounces) olive paste

12 flour tortillas

FOR THE TOPPINGS:

2 cups Sour Cream (page 88)
3 cups Shredded Lettuce (page 88)
1 tablespoon balsamic or sherry vinegar
2 tablespoons olive oil

If using fresh steak, pan fry as in the basic recipe, page 189.

Remove to a platter and let rest 15 minutes for the juices to settle while preparing the remaining ingredients. Slice crosswise into ⅛-inch-thick strips just before assembling the tacos. If using leftover roast beef, slice crosswise into ⅛-inch-thick strips. Sauté in a little olive oil just until heated, less than 1 minute.

Drain the red peppers and cut lengthwise into long thin strips. Drain the pepperoncini and cut into ⅛-inch-wide rounds.

Place the shredded lettuce in a bowl. Add the vinegar and oil and toss.

Just before serving, crisp the tortillas (page 80).

To assemble the tacos, spread about ½ tablespoon olive paste over the bottom of a hot tortilla. Arrange steak strips over the olive paste. Spread some red pepper and pepperoncini over the steak. Top with the dressed lettuce and a dollop of Sour Cream. Fold and serve.

Tacos of Grilled Beef Fajita Marinated in Lime and Onion Juice with Grilled Green Onions

FOR THE MARINADE:
1 large onion (about 10 ounces)
½ cup lime juice (about 3 medium limes)

2½ to 3 pounds skirt steak

FOR THE TOPPINGS:
3 bunches small green onions
2 limes

18 corn tortillas
1½ cups Tomatillo Sauce (page 85) or Chive Salsa (page 83, optional)

Plenty for 6

20 to 40 minutes

A real fajita taco—the way you would get a steak taco off a smoky charcoal grill in Mexico— is so flavorful it is best just wrapped in a warm, soft tortilla with grilled green onion and sprinkled with lime. If you like the tang of double onion and double lime, pour the remaining marinade over the meat after it is cooked.

In a food processor or on a grater set over a bowl, fine grate the onion to a pulp. Remove the pulp to a nonreactive baking pan. Stir in the lime juice. Place the skirt steak in the marinade and turn to coat. Marinate for at least 30 minutes at room temperature, turning once, or up to 2 days in the refrigerator, turning several times.

Prepare the grill (page 144).

When the grill is ready, place the skirt steak on the rack directly over the coals and cook 4 to 5 minutes. Turn and cook 4 to 5 minutes more. If there is room on the grill, add the green onions when you turn the skirt steak and grill for 2 minutes, until wilted and partially blackened. (If there is not room, grill the green onions after the steak is done.) Remove the skirt steak and green onions to a platter and let the steak rest 10 minutes before cutting.

Cut each lime into 10 thin wedges.

Just before serving, dip the tortillas in a little of the Tomatillo Sauce or Chive Salsa if using. Warm the tortillas until soft (page 80).

To assemble the tacos, cut the skirt steak diagonally across the grain into ¼-inch-thick slices. Place 4 to 5 slices of steak on the bottom of a hot corn tortilla. Arrange 2 green onions over the steak slices. Squeeze the juice of 1 lime wedge over the onions. Fold and serve with the Tomatillo Sauce or Chive Salsa.

NOTES AND AFTERTHOUGHTS

1. Flank steak is also suitable for this recipe, although it doesn't absorb the marinade quite as well.

2. Sour cream is also a good embellishment for this taco.

3. Beef fajita and its grilled onion accompaniment can be pan fried as well as grilled. The timing is the same.

4. If you have that wonderful Mexican spice *achiote,* sprinkle some on the green onions after grilling them.

Pork Carnitas Tacos

3 pounds boneless pork butt
4 garlic cloves
2 teaspoons fresh thyme leaves or ½ teaspoon dried
1 bay leaf
⅓ cup white wine
1 teaspoon freshly ground black pepper
¾ teaspoon salt
½ cup water

18 corn tortillas
2 cups Tomato Salsa (page 82)

FOR THE TOPPINGS:

2 cups Guacamole (page 86)
2 cups Sour Cream (page 88, optional)

Plenty for 6

3½ hours

On Saturday morning in the little towns throughout Mexico and the Southwest, and in the Latin districts of larger cities, everybody waits around the butcher shop. The red flag goes up, meaning meat is about to appear, then around noon out come the carnitas, roasted pork in little bites. That, together with a slice of avocado and tomato salsa, is the favorite snack of everyone. The children love the pieces of skin, which come out first. The adults wait for the succulent meat. The bits of pork are incredible wrapped in a tortilla.

If you've ever wondered how carnitas develops such a rich flavor, it's in the cooking. Carnitas is started with a very little liquid to keep the meat from sticking at first. From then on, once the temperature is up, the meat stews in its own fat until it's done to a tender succulence. Traditionally, unless very fat pork is used, extra pork fat is added to insure plenty of juices for the meat to cook in. In our recipe, we use no extra fat. Instead we add a small amount of water for the last hour of simmering so the meat won't stick once its own fat is absorbed.

Cut the pork across the grain into ½-inch-wide "steaks." Stack the slices in 3 piles, then cut each stack crosswise into ½-inch-wide strips.

Place the pork strips in a large heavy casserole or stockpot. Peel the garlic cloves, cut them into 4 pieces each, and add to the pot. Add the thyme, bay leaf, wine, pepper, and salt. Place over medium heat and bring the liquid to a boil. Stir to mix well, partially cover, and cook over low heat 2 hours.

After 2 hours, remove the cover and add ½ cup water. Increase the heat to medium high and continue cooking 1 hour, stirring every 10 minutes. Reduce the heat if the pork begins to burn. Discard the bay leaf.

Just before serving, warm the tortillas until soft (page 80).

To assemble the tacos, place a heaping ⅓ cup shredded pork on the bottom of a hot tortilla. Top with 1½ tablespoons salsa, the same amount of guacamole, and a few dollops of Sour Cream, if using. Fold and serve.

NOTES AND AFTERTHOUGHTS

1. Carnitas is the same everywhere, but the salsas vary. Indeed, carnitas goes with any salsa, so don't hesitate to try whatever you have on hand.

2. In a strictly authentic version of carnitas, the pork would be long simmered in fat instead of wine and water. While the fat adds a wonderful flavor to the meat, it also adds unhealthful lard, so we have modernized the recipe.

Pork Tenderloin, Chili, and Watercress Tacos with Pumpkin Seed Topping

3 pork tenderloins (about 12 ounces each)
Salt
Freshly ground black pepper
2 tablespoons olive or peanut oil

FOR THE TOPPINGS:

2 cups fresh watercress leaves
2 red Fresno or Santa Fe Grande or 3 red serrano chili peppers
2 bunches green onions
¼ teaspoon salt

2 teaspoons vegetable or peanut oil
⅔ cup shelled pumpkin seeds

12 corn tortillas
2 cups Sour Cream (page 88)

Plenty for 6

20 to 40 minutes

Pumpkins are one of the oldest New World crops, cultivated both for their pulp and for their seeds for 9,000 years. In Mexican cooking, pumpkin seeds, called *pepitas*, remain a common ingredient. The roasted seeds are not only delicious, but are full of protein.

Pat the pork tenderloins dry with a paper towel. Lightly salt and pepper them on all sides. Heat the oil in a skillet large enough to hold the pork tenderloins in a single uncrowded layer. Add the pork and cook 20 minutes over medium-high heat, turning one quarter turn every 5 minutes. Remove to a platter, and let rest at least 15 minutes before slicing.

While the pork cooks, wash and spin dry the watercress. Rough chop and place in a medium bowl. Trim the tops off the chilies, then mince the peppers. Add to the watercress in the bowl. Remove the root ends and limp tops from the green onions and cut them into very thin rounds. Add to the bowl. Sprinkle on the salt and mix.

Heat the vegetable oil in a medium skillet. Add the pumpkin seeds and stir over medium-high heat until the seeds are browned and they exude a nutty aroma. Remove the toasted seeds to a plate.

Just before serving, crisp the tortillas (page 80).

To assemble the tacos, cut the pork crosswise into ⅛-inch-thick slices. Arrange 6 or 7 slices down the center of a hot tortilla. Spread 2 tablespoons or so of the watercress, green onion, and chili mixture over the pork. Top with 2 dollops of Sour Cream. Sprinkle about ½ tablespoon pumpkin seeds over all. Fold and serve.

NOTES AND AFTERTHOUGHTS

You can make this taco with leftover pork, too. Cut the pork into thin slices or strips and fry it in a little oil until slightly crispy to simulate a quick carnitas.

Nobody, but nobody made a stewed chicken taco with a dipped tortilla like Josefina. Originally from the Jalisco area of Mexico, now a resident of Los Angeles, Josefina could cook up a storm. Everybody who discovered Josefina's place returned. That is, when there *was* a Josefina's place. Every now and then Josefina would get a yearning to see the rocky terraces of her home again and would close her place down. Sure enough, some incalculable months later, she'd appear again. Under another version of her name, she'd open her doors once more. In all the years in Los Angeles, she never learned English, but she knew every customer. Then one day, her restaurant disappeared for good . . . before we got her recipe! This version with its potatoes and dried chilies is, we think, almost a duplicate.

Stewed Chicken Tacos with Tomatillo-Dipped Tortillas

1½ chickens (about 5½ pounds)
6 large garlic cloves
2 dried ancho chilies
1½ pounds fresh tomatoes, or 1 cup canned crushed tomatoes in puree
2 teaspoons salt
8 cups water (approximately)
2 large white potatoes (about 1 pound)

18 corn tortillas
2 cups Tomatillo Sauce (page 85)

Cut the chicken into quarters and remove the excess fat. Place the pieces, meat side down, in a large pot. Peel the garlic and cut each clove into quarters. Add to the chicken. Remove the seeds and core from the chilies, then cut the chilies into ½-inch-wide strips. Add to the pot.

If using fresh tomatoes, cut the tomatoes into quarters and add them to the pot. If using canned tomatoes, add them and the puree to the pot.

Sprinkle the salt into the pot. Add just enough water to cover the chicken. Bring to a boil. Reduce the heat to maintain a simmer, cover partially, and cook 35 to 40 minutes, until the leg and thigh joint can be separated easily and the meat is no longer pink. Remove the pot from the burner. Remove the chicken to a bowl and let the chicken and broth cool for 15 minutes.

When the broth is cool, remove and discard the layer of fat from the surface.

Cut the potatoes into ¼-inch dice. Bring the broth to a boil. Add the potatoes, reduce the heat, and simmer for 10 minutes.

While the potatoes cook, separate the chicken meat from the fat and bones. When the potatoes are done, return the chicken meat to the pot.

Just before serving, dip the tortillas in the Tomatillo Sauce. Crisp the dipped tortillas (page 80).

To assemble the tacos, spread ⅓ to ½ cup of the chicken stew over a hot tortilla. Top with a dollop of Tomatillo Sauce. Fold and serve.

Tacos of Chicken Fajita Rolled in Chili Flakes and Marjoram

5¼ pounds bone-in chicken breasts, or 3¾ pounds boneless
1 tablespoon dried chili flakes
½ tablespoon dried marjoram leaves
4 tablespoons oil

18 corn tortillas

FOR THE TOPPINGS:

3 cups Shredded Cheese (page 88)
2 cups Sour Cream (page 88)
2 cups Melon and Jalapeño Salsa (page 84)
4 cups Shredded Lettuce (page 88)

Plenty for 6

20 minutes or less

Bone the chicken breasts if they aren't already boned. Mix the chili flakes and marjoram together in a small bowl. Spread a little of the mixture on a cutting board. Place 1 or 2 chicken breasts over the chili marjoram mixture and pound the chicken with a mallet or other heavy object. Turn and pound the other side until the breasts are ¼ inch thick.

Remove the pounded chicken to a plate. Sprinkle more of the mixture on the board and continue pounding until all the pieces are flattened.

Divide the oil between 2 heavy skillets and heat until the oil smokes. Divide the chicken breasts between the pans and cook 2 minutes. Turn and cook 2 minutes on the other side. Remove the cooked breasts to a cutting board and continue until all the chicken breasts are cooked. Slice them crosswise into ⅓-inch-wide strips.

Just before serving, warm the tortillas until soft (page 80).

To assemble the tacos, place a few of the chicken strips on the bottom of a hot tortilla. Sprinkle on about ⅓ cup shredded cheese. Spoon 1½ tablespoons Sour Cream over the cheese. Top with the salsa and shredded lettuce. Fold and serve.

NOTES AND AFTERTHOUGHTS

1. If small scraps come off the chicken or cling to the mallet while you are pounding, knead them into a flat patty and fry them like the other pieces.

2. The chicken in this taco is delicious grilled on a barbeque as well as fried.

Turkey Tacos with Salsa and White Wine

Plenty for 6

20 to 40 minutes

We make turkey tacos frequently. **Our children moan and complain if two weeks go by without them. On school or work nights when time is short, serve them with just cheese, lettuce, tomato, and salsa. But when you have time or company is coming, there's nothing as good as a turkey and potato taco with guacamole and sour cream. You'll love their homey splendor—and you'll never wonder what to do with leftover turkey again.**

2 large onions (about 1¼ pounds)
2 to 4 garlic cloves
3 tablespoons oil
2 ½ pounds freshly ground turkey, or 6 cups diced cooked turkey
3 to 6 tablespoons Tomato, Chive, or Corn and Red Bell Pepper Salsa (page 82 to 84)
⅔ cup white wine
1 teaspoon salt

18 corn tortillas

FOR THE TOPPINGS:

3 cups Shredded Cheese (page 88)
2 cups Diced Tomatoes (page 87)
2 cups Tomato, Chive, or Corn and Red Pepper Salsa (page 82–84)
4 cups Shredded Lettuce (page 88)
4 cups Fried Potatoes (page 87, optional)
2 cups Guacamole (page 86, optional)
2 cups Sour Cream (page 88, optional)

Peel the onions and chop into ¼-inch dice. Peel and rough chop the garlic. Heat the oil in a large skillet. Add the onions and garlic and cook over medium heat until the onions are translucent, about 5 minutes.

Add the turkey and brown thoroughly. (If you are using ground turkey, break up the meat as it cooks.) Add 3 to 6 tablespoons salsa, along with the wine and salt. Stew together about 15 minutes, or until most of the liquid has been absorbed. Turn off the heat, cover, and set aside.

Just before serving, crisp the tortillas (page 80).

To assemble the tacos, put about ⅓ cup of the turkey filling in the middle of a hot tortilla. Sprinkle on ⅓ cup of the shredded cheese. Add 1½ tablespoons diced tomatoes. Top with 1½ tablespoons salsa and shredded lettuce. If using, layer fried potatoes and guacamole under the lettuce, and Sour Cream on top. Fold and serve.

NOTES AND AFTERTHOUGHTS

1. Turkey tacos go with any and every topping and any and every salsa. Part of their fun is varying the toppings and salsas every time you make them.

2. The filling for turkey tacos will dry out if it's overcooked. You can always add a little more wine or some water to perk it up.

3. Turkey taco filling freezes well. You can save time on what is already a quick recipe by making a double batch and storing half. It lasts in the refrigerator for about 3 days and in the freezer for months.

Fried Fish and Roasted Red Bell Pepper Tacos

4 tablespoons olive or peanut oil
2 pounds tuna, red snapper, swordfish, halibut, shark, or sea bass fillets or steaks,
cut about ½ inch thick
Salt
Freshly ground black pepper
¼ cup lemon juice

12 flour or 18 corn tortillas

FOR THE TOPPINGS:

2 large or 3 medium red bell peppers (about 1 pound), or 2 jars (6 ounces each)
roasted red peppers
¼ cup cilantro
2 tablespoons olive oil
¼ cup chopped fresh parsley
4 cups Shredded Lettuce (page 80)
2 cups Tomato, Chive, or Melon and Jalapeño Salsa (pages 82 to 84)

Divide the 4 tablespoons olive or peanut oil between 2 large skillets. Set over medium heat until the oil begins to smoke. Add the fish and fry until moist and just cooked through, 4 to 6 minutes per side, depending on the fish. Lightly salt and pepper each side as you go.

Remove the fish to a plate and set aside to cool. When cool, remove any bones. Break the fish into chunks and toss with the lemon juice.

To roast and peel the red bell peppers, see page 47. If using jarred roasted red peppers, drain them. Cut the red peppers into strips about ⅛ inch wide. Place the strips in a small bowl and toss with the cilantro, olive oil, and parsley.

Just before serving, crisp the tortillas (page 80).

To assemble the tacos, place about ⅓ cup of the fish on the bottom of a hot tortilla. Top with a tablespoon or so of the red peppers, some shredded lettuce, and finally as much salsa as you want. Fold and serve.

Plenty for 6

20 to 40 minutes

Just as there are fish sandwiches, there are fish tacos. And what better way to stretch a fish dish and make it tantalizing for people who think they don't like fish? Any meaty fish—halibut, tuna, red snapper, swordfish, shark, mahi mahi—fried, baked, grilled, or leftover, will make a top-notch taco.

Every now and then, we can't resist buttering the tortillas, even for a taco dish. This is one of those instances because there is no salsa to add moisture to the taco and besides, the butter melting between the cheese and cream and tortilla is irresistibly good!

Salmon with Lime, Cheese, and Sour Cream Tacos

2 tablespoons olive oil
2 pounds salmon steaks or fillets
2 large garlic cloves
4 tablespoons lime juice
½ cup white wine

12 flour tortillas
Butter, for the tortillas

FOR THE TOPPINGS:

3 ounces Feta cheese, preferably Bulgarian or Corsican
2 cups Sour Cream (page 88)
3 Anaheim chilies, or 2 medium green bell peppers
12 green onions
1 cup cilantro leaves

Divide the olive oil between 2 large nonreactive skillets. Set over medium heat until the oil begins to smoke. Add the salmon and cook 4 minutes. Peel the garlic and cut into thin slivers. Turn the salmon and divide the garlic, lime juice, and wine between the pans. Cook 4 minutes more. Remove to a plate and set aside to cool.

Crumble the Feta into a small bowl; mash with a fork. Add the Sour Cream and mix to blend. Set aside.

Remove the seeds and core from the Anaheim chilies. Cut the chilies into ⅛-inch-thick rounds, or the bell peppers into ⅛-inch-thick half rounds. Place in a bowl. Trim off the root ends and limp green tops from the green onions. Cut into thin rounds and add to the bowl. Rough chop the cilantro and add to the bowl. Toss together.

When the salmon is cool, remove any bones. Break the salmon into chunks.

Just before serving, warm the tortillas until soft (page 80). Butter them right away while still hot.

To assemble the tacos, spread 2 tablespoons Feta cheese mixture over the bottom of a hot buttered tortilla. Arrange ⅓ cup salmon chunks over the cheese. Top with the chili, green onion, and cilantro mixture. Fold and serve.

NOTES AND AFTERTHOUGHTS
You can cook the salmon in the oven as in the baked salmon recipe, page 250. Or, you can use leftover salmon.

Lobster or Crab Tacos with Pan-Grilled Green Onions

6 live lobsters (about 1¼ pounds each), 3 pounds lobster tails, or 3 pounds
    crabmeat
½ cup lime juice
3 tablespoons chopped cilantro
3 bunches green onions
Oil to coat the frying pan
2 tablespoons lime juice

18 corn tortillas

FOR THE TOPPINGS:
2 cups Tomatillo Sauce (page 85)
2 cups Sour Cream (page 88)

Plenty for 6

40 to 60 minutes

Although more expensive and not as much fun, buying lobster tails is a simpler, faster way to get enough meat for this recipe. Of course, you can use live crab in season. Four Dungeness crabs should yield enough meat for this recipe.

If you are using live lobsters, bring 2 large pots of water to a boil. Drop 1 or 2 lobsters into each pot, cover, and return to a boil. Cook 11 minutes, or until the small legs pull off easily. Remove the lobsters and rinse in cold water to cool. Continue with another round until all the lobsters are cooked.

When the lobsters are cool enough to handle, pull off the small legs (called swimerettes), and the 2 large front claws. Set the swimerettes aside for another purpose. Break the lobster body at the joint between the tail and upper body. With the point of a knife, split the shell down the center on the underside of the tail. Remove the meat from the tail. Cut the tail meat into 1-inch chunks, and place in a bowl. Crack the large claws with a nutcracker or hammer and remove the meat with a fork. Add the claw meat to the bowl. Remove from the upper body the green part, which is the liver, the marrow-like white part, and the pink to orange colored coral. Set aside in a separate bowl.

If you are using frozen lobster tails, defrost them. Drop into boiling water, cover and return to a boil. Cook 5 to 6 minutes, and drain. When cool, split the tails, remove the meat, and cut the meat into chunks.

If you are using crabmeat, place it in a frying pan and stir over medium heat 2 minutes to warm.

Add the ½ cup lime juice and the chopped cilantro to the lobster or crabmeat in the bowl and toss.

To make the pan-grilled green onions, trim the root ends and limp green tops off the green onions. Cut into 1-inch lengths.

Coat a cast iron or other heavy skillet with a thin film of oil. Wipe out any excess. Set the pan over high heat until the oil begins to smoke. Add the green onions and stir for 2 to 3 minutes, until the onions are quite wilted and blackened in spots. Remove to a platter and sprinkle with the 2 tablespoons lime juice.

Just before serving, dip the tortillas in the Tomatillo Sauce, and then crisp them (page 80).

(continued)

To assemble the tacos, spread ⅓ to ½ cup lobster or crabmeat on the bottom of a hot, dipped tortilla. Cover with green onions. Top with a dollop each of Tomatillo Sauce and Sour Cream. Fold and serve. If you like, garnish with the reserved liver, marrow, and coral on the side.

NOTES AND AFTERTHOUGHTS

1. Enough lobster tacos for 6 people for a whole meal entails a fairly outrageous extravagance. To modify the expense, make them part of a taco smorgasbord, with one lobster taco each, and perhaps a stewed vegetable taco and a beef fajita taco to round out the table. Or make some lobster and some crab tacos. They're equally delicious.

2. Angler, popularly called the poor man's lobster meat, makes a good substitute for the lobster in this recipe.

FRIED POTATO TACOS

Potatoes, along with corn, tomatoes, and squashes, are one of the great native crops of America. Throughout North, Central, and South America—where there are over 400 varieties—you get them cooked and served in every fashion. One of the best ways is south-of-the-border style, fried, wrapped in a hot tortilla with perhaps another fresh ingredient, and doused with a hit of hot sauce.

Fried potato tacos are ubiquitous in Mexico. In a little village off Lake Pátzcuaro, you might find a peasant woman selling them off her kettlelike brazier in the corner of the square when everyone takes an evening promenade—men walking one direction around, women walking the other. If you ride the narrow gauge railroad train across the volcanos to Uruapan, you will find the fried potato tacos with little green bananas, handed through the train windows in exchange for a peso. You can find them fried with chilies everywhere.

Fried potato tacos make a champion lunch or breakfast as well as dinner. Instead of bacon and eggs, have a Fried Potatoes and Eggs or Chili Strips and Canadian Bacon taco. Instead of corn flakes, you can have a tortilla toasted and filled with fried potatoes and banana.

Fried Potatoes and Eggs Northern Style

4 cups Fried Potatoes (page 87)
12 eggs
6 tablespoons vegetable or peanut oil or butter
4 tablespoons water

18 corn or 12 flour tortillas

FOR THE TOPPINGS:

3 cups Shredded Cheese (page 88)
2 cups Ancho Chili Sauce (page 85)

Make the Fried Potatoes. Remove them to paper toweling to drain.

In the same frying pan, heat 3 tablespoons of the oil or butter. Break 6 eggs into the pan. Immediately drizzle 2 tablespoons water all around the outer edge of the pan. Cover tightly and cook on medium-low heat 2 minutes. Carefully remove the cooked eggs to a plate. Add the remaining 3 tablespoons of oil and cook the remaining six eggs as above.

Just before serving, crisp the tortillas or warm them until soft (page 80).

To assemble the tacos, place ½ cup of the fried potatoes on the bottom of a hot tortilla. Place a soft fried egg over the potatoes. Top with ¼ cup shredded cheese and 1½ tablespoons Ancho Chili Sauce.

NOTES AND AFTERTHOUGHTS

If you're in the mood for a travel adventure, try different sauces progressing southward. Southern-style Fried Potatoes and Egg Tacos would have fresh Tomato, Chive, or Corn and Red Pepper Salsa. Still farther south, they would have Tomatillo Sauce.

Plenty for 6

20 to 40 minutes

Drizzling water around the outer edge of the fried eggs and then cooking them with a tight cover is a way to get beautiful, pink-topped eggs without standing by, spoon in hand, and basting them. It also keeps the eggs soft— whites and all. The eggs should be a bit runny for Fried Potatoes and Egg tacos so the egg will seep into the potatoes.

Fried Potatoes, Chili Strips, and Canadian Bacon

4 cups Fried Potatoes (page 87)
3 medium poblano chili peppers (about 10 ounces)
6 ounces Canadian bacon

18 corn or 12 flour tortillas

FOR THE TOPPINGS:

2 cups Diced Tomatoes (page 87)
2 cups Sour Cream (page 88)

Chop the potatoes as in the Fried Potatoes recipe. Begin frying the potatoes while preparing the chili peppers and Canadian bacon.

Remove the stems and cores from the poblano chilies. Cut lengthwise into ⅛-inch-wide strips. Cut the Canadian bacon into ⅛-inch-wide strips.

(continued)

Plenty for 6

20 to 40 minutes

Poblano chilies are the big, green, mildly hot ones—they look a bit like a flattened, pointed bell pepper with a stem— that are used for *chilies rellenos.* If you can't find them, you could use the other large mild chili, Anaheim, or even green bell peppers.

When the potatoes have cooked 10 minutes, add the chilies to the pan and cook 5 minutes. Add the Canadian bacon strips to the pan and cook 5 minutes more.

Just before serving, heat the tortillas. They can be soft or crispy, see page 80.

To assemble the tacos, spread ½ cup of the potato, chili, and Canadian bacon mixture on the bottom of a hot tortilla. Top with 1½ tablespoons Diced Tomatoes and a few dollops of Sour Cream. Fold and serve.

NOTES AND AFTERTHOUGHTS
This taco doesn't really need a salsa, but if you're a salsa-holic, try the Tomato or Chive Salsa or the Tomatillo Sauce.

Fried Potatoes and Bananas

6 cups Fried Potatoes (page 87)
½ cup pine nuts
3 large or 4 small bananas (about 1¼ pounds)

18 corn or 12 flour tortillas

FOR THE TOPPINGS:
2 cups Chive Salsa, Melon and Jalapeño Salsa, or Tomatillo Sauce (pages 83, 84 and 85)
2 cups Sour Cream (page 88)
2 cups sliced avocado (optional)

Prepare the Fried Potatoes recipe. Remove to paper towels to drain.

In the same skillet you used for the potatoes, toast the pine nuts over medium heat, stirring constantly, about 1½ minutes.

Peel the bananas and slice crosswise into ⅜-inch-thick rounds. Add the bananas to the pan and stir 30 seconds. Remove the pine nuts and bananas to a plate or bowl.

Just before serving, heat the tortillas. They can be soft or crisp (page 80).

To assemble the tacos, place ½ cup of the fried potatoes on the bottom of a hot tortilla. Arrange about 2 tablespoons of the pine nut and banana mixture over the potatoes. Top with whatever salsa or sauce you are using, the Sour Cream, and optional avocado slices. Fold and serve.

Plenty for 6

20 to 40 minutes

Throughout Central and South America banana-like plantains are as common as bananas and are cooked and served daily just like a vegetable. Slightly less sweet than bananas, plantains fry up firmer and make a delightful variation in this taco. Plantains are available in many markets, especially those catering to a Latin American clientele.

Vegetables Stewed with White Wine Tacos

3 ears fresh corn or 1½ packages (10 ounces each) frozen petite corn
5 medium red or white potatoes (about 1½ pounds)
1 large or 2 medium onions (about ¾ pound)
6 medium tomatoes (about 1½ pounds)
3 medium zucchini (about ¾ pound)
1 jalapeño pepper
1 teaspoon dried oregano
1½ teaspoons salt
¾ cup white wine
¼ cup chopped cilantro leaves

12 flour tortillas

FOR THE TOPPINGS:
3 cups Shredded Cheese (page 88)
2 cups Tomato or Chive Salsa or Tomatillo Sauce (pages 82, 83, 85)
2 cups Sour Cream (page 88, optional)
2 cups Guacamole (page 86, optional)

If you are using fresh corn, bring a large pot of water to boil. Shuck the corn. Add to the boiling water and cook 5 minutes. Drain and cool. Cut the kernels off the cobs.

Cut the potatoes into quarters. Cut the quarters into ¼-inch-thick quarter rounds. Cut the zucchini lengthwise in half, then cut the halves into ¼-inch-thick half rounds. Cut the onion and tomatoes into ½-inch dice. Mince the jalapeño pepper.

In a large nonreactive pot or in a saucepan, combine fresh-cooked or frozen corn kernels, potatoes, onions, tomatoes, zucchini, jalapeño, oregano, salt, and wine. Cook, stirring once or twice, over medium-high heat, about 15 minutes, or until the potatoes are done. Stir in the cilantro and remove from the heat.

Just before serving, crisp the tortillas (page 80).

To assemble the tacos, place ½ cup of the stewed vegetables on the bottom of a hot tortilla. Sprinkle on ¼ cup Shredded Cheese. Top with 1½ tablespoons salsa or sauce. Add 1½ tablespoons Sour Cream and/or Guacamole, if using.

NOTES AND AFTERTHOUGHTS
Rather than frozen corn, you might substitute lima beans or fresh peas. In this case, the Corn and Red Bell Pepper Salsa (page 84) would be good with this taco.

Plenty for 6

20 to 40 minutes

The mysterious and remarkable flavor in this filling comes from stewing the vegetables in white wine only, no oil or water whatsoever, and finishing the array with a nuance of cilantro. Done this way, the vegetables are so extraordinary you will want to serve them not only as a taco filling with cheeses and salsa, but as a vegetable accompaniment to many other dishes. Try them especially with grilled or stovetop meats and poultry.

QUESADILLAS OR CHEESE TACOS

Quesadillas are different from other tacos. They are filled and folded first. Then they are crisped. Since you don't open them up again to add toppings, they are smaller than other tacos, and you will need one or two more per person to make a satisfying meal. Like fried potato tacos, quesadillas are eminently versatile. The number of ways you can diversify them is limited only by what you think might meld well with cheese.

Basic Quesadillas

Plenty for 6

20 minutes or less

Quesadillas make a great nibble as well as a meal. Quicker than a tuna melt, healthier than a Twinkie, and better than a grilled cheese sandwich, they don't take outside buttering, foil wrapping, or a weight to press them down. You can even make them in a toaster oven if you don't want to use a frying pan.

8 to 9 cups Shredded Cheese (page 88)
3 cups Tomato Salsa (page 82) or Diced Tomatoes (page 87)
24 corn or 18 flour tortillas
About 1½ cups vegetable or peanut oil

Spread the cheese evenly over half of a tortilla. (Corn tortillas take ⅓ cup cheese per quesadilla. Flour tortillas take ½ cup cheese per quesadilla.)

Spread about 1½ tablespoons Tomato Salsa or Diced Tomatoes over the cheese. Fold the tortilla in half.

In a frying pan, heat enough oil to coat the bottom of the pan. Place 1 or more folded tortillas in the pan and cook 1 minute over medium heat. Turn and cook 1 minute more on the other side.

VARIATIONS

Before folding and frying each quesadilla, add to the cheese:

SALSA: Tomatillo Sauce, Chive Salsa, or Corn and Red Bell Pepper Salsa.

CHOPPED VEGETABLES: 1 tablespoon or so chopped onion, green onion, bell pepper, olive, radish, artichoke heart, sorrel, or just about any other vegetable, with or without a salsa.

HERBS: About ½ teaspoon chopped fresh, or ¼ teaspoon dried, oregano, marjoram, sage, mint, basil, thyme, or dill.

NUTS AND SEEDS: 1 teaspoon toasted pumpkin seeds or pine nuts.

GOAT CHEESE AND WALNUTS: Stretching the idea of the quesadilla to include a version you might find in Los Angeles, New York, Paris, Rome, or the Zona Rosa District of Mexico City, mix 2 tablespoons crumbled goat cheese with the shredded cheese topping and sprinkle ½ tablespoon chopped walnuts over the cheese.

NOTES AND AFTERTHOUGHTS

Since quesadillas are fried with the cheese stuffing and must stay in the pan long enough for the cheese to melt, they take a little more oil than do the tortillas for other tacos to keep them from burning.

Mu Shu-Style Tacos with Mock Hoisin Sauce

1½ pounds boneless pork butt or shoulder
3 tablespoons dry sherry
3 tablespoons soy sauce
Mock Hoisin Sauce (page 106)
12 green onions
1 cup cilantro leaves
4 eggs
3 tablespoons peanut oil
1½ tablespoons sesame oil
2 cups fresh bean sprouts

12 flour tortillas

Shred the pork into thin strips ¼ inch thick by ½ inch wide and ½ inch long.

Mix the sherry and soy sauce together in a shallow bowl. Add the pork strips and turn to coat. Set aside to marinate for 20 to 30 minutes.

Make the Mock Hoisin Sauce.

Trim off the root ends and limp green tops from the green onions. Cut the onions lengthwise into thin shreds. Set aside on a plate along with the cilantro leaves.

Break the eggs into a small bowl and beat lightly.

When the pork is marinated, heat the peanut and sesame oils in a heavy skillet over high heat until the oil begins to smoke. Add the pork strips and bean sprouts and stir fry for 1 minute. Add the eggs and cook, stirring, for 30 seconds more. Remove from the heat.

Just before serving, warm the tortillas until soft (page 80).

To assemble the tacos, spread about 1 tablespoon of Mock Hoisin Sauce across a hot tortilla. Place about ⅓ cup of the meat mixture on top of the sauce. Top with 5 or 6 green onion strips and several cilantro leaves. Fold and serve.

NOTES AND AFTERTHOUGHTS

Mu Shu pork often has bamboo shoots and varieties of mushrooms in it or perhaps the fresh vegetable of the day, a little cabbage or bok choy. If you like these ingredients, you might want to add them. It will make a heftier taco.

(continued)

Plenty for 6

20 to 40 minutes

One of the most popular Chinese dishes is Mu Shu Pork. When we noticed our favorite "low rent" Chinese restaurant using tortillas instead of making their own crepes, we knew we had another taco we could make at home. The only problem was the hoisin sauce. The packaged varieties invariably have monosodium glutamate, an additive we try to avoid. We started experimenting. Hoisin looks pruny. It tastes pruny. A little garlic and soy and we came up with a homemade version. It stores in the refrigerator, still fresh for many a Mu Shu taco later.

Mock Hoisin Sauce

¾ cup pitted prunes (about ½ pound)
2 cups water
3 large garlic cloves
1½ tablespoons soy sauce
1½ tablespoons dry sherry

Place the pitted prunes and water in a small saucepan. Peel and sliver the garlic cloves and add to the pan. Cover the pan and simmer over medium heat 12 minutes, until the prunes are tender.

Pour the mixture into a food processor or blender. Add the soy sauce and sherry and puree until smooth. The sauce should be thick enough to peak, but runny enough to spread.

Vietnamese-Style Tacos with Shrimp, Noodles, Lettuce, and Dipping Sauce

Vietnamese-Style Dipping Sauce (page 107)
1 pound tiny cooked bay shrimp
¼ pound angel hair pasta or bean thread noodles (*sai fun*)
1 tablespoon sesame or sesame chili oil
2 medium cucumbers (about ¾ pound)
12 large red leaf or curly leaf lettuce leaves
1½ cups fresh basil leaves
4 cups bean sprouts (about 12 ounces)

12 flour tortillas

We've been blessed in recent years with yet another cuisine blending into ours. And readily, too, for like our modern cuisine, Vietnamese food is made up mainly of barbecues, pastas, soups, and salad dishes. This taco is like a rolled up shrimp salad. It is perfect for a light dinner, or you might also use it as an hors d'oeuvre or cocktail snack before a more elaborate dinner.

Bring a large pot of water to a boil for the pasta.

Meanwhile, make the Vietnamese-Style Dipping Sauce.

Place the shrimp in a colander and rinse under cold water. Pat dry with paper towels. Place the shrimp in a bowl and toss with ¼ cup of the dipping sauce.

When the water boils, drop in the pasta or bean thread noodles and cook until just tender to the bite. (The directions on the package will probably specify too long a cooking time, so test a piece after 4 minutes.) When done, drain the noodles in a colander. Place them in a medium bowl and toss with the sesame oil.

Wash the cucumbers. With a potato peeler, peel lengthwise in alternating strips ¼ to ½ inch wide to create a striped effect. Quarter the cucumbers lengthwise. Cut the quarters crosswise into ⅛-inch-thick quarter rounds.

Wash the lettuce leaves and pat them dry. Cut the larger basil leaves, more than 1 inch long, into 2 or 3 pieces, depending on the size. Leave smaller ones whole.

Arrange cucumber slices, lettuce, basil, and bean sprouts on a platter.

Just before serving, crisp the tortillas (page 80).

To assemble the tacos, place a large lettuce leaf on a hot tortilla. Spread about ¼ cup of the pasta over the lettuce leaf. Arrange 2 heaping tablespoons shrimp over the lettuce and noodles. Arrange about 2 tablespoons cucumber slices, ¼ cup bean sprouts, and several basil leaves over the shrimp. Spoon 2 tablespoons dipping sauce over all. Fold and serve.

NOTES AND AFTERTHOUGHTS
Sesame chili oil and bean thread noodles, called *sai fun,* are available in Oriental markets or the Oriental foods section of many supermarkets.

Vietnamese-Style Dipping Sauce
6 green onions
2 red Fresno or Santa Fe Grande or 3 red serrano chili peppers
1 cup vinegar, preferably rice wine, white wine, or cider
½ cup water

Plenty for 6

Makes 1½ cups

Trim the root ends and limp green tops off the green onions. Slice the onions into very thin rounds. Place in a medium bowl.

Remove the stems from the chili peppers and slice into very thin rounds. Add to the green onions.

Add the vinegar and water and mix.

NOTES AND AFTERTHOUGHTS
To serve the dipping sauce in authentic Vietnamese fashion, each person should have an individual small bowl.

COOL SALADS TO GO WITH HOT TACOS

Tacos are full meals in themselves and don't require side dishes to be filling. But occasionally you may want a more elaborate spread for a fancy taco party or simply to soothe the spiciness of tacos with a cooling antidote.

Orange and Curly Endive Salad

6 medium navel, Valencia, or blood oranges (about 1½ pounds)
1½ cups shredded curly endive
FOR THE DRESSING:
½ teaspoon dried mustard
½ teaspoon dried marjoram
2 teaspoons chopped orange peel
1 tablespoon lemon juice
½ tablespoon balsamic or red wine vinegar
2 tablespoons walnut oil, or 1 tablespoon peanut oil plus 1 tablespoon sesame oil

Make the dressing first. In a bowl, mix together the dry mustard, marjoram, orange peel, lemon juice, vinegar, and oil.

Peel the oranges and slice into ¼-inch-thick rounds. Stack the rounds and cut them into quarter rounds. Place them in a salad bowl.

Just before serving, add the shredded endive and dressing to the bowl. Toss.

Wilted Cucumber Salad

6 medium cucumbers (about 2 pounds)
2 teaspoons salt
2 tablespoons cider vinegar
2 teaspoons fresh oregano leaves or ½ teaspoon dried

Peel the cucumber. Cut into ⅛-inch-thick rounds. Place in a large bowl, sprinkle on the salt, and toss. Set aside to wilt about 20 minutes.

Drain the cucumbers. Squeeze out the excess liquid with your hands or in a dish towel.

Place the cucumbers in a clean bowl. Toss with the vinegar and oregano.

Plenty for 6
Makes about 8 cups

20 minutes or less

Oranges were brought to Mexico by the Spanish conquistadors and spread rapidly across the new world, perhaps because they go so well with chilies. You can occasionally find packaged fresh lima beans in the produce section of your market. But like black-eyed peas, they are very perishable. This salad is particularly refreshing with hot tacos.

Plenty for 6
Makes 4½ cups

20 to 40 minutes

Salting the cucumbers before dressing them leeches out much of their water and intensifies the cucumber taste. It is not particularly a way to eliminate bitterness. Although bitterness has largely been bred out of modern cucumber strains, the only way to ensure no bitterness in your cucumber salad is to taste each one and, if you come across a bitter one, toss it out.

Grated Carrot, Lemon, and Cumin Salad

1½ pounds medium carrots
½ cup lemon juice
2 tablespoons lime juice
¼ teaspoon ground cumin
3 tablespoons chopped cilantro or parsley leaves
¼ teaspoon salt

Peel the carrots. Grate in a food processor or through the large holes of a hand grater.

Place the carrots in a large bowl. Add the lemon juice, lime juice, cumin, cilantro, and salt. Toss.

Lima Bean and Chick Pea Salad

1 package (10 ounces) frozen baby lima beans
1 can (15½ ounces) chick peas
1 teaspoon very thinly shredded fresh sage leaves or ¼ teaspoon dried rubbed sage
2 tablespoons thinly shredded fresh mint leaves
⅓ cup chopped fresh parsley leaves, preferably Italian
½ teaspoon salt
2 tablespoons balsamic or red wine vinegar
4 tablespoons lemon juice
1 tablespoon olive oil

Bring 1 cup of water to a boil in a small saucepan. Drop in the frozen lima beans, cover, and cook 8 minutes. Drain in a colander and set aside to cool.

Drain the chick peas.

Line a medium bowl with a dish cloth or paper towel. Add the lima beans and chick peas and let sit 30 seconds to absorb any remaining moisture. Remove the paper towel, leaving the beans in the bowl.

Add the sage, mint, parsley, and salt, and toss well. Add the vinegar, lemon juice, and oil. Toss again.

Plenty for 6
Makes 4 cups

20 to 40 minutes

Plenty for 6
Makes 3½ cups

20 minutes or less

The instructions on frozen vegetable packages inevitably direct you to cook the vegetables too long.

Check the instructions, then seriously reduce the cooking time for all frozen vegetables.

You can occasionally find packaged fresh lima beans in the produce section of your market. But like black-eyed peas, they are very perishable. Check the package for any trace of juice. If the beans are not perfectly dry, they have most likely started to sour.

Canned vegetables packed in brine, such as chick peas, or cooked vegetables boiled in water, such as lima beans, need to be quite dry to absorb a salad dressing. Pat them dry with a dish cloth or paper towel after draining.

GOOD OLD
SPAGHETTIS
AND FRESH
NEW PASTAS

Three things rank supreme in making a good spaghetti dish. The sauce has to be rich whether it is thick or thin because pasta noodles are essentially bland. The sauce has to be "wet." It can consist of cream, oil, tomatoes, or pan juices, but it must flow like lava from Vesuvius over the noodles. Hunks of dense meats, fish, and vegetables don't work. They defy the lightness and separateness of the noodles, and they are tough, whereas noodles are soft. Better to use tidbits and soft delicacies—scallops, clams, ground meats, little bits of pork, salmon, or bacon, smatterings of red pepper, peas, yam.

The noodles should be cooked only until just done. *Al dente* is the Italian way of describing how the noodles are when they are perfect—cooked through, but still toothsome. Soggy noodles cannot buoy the sauce. They lie on the platter or in the bowl like albino eels, letting the savories float in between and by, not offering them up as the best dish you've ever seen and eaten. And pasta can be the best dish you've ever seen and eaten.

From red sauce and meatballs, Chef Boy-ar-Dee, and Kraft Macaroni, spaghetti in our kitchens has undergone an amazing evolution. Spaghetti isn't new to us. It's been part of our cuisine since the first Italian immigrant after Amerigo Vespucci. Every town across the nation has its Italian restaurant. Every mom has spaghetti among her offerings. But we've learned a lot about noodles in the last few decades, and we've incorporated many new ideas. We even call spaghetti pasta.

What suave Italian restaurants and trendy California ones started doing with pasta, we quickly adapted. Even at home, we make cheese sauces, white sauces, olive oil sauces. We use baby vegetables, chard, clams, mussels, duck, and just plain herbs. Kids love pasta. Friends love pasta. We love pasta because it's done in 20 minutes. It's always appealing. It's warm, it's soothing, and it's a meal.

We offer here 18 pasta dishes. Some of them are classics. Some of them are new. Some can be done in 10 minutes. Some take a little longer. Some are based on sauces that can be made months ahead and frozen to pull out and reheat. Practically none takes much in the way of ingredients. A cup of cream (unopened, you can keep a carton for weeks, and having one in the refrigerator means you can always make a pasta), a couple of tomatoes, half a pound of cheese, a few slices of bacon, a cup of nuts, garlic, some salmon, a leek, some ginger.

There are good packaged noodles in the markets that are dandy to use, but mostly, we would like to encourage you to make your own homemade noodles. We tell you how to do it quickly, with a fail-safe method that measures exactly for the number of people you are feeding. In most of our recipes, we call for tossing the noodles in sauce relatively rapidly to prevent their sticking together in great communal noodle spirit. If you are going to let cooked pasta sit for any length of time, oil or butter it. For double

For two oven-baked pastas, see the Corsican Lasagne (page 255) and Lasagne with Chard, Turnips, Pine Nuts, Ricotta, and Fontina (page 253). Corsican Lasagne also has a terrific red sauce that can be lavishly bestowed upon spaghetti, manicotti, ravioli, mesaluna, agnolotti, cappelletti, conchiglie, rigatoni, spaghettini, tortellini, or any other pasta, stuffed or otherwise.

protection you might also pour a dollop of oil in the boiling water when cooking the pasta.

If you are using olive oil as your sauce base, we recommend a good-quality extra-virgin oil. Good extra-virgin olive oil has a more assertive flavor that suits pasta and leaves no bitter aftertaste. If you are using heavy cream, try to purchase one with no preservatives from among those displayed in your dairy counter. It will probably be ultra-pasteurized to extend shelf life, but that's preferable to having stabilizing additives.

You can toss spaghettis and other pastas in a big bowl, serve them on a platter, dish them out onto individual plates, or send the bowl of noodles around first followed by the bowl of sauce and a big ladle after. We suggest a way to serve each of our pasta dishes. But the trick always with pasta, in both what you put in it and how you serve it up, is—suit your fancy.

EQUIPMENT

To make your own noodles, it's very helpful to have a pasta machine, but it isn't necessary. The dough can be kneaded quickly on a table and rolled out with a rolling pin. We still like good, old hand-cranked pasta machines for less fuss. It should have a way to tighten the rollers so you can roll out the dough thinner and thinner.

In addition, you need a large pot for cooking the noodles (they need plenty of water to turn out fluffy). Also a colander—or a very large sieve—is important for draining the pasta. A pair of short-handled tongs helps catch a serving of noodles from the pile, but two forks will do. ∎

Basic Pasta Dough

All pastas, and noodles too, come from the same basic pasta dough. Ours is an egg dough. Once the pasta is rolled into sheets and dried for a few minutes, you can cut it into any shape you desire: spaghetti, vermicelli, linguine, lasagne, or even angel's hair.

eggs: 1 per person plus 1 extra "for the house"
water: ½ eggshell full for every 2 eggs
nutmeg: ⅛ teaspoon for every 6 eggs
salt: 1 pinch per egg
white pepper: ½ pinch per egg
flour: depending on the eggs
olive oil or butter, for coating the noodles

Break the eggs into a large bowl. Add the water, nutmeg, salt, and pepper and beat lightly.

Slowly begin to add flour by the cupful to the egg mixture. Stir with a fork. Add flour in decreasing amounts until you cannot stir the dough with the fork any more and the dough forms into a sticky ball. Place the ball on a floured surface.

Kneading with your hands, continue to add flour in approximately ¼-cup amounts, until the dough no longer clings to your fingers. Divide the dough into balls about the size of baseballs.

Flatten and press each ball with your hand, lightly sprinkling with flour as you go, until the dough no longer sticks to your hand and no sticky spots open up as you flatten out the dough. The trick to light noodles is to stop kneading as soon as you have reached this point.

With a rolling pin or through the largest opening of a pasta machine, roll out the flattened dough as you would a pie crust. If any sticky spots still open up, work more flour into the dough by hand. Continue to roll out the dough with the rolling pin or through narrower and narrower openings of the pasta machine, until it is ¹⁄₁₆ inch thick or less, depending on your taste. Sprinkle with flour occasionally as you go.

Hang the rolled-out sheets of dough over a string or rack, or lay them out over a table to dry. Dry 10 to 20 minutes, but no longer or they will be too dry to cut without breaking. When the pasta has dried slightly, it is ready to cut and cook.

By hand or with a pasta machine, cut the sheets of dough into whatever width noodles you want.

To cook the pasta, bring a large pot of water to boil. Add 1 tablespoon olive oil to the water to keep the noodles from sticking together. Drop the noodles into the boiling water and cook 3 to 4 minutes. Drain briefly, then put the noodles in a bowl. Add olive oil or butter to coat lightly and toss. The noodles are now ready for whatever sauce you want or to eat as is.

(continued)

Plenty for however many are eating

20 minutes or less

We know, there are no exact amounts in this recipe. That's because the number of eggs depends on the number of people. The amount of flour and water depends on the number of eggs, and so does the nutmeg. BUT IT ALWAYS WORKS. By using an egg per person, you never get too much or too little. The shell of the egg perfectly measures the necessary water. The egg for the house gives that sometimes needed little bit extra. You never over- or under-measure the flour because of a stated cup measure that doesn't match the egg size. The process is extraordinarily simple and fast. More than fast, it's the best noodle recipe ever. So don't be timid. Count heads, crack eggs, and have at it.

When the sheets of homemade pasta dough have dried 10 to 20 minutes, you can lay them on a length of plastic wrap to cover, roll or fold the covered sheets into a size easy to store, and refrigerate up to 3 days or freeze for longer. The pasta should not be cut before storing, though, because it will dry out too much.
continued

On the other hand, if you would like to make a supply of dried pasta, cut the slightly dried dough sheets into whatever width you want, spread the noodles out to dry completely (a few hours), then store in a tightly covered container in the pantry. Dried pasta takes 5 to 6 minutes longer to cook.

Plenty for 15 or so
Makes 13 cups

3½ hours

The surprise in this vegetable tomato sauce is its zucchini base. More than onions and carrots, the zucchini imbues the sauce with an extra special, deep vegetable essence. Like the quicker marinara sauce, so well known by lovers of Italian cuisine, this longer-cooking fresh tomato sauce is notable for its versatility. You can put meats or fish *in* it to serve over pasta. It can also be used as a sauce or condiment for pork, lamb, or beef roast, Desperation Chicken (page 195), roast chicken or game hens, as well as over rice, potatoes, grilled foods, steamed vegetables, or on pizza.

Fresh tomatoes vary enormously in their water content. If after 3 hours, watery liquid remains on top of the sauce and there is still a good deal of steam escaping, it has not thickened enough. Continue simmering a little longer until the steam is mostly gone; the oil, not water, has risen

NOTES AND AFTERTHOUGHTS

1. If you are making fresh pasta for more than 10, you might want to add a second extra egg "for the house" in case there are big eaters in the crowd.

2. We call for white pepper in the noodle dough because it preserves the clean, white look of the pasta. If you don't keep white pepper in your pantry, black will do, but will speckle the noodles.

Basic Red Zucchini Tomato Sauce

2 medium onions (about 14 ounces)
8 medium zucchini (about 2 pounds)
2 carrots (about 4 ounces)
1 medium green bell pepper (about 6 ounces)
4 medium garlic cloves
½ cup olive oil
20 to 24 medium tomatoes (about 6 pounds)
2 cups red wine
1 teaspoon dried basil
1½ teaspoons fresh marjoram leaves or ½ teaspoon dried
1 medium bay leaf
1 teaspoon salt
1 small dried red chili pepper (optional)

Peel the onion. Wash and trim the ends from the zucchini and carrots. Remove the stem and core from the bell pepper. Peel the garlic.

By hand or in a food processor, medium chop the onion, zucchini, carrots, bell pepper, and garlic.

Heat the oil in a 5-quart or larger pot or sauté pan. Add the chopped vegetables. Sauté, over medium-high heat, stirring occasionally, for 30 minutes.

Cut the tomatoes into quarters.

Add the tomatoes, red wine, basil, marjoram, bay leaf, salt, and red pepper to the pot. Bring to a boil. Reduce the heat to low, and simmer 2½ hours.

VARIATIONS

EGGPLANT: For a more intriguing vegetable spaghetti sauce, use ½ an eggplant, chopped medium fine, in place of 2 of the zucchini. Sauté the eggplant along with the zucchini, onions, peppers, and garlic.

MUSHROOMS: Mushrooms also deepen the flavor of a tomato sauce. Add ½ pound cleaned and sliced mushrooms along with the zucchini, onions, peppers, and garlic.

ANCHOVY: Add 6 whole salt-packed anchovies, deboned and rinsed of all their salt, or 12 flat fillets to the sauce along with the wine, tomatoes, and herbs.

HAM, PROSCIUTTO, OR BACON: Sauté 2 cups medium-chopped ham, prosciutto, or bacon in the olive oil for 5 minutes before adding the vegetables.

SAUSAGE: Add 1 pound Quick Sweet Sausage (page 62), Sausage Burger (page 155), or purchased fresh Italian sausage after sautéing the vegetables. Brown, then add the wine, tomatoes, and herbs.

Spaghetti with Basic Red Zucchini Tomato Sauce

1½ pounds spaghetti

4½ cups Basic Red Zucchini Tomato Sauce (page 117)
1 cup grated Parmesan, Romano, or aged Asiago cheese

Bring a large pot of water to boil. When the water boils, cook the spaghetti. Drain briefly.

Meanwhile, heat the Basic Red Zucchini Tomato Sauce.

To assemble the pasta, spread the noodles on a large platter. Spoon the sauce over the noodles, sprinkle the cheese over the top, and serve.

VARIATIONS

MEATBALLS: Cook Turkey and Pistachio Meatballs (page 130) or Pork, Onion, and Caper Meatballs (page 125) just until done, then add to the sauce right before serving or arrange on top of the sauced pasta.

SHELLFISH: Cook scallops, shrimp, mussels, or clams separately. Spoon the sauce over cooked pasta and arrange the shellfish on top.

SQUID: Add tentacles and strips of fresh, cleaned squid to the sauce and cook 5 minutes. Serve right away.

NOTES AND AFTERTHOUGHTS

1. By using the variations listed above for the sauce or the dish, this pasta becomes spaghetti and meatballs, seafood spaghetti, sausage, bacon, or what-have-you spaghetti. It's wonderful every way.

2. Of course, you can vary the pasta also. It doesn't have to be spaghetti. It can be linguine, manicotti, rigatoni, angel hair, or some other shape that captures your fancy.

to the top; and the sauce is bubbling like lava. On the other hand, if the sauce meets this description before 3 hours of cooking, turn it off.

Plenty for 6

20 minutes of less

Plenty for 20
Makes 15 cups

5½ to 6 hours

A good Bolognese sauce does take 5 hours to cook, but it is incredibly delicious. If you have a day at home for the simmering and a food processor to help chop the vegetables (though it takes little time by hand), the sauce is no trouble to make. Another payoff is how well it stores: well enough to stay ahead of the what's-for-dinner game for weeks. Susanna makes a huge batch in an 18-quart sauté pan and freezes the sauce in containers varying in size from enough for 2 to enough for 10.

There are two tricks involved in making this an exceptionally fine and rich sauce. The first is to reduce the vegetables to an unrecognizable state. No skimping on this step. It's the caramelized vegetables that form the deep, robust essence of the sauce. The second trick is to stir in the milk at the very last, just as the sauce is done. The milk amalgamates the savory oils that have risen to the top and pulls them back thoroughly into the sauce.

Basic Meat Sauce Bolognese

2 medium onions (about 14 ounces)
6 medium garlic cloves
2 celery ribs (about 6 ounces)
3 carrots (about 6 ounces)
½ cup olive oil
1 pound ground round or ground chuck
½ pound ground veal or ground turkey
½ pound ground pork
5 cans (28 ounces each) crushed tomatoes in puree
1 can (6 ounces) tomato paste
2½ cups red wine
1 bay leaf
1 tablespoon fresh oregano leaves or 1 teaspoon dried
1 tablespoon fresh thyme leaves or 1 teaspoon dried
½ teaspoon salt
½ cup milk

Peel the onion and garlic cloves. Wash the celery and carrots. By hand or in a food processor, medium chop the onion, garlic, celery, and carrots.

Heat the oil in a 5-quart or larger heavy nonreactive pot or sauté pan. Add the chopped vegetables. Sauté over medium heat until the vegetables are dark brown and crispy, no longer cover the entire bottom of the pan, and only a few carrot pieces are recognizable, about 1 hour. Stir occasionally for the first 20 minutes, and then more often for the remaining 40 minutes. Reduce the heat if the vegetables begin to burn.

When the vegetables are thoroughly crisped, add the ground beef, veal or turkey, and pork. Cook, stirring to crumble completely, until well browned, about 10 minutes.

Add the tomatoes, tomato paste, wine, bay leaf, oregano, thyme, and salt. Bring to a boil over medium heat, stirring occasionally, about 45 minutes to 1 hour. (It will take this long to come to a boil.)

Reduce the heat to maintain a gentle simmer with occasional bubbles rising to the top and cook 3 to 3½ hours more. Stir from time to time to make sure the sauce doesn't stick to the bottom of the pot.

When the sauce is done, the oil will have risen to the top and a crust will have formed over the surface. No steam will be escaping, and the color of the sauce will be a deep red-brown. Stir in the milk, blending thoroughly. Remove from the heat.

NOTES AND AFTERTHOUGHTS
If you don't want to deal with the volume of sauce in this recipe, cut the amounts in half. The cooking time is the same.

VARIATIONS

BACON: Use ½ pound sliced bacon, cut into ¼-inch-wide pieces, in place of the pork.

CHICKEN LIVERS: Add ¼ pound chopped fresh chicken livers along with the other meats.

SAUSAGE: Use ½ pound fresh Italian-style sausage in place of the pork.

MUSHROOMS: Add 1 pound sliced mushrooms along with the meats.

WHITE WINE: Use 2½ cups white wine in place of the red wine.

Pasta with Basic Meat Sauce Bolognese

1½ pounds spaghetti, fettuccine, rigatoni, ravioli, or any other shaped pasta

4½ cups Basic Meat Sauce Bolognese (page 118)
3 tablespoons butter (optional)
1 cup grated Parmesan, Romano, or aged Asiago cheese

Plenty for 6

20 minutes or less

Bring a large pot of water to boil. Cook the pasta noodles and drain briefly.

While the noodles cook, heat the Basic Meat Sauce Bolognese.

To assemble the dish, spread the noodles on a large platter or divide among 6 individual plates. Top with the Bolognese sauce, using about ¾ cup per person. If using butter, divide into 6 pieces and place on top of the sauce. Sprinkle grated cheese over all and serve.

NOTES AND AFTERTHOUGHTS

The butter is in case you want to serve the pasta Bolognese in true Bolognese style. The butter melts into the sauce, gilding it with still more richness.

The Good & Plenty Cafe sits next to a new and vital art gallery on the grounds of the California College of Arts and Crafts. "Starving" students are plentiful among our clientele. To sate their hunger, accommodate their pocketbooks, and often simply soothe their longing for home cooking, we frequently offer good old macaroni and cheese. The method of mixing the cheese into cream and butter—Italian style—and heating the mixture until the cheese is blended in is much faster than the better known way of baking the noodles and cheese in a casserole. If you don't want to sacrifice the crispy crust, you can top the Alfredo with some grated cheddar and bread crumbs, and slip it into a hot oven for 20 minutes until the top browns—as we do at the Good & Plenty.

Pasta and Cheese Alfredo

1½ pounds pasta, any shape

4 tablespoons butter
1½ cups heavy cream
1 cup grated Parmesan cheese

Bring a large pot of water to boil. Cook the pasta and drain in a colander, and set aside.

In the same pot you used for the pasta, melt the butter over medium heat until it begins to foam. Add the cream and cheese and stir.

Return the pasta to the pot and stir to coat well. Serve.

NOTES AND AFTERTHOUGHTS
If you want your cheese sauce a little thicker, beat the cream until thickened but not stiff before adding it to the butter.

VARIATIONS

CHEESE: Vary the cheeses in your cheese sauce. Use only ½ cup grated Parmesan and add 2 ounces other cheese such as grated cheddar, Fontina, or Swiss-type cheese, or crumbled Feta, Gorgonzola, Roquefort, Bavarian Blue, or chèvre into the cream mixture. Stir until melted and smooth.

BACON: Make an Alfredo-carbonara combo. Cut bacon slices into ½-inch-wide pieces and fry until crisp. Stir into the pasta just before serving.

COLD CUTS: Cut salami, prosciutto, capocolo, or cooked ham into strips and stir into the pasta just before serving.

SAUSAGE: Sauté Quick Sweet Sausage (page 65), Sausage Burger (page 155), or purchased fresh sausage and crumble it into the pasta. Stir to mix and serve.

SHELLFISH: Stir cooked and shelled clams, mussels, or shrimp into the pasta just before serving.

ANCHOVIES: Clean and debone salt-packed anchovies, mince the fillets, and stir them into the sauce before tossing with the pasta.

GARLIC: Press 1 to 3 cloves garlic into the sauce before tossing with the pasta.

MUSHROOMS: Sauté sliced mushrooms in a little butter and lemon juice and stir into the sauce before serving.

TOMATOES: Stir peeled or unpeeled diced fresh tomatoes into the sauce just before serving.

BLANCHED VEGETABLES: Briefly boil bite-size pieces of cauliflower, summer squashes, green beans, broccoli, julienned strips of carrot, peas, or use a mixture. Stir into the pasta just before serving.

HERBS: Stir chopped fresh herbs into the sauce before tossing with the pasta.

CHILI PEPPERS: Slice fresh chili peppers into thin rounds and stir into the sauce before tossing with the pasta.

NUTS AND SEEDS: Toast sliced almonds, chopped walnuts, pine nuts, or pumpkin seeds and sprinkle them over the pasta just before serving.

Quick Tomato and Bacon Spaghetti *Amatriciana*

2 pounds spaghetti, vermicelli, or linguine

1½ medium onions (about 10 ounces)
1½ serrano chili peppers
2 tablespoons olive oil
3 small dried red chili peppers
¾ pound sliced bacon
8 medium tomatoes (about 2 pounds)
¾ cup white wine
2 tablespoons chopped fresh parsley leaves
1 tablespoon chopped lemon peel

Bring a large pot of water to a boil. Cook the pasta. Drain briefly, return it to the pot, and set aside in a warm place.

Meanwhile, peel the onions and cut lengthwise into quarters. Cut the quarters crosswise into ⅛-inch-thick quarter rounds. Remove the stems from the serrano chilies. Cut the chilies into ⅛-inch-thick rounds.

Heat the olive oil in a large skillet until the oil begins to smoke. Add the onions, chilies, and the whole dried red chili peppers. Cook over medium heat 10 minutes.

Cut the bacon crosswise into ½-inch-wide pieces. Add to the skillet and cook, stirring occasionally, 10 minutes.

Rough chop the tomatoes into ½- to ¾-inch chunks.

Discard the dried peppers. Add the tomatoes and wine to the skillet. Increase the heat to medium high and cook 5 minutes.

To assemble the pasta, place the noodles on a large platter. Spoon the sauce over the top. Sprinkle on the parsley and lemon peel and serve.

NOTES AND AFTERTHOUGHTS

1. If you can get the peppery Italian bacon called pancetta, use it instead of bacon for this dish.

2. If you can't find the little serrano chili peppers, use a jalapeño instead. If you can find no fresh chilies at all, use 1 more dried chili.

Plenty for 6

20 to 40 minutes

There is some controversy over what the word *amatriciana* in the title of this dish means. Some people, including Ada Boni, say the reference to ladies of the night is a misconception, and that *amatriciana* comes from the village named Amatrice in the Sabine hills near Rome where the dish originated. Others think it comes from the Latin for prostitute, as the dish is often also called *pasta putanesca*, the modern term for members of that profession. Whichever interpretation you choose, the dish is a spicy Roman-style pasta that you make in a jiffy. It always includes bacon and a little hot red pepper. Under either name you might find it in the simple version we have here or with the addition of olives and capers.

Quick Spaghetti with Fried Tomatoes, Cabbage, Garlic, Capers, and Cream

Plenty for 6

20 minutes or less

Fry tomatoes and cabbage, heat a creamy sauce, serve it over a bed of steaming noodles. It's a hot twist on the idea of cole slaw! Even those who are not fond of cabbage relish this dish.

1½ pounds spaghetti, vermicelli, or linguine

4 medium tomatoes (about 1 pound)
1 medium head green cabbage (about 2 pounds)
2 medium garlic cloves
2 tablespoons olive oil
2 tablespoons capers
1½ tablespoons chopped fresh tarragon leaves or 1½ teaspoons dried
2 cups heavy cream

Bring a large pot of water to boil. Cook the pasta, drain briefly, and return it to the pot. Set aside.

Meanwhile, cut the tomatoes in half, then slice into ¼-inch-thick half rounds. Cut the cabbage into quarters and remove the core. Slice crosswise into ¼-inch-thick strips. Peel the garlic cloves and rough chop.

Heat the oil in a large skillet until the oil begins to smoke. Add the tomatoes and fry over medium-high heat, turning once, 5 minutes. Remove the tomatoes and set aside.

Add the cabbage and garlic to the skillet. Sauté 8 to 10 minutes, until the cabbage is wilted and slightly browned.

Return the tomatoes to the skillet. Stir in the capers and tarragon. Add the cream. Bring to a boil and remove from the heat.

To assemble the pasta, place the noodles on a platter. Spoon the tomato and cabbage mixture over the top. Serve.

Pasta Primavera with Cauliflower, Peas, Squash, Tomatoes, and Basil

1 pound spaghetti, vermicelli, or linguine

6 medium tomatoes (about 1½ pounds)
1 pound cauliflower (about ½ regular head, or 2 heaping cups florets)
7 small crookneck or yellow zucchini squash (about ¾ pound)
1½ pounds peas in their pods (or about 1½ cups shelled peas)
3 medium garlic cloves
1½ cups shredded fresh basil leaves
¾ teaspoon salt
1 cup olive oil
⅔ cup grated Parmesan, Romano, or aged Asiago cheese

Plenty for 6

20 minutes or less

Victoria once cooked for the family of an Italian-American film director, whose house was always teeming with activity. To stave off the hungry hordes, he taught her classic Pasta Primavera. It has only tomatoes, garlic, and basil, and is quick to put together on the spur of the moment, to serve anytime. On her first try, the director berated Victoria for overchopping the basil. "That's the trouble with you French cooks—you overprocess everything," he teased. He was right. The trick to the elegance of this dish is to keep it simple and country style. Briefly cook the vegetables, roughly chop the tomatoes and basil, press the garlic into the dish, and pour plenty of good, extra-virgin olive oil over all. Although he would not approve of the adulterated version of Primavera here (all those other vegetables tossed in), cauliflower, squash, and peas make a meal out of what, to a good Italian, is only a first course.

Bring 1 large and 1 medium-size pot of water to boil. When the large pot of water boils, cook the pasta. Drain briefly and return the pasta to the pot. Set aside in a warm place.

When the medium-size pot of water boils, drop in the tomatoes. Count to 10 and remove the tomatoes, reserving the water. Rinse the tomatoes in cool water, then peel them. Cut the tomatoes into ½-inch dice.

Remove the core from the cauliflower. Slice the cauliflower into bite-size florets. Slice the crookneck squash into ⅛-inch-thick rounds. Shell the peas. Peel the garlic cloves.

Drop the cauliflower and squash into the reserved pot of boiling water. Slowly count to 20, and add the peas. Slowly count to 20 again, then drain the vegetables. Pat dry with paper towels.

To assemble the pasta, place the noodles in a large bowl. Press the garlic over the noodles. Add the tomatoes, cooked vegetables, basil, salt, and oil; toss. Serve with the grated cheese on the side.

NOTES AND AFTERTHOUGHTS

Primavera means "spring" in Italian, and this dish is called Pasta Primavera because the vegetables that garnish the pasta are as fresh as spring. Barely blanched, they are brought to full flavor with olive oil alone. You can substitute green beans, broccoli, zucchini, or other summer squashes in season, but to keep the springlike quality of the dish, vegetables should be of the fresh-from-the-garden type. Winter vegetables are too heavy.

Spaghetti with Pork, Onion, and Caper Meatballs and Gorgonzola Cream

1½ pounds spaghetti, vermicelli, or linguine
1 tablespoon olive oil

1 batch Pork, Onion, and Caper Meatballs (page 125)
6 ounces Gorgonzola cheese
3 tablespoons butter
1½ cups heavy cream

Bring a large pot of water to boil. Cook the pasta. Drain briefly, return to the pot, and toss with the olive oil. Set aside in a warm place.

Meanwhile, make and cook the Pork, Onion, and Caper Meatballs.

Combine the Gorgonzola, butter, and cream in a saucepan. Stir with a wooden spoon over medium heat, melting the butter and mashing the cheese, until the sauce is smooth.

To assemble the dish, pour the sauce over the noodles in the pot and toss together. Spread the noodles and sauce on a large platter. Arrange the meatballs over the top. Serve.

NOTES AND AFTERTHOUGHTS
Spaghetti in Gorgonzola cream sauce without the meatballs is a variation of Pasta and Cheese Alfredo and makes a delicious side dish or small first course.

Pork, Onion, and Caper Meatballs

½ medium onion (about 3 ounces)
3 tablespoons capers
¾ pound ground pork
3 tablespoons fresh Bread Crumbs (page 136)
1 tablespoon tomato paste
1 egg
¼ teaspoon ground nutmeg
¼ teaspoon salt
¼ teaspoon freshly ground black pepper
1 to 2 teaspoons oil

Makes 68 tiny meatballs

Peel the onion. With a chef's knife or a food processor, fine chop the onion and capers. Place in a mixing bowl and add the pork, bread crumbs, tomato paste, egg, nutmeg, salt, and pepper. Mix well.

Using about 1 teaspoon of the mixture, roll meatballs the size of marbles or large cherries.

To cook the meat balls, coat a large skillet with 1 teaspoon oil. Add as many meatballs as will fit in a single uncrowded layer, and cook 5 mintues over medium heat, turning once. Remove the cooked meatballs and continue with another round until all are done.

NOTES AND AFTERTHOUGHTS

1. Pork, Onion, and Caper Meatballs can be made up to 2 days in advance. Place on a plate, cover with plastic wrap, and refrigerate. Cook just before serving.

2. Small, bite-size meatballs work best with the extremely rich Gorgonzola cream sauce. For other dishes, the size of the meatballs can be varied.

Cold Noodles, Crispy Fried Pork, and Bean Sprouts with Hot Peanut Sesame Sauce

Plenty for 6

20 to 40 minutes

For those who find themselves forever heading to their favorite Chinese eatery for cold peanut noodles or shredded chicken peanut salad, this is it! Our version of the sauce is slightly thicker and more peanutty. We have complemented the dish with sweet crispy pork instead of chicken, but you could use chicken, hot or cold, and add lettuce or cabbage should you desire.

2 pounds vermicelli or rice noodles
2 tablespoons peanut oil

3 cups Hot Peanut Sesame Sauce (page 127)

1 pound pork tenderloin
⅓ cup shelled peanuts
2 tablespoons peanut oil
½ cup sherry
2 teaspoons sugar
1 teaspoon chili oil
2 cups fresh bean sprouts (about 6 ounces)
¼ cup cilantro or Italian parsley leaves

Bring a large pot of water to boil. Cook the vermicelli or rice noodles. Drain the noodles and toss them with 2 tablespoons of the peanut oil. Cover and refrigerate until chilled.

Meanwhile, make the Hot Peanut Sesame Sauce.

Slice the pork tenderloin into ¼-inch-thick rounds. Cut the rounds into ¼-inch-wide strips. Medium chop the peanuts in a food processor or by hand.

Heat the second 2 tablespoons peanut oil in a heavy skillet until the oil begins to smoke. Add the pork and cook over high heat 1 minute. Add the sherry and cook until evaporated, about 2 minutes. Add the chopped peanuts, sugar, and chili oil. Cook, stirring constantly, for 2 to 3 minutes until the pork strips are crisped and the peanuts are browned.

To assemble the dish, toss the cold noodles with two thirds of the Hot Peanut Sesame Sauce. Arrange the noodles down the center of a large platter. Top the noodles with the bean sprouts and cilantro. Arrange the hot pork and peanut mixture around the edges of the noodles. Serve the remaining sauce on the side.

NOTES AND AFTERTHOUGHTS

1. This dish can be divided into very simple parts, most of which can be made well ahead of time. The Hot Peanut Sesame Sauce keeps well for weeks so aficionados can make large batches to have on hand in the refrigerator. The noodles can be made in the morning or the night before. You can even sauté the pork ahead instead of just before serving, assemble the entire dish in advance, and serve it chilled.

2. Chili oil (also called red pepper oil, or hot sesame oil) can be found in the Oriental food markets or the international food section of most supermarkets. It is oil that's been infused with chili pepper or cayenne, to

make it mildly, but not fiery, hot. You often find it on the table in Chinese restaurants, to be used as dipping sauce for dumplings.

3. You can make this dish with chicken instead of pork.

Hot Peanut Sesame Sauce

Makes 3 cups

2 tablespoons grated fresh gingerroot
2 tablespoons peanut oil
2½ tablespoons rice vinegar
2 teaspoons sugar
¼ cup sesame seed
⅔ cup peanut butter, preferably unsweetened chunky style
8 tablespoons soy sauce
⅔ cup water
2 tablespoons sesame oil
2 teaspoons chili oil
2 teaspoons freshly ground black pepper

In a small bowl, combine the ginger, peanut oil, rice vinegar, and sugar. Set aside to marinate at least 15 minutes.

Place the sesame seeds in a small ungreased frying pan and toast over medium low heat, stirring occasionally, for 3 to 4 minutes. When browned, crush a bit with the back of a spoon.

Put the peanut butter into a bowl. Add the soy sauce, 1 tablespoon at a time, blending thoroughly after each addition and stirring until smooth. Stir in the water, sesame oil, chili oil, black pepper, and toasted sesame seeds.

Add the ginger and marinade to the peanut-sesame mixture. Stir to blend well.

NOTES AND AFTERTHOUGHTS

1. If you have time, marinate the ginger for an hour or even longer before adding it to the rest of the ingredients.

2. When toasting sesame seeds, the frying pan must be kept at medium-low heat. Otherwise, the seeds pop like popcorn and spatter everywhere.

3. You can use white wine vinegar if you don't have rice vinegar, but add a smaller amount. Rice vinegar is very mild.

4. Avoid using brands of peanut butter that have sugar added. Other than making the peanut butter more attractive to children, the sugar is completely unnecessary. Peanut butter made with just ground peanuts is sweet enough on its own.

Pasta with Crispy Fried Pork, Yams, Walnuts, White Wine, and Cream

Plenty for 6

20 to 40 minutes

1½ pounds spaghetti, vermicelli, or linguine
1 tablespoon peanut oil
¼ teaspoon salt

1½ pounds yams
5 tablespoons peanut oil
⅓ cup chopped walnuts
1½ pounds boneless, well-trimmed pork loin chops
12 medium garlic cloves
1 tablespoon fresh thyme leaves or 1 teaspoon dried
½ teaspoon fennel seed
⅜ teaspoon freshly ground black pepper
⅜ teaspoon salt
½ cup white wine
1 cup heavy cream
⅓ cup chopped fresh parsley
3 tablespoons grated Parmesan, Romano, or aged Asiago cheese

Bring a large pot of water to boil. Cook the pasta. Drain briefly and toss with the 1 tablespoon peanut oil and ¼ teaspoon salt. Set aside in a warm place.

Peel the yams with a potato peeler and cut lengthwise into quarters. Cut the quarters into ⅛-inch-thick quarter rounds.

Heat 3 tablespoons of the peanut oil in a large skillet. Add the yams and fry, stirring occasionally, over medium to medium-high heat for 5 minutes. Add the walnuts and cook 5 minutes more. Remove the yams and walnuts to a plate, and reserve the pan for cooking the pork.

Cut the pork chops lengthwise into ⅛-inch-thick strips. Peel the garlic cloves and cut them crosswise into very thin slices.

Heat the remaining 2 tablespoons peanut oil in the reserved skillet until the oil begins to smoke. Add the pork, garlic, thyme, fennel seed, black pepper and ⅜ teaspoon salt. Fry over high heat, stirring often, for 5 minutes.

Add the wine, and bring to a boil. Cook about 2 minutes, until the alcohol burns off and the wine has almost evaporated. Stir in the cream and bring to a boil. Remove from the heat.

To assemble the dish, place the noodles in a large bowl. Add the yams and walnuts, pork strips and cream sauce, and the parsley. Toss. Sprinkle the grated cheese over the top and serve.

Spaghetti with Chicken, Pecans, and Cream

1½ pounds spaghetti, vermicelli, or linguine

2 tablespoons plus 2 teaspoons peanut oil
3 chicken breasts, preferably with bone in (about ¾ pound each)
6 celery ribs
3 red serrano chili peppers
1 cup pecan halves (about 4 ounces)
1 tablespoon fresh thyme leaves or 1 teaspoon dried
6 tablespoons capers
½ teaspoon salt
3 tablespoons chopped fresh chives
2 cups heavy cream

Bring a large pot of water to boil. Cook the pasta. Drain briefly, return to the pot, and set aside in a warm place.

Meanwhile, heat 2 tablespoons of the peanut oil in a large skillet until the oil begins to smoke. Remove the skin from the chicken breasts. Place the breasts, meat side down, in the skillet. Cook over medium-high heat 12 minutes. Turn and cook 12 minutes on the other side.

While the chicken cooks, cut the celery crosswise into ¼-inch-wide pieces. Remove the stems from the chilies. Cut the peppers lengthwise into very thin slivers. Cut the pecan halves into large pieces.

Heat the 2 remaining teaspoons peanut oil in a small frying pan. Add the pecans and stir over medium-high heat 2 minutes, until browned.

When the chicken has cooked for 20 minutes, add the celery and thyme to the skillet. Continue cooking for the remaining 4 minutes.

When the chicken is done, remove it to a plate, leaving the celery in the skillet. Add the pecans, chili pepper, capers, salt, and half of the chives to the skillet and set aside off the heat.

Remove the bones from the chicken breasts. Cut the meat into 1-inch-long, ¼-inch-wide strips. Add the chicken strips to the skillet.

Whip the cream until slightly thickened but not stiff. Add to the skillet, and bring to a boil. Immediately remove from the heat.

To assemble the dish, pour the chicken and sauce over the pasta and toss. Sprinkle on the remaining 1½ tablespoons chives and serve.

NOTES AND AFTERTHOUGHTS
If you can't find serrano chili peppers, use 1 fresh jalapeño or 3 small dried red chili peppers.

Plenty for 6

20 to 40 minutes

Chicken, fish, or meat sometimes work better with pasta if you head for an Oriental style or if you add other tangy touches such as we've done here with pecans, red peppers, capers, and chives.

Pecans, the fruit of a species of hickory tree native to the Mississippi River valley, are America's one true nut. Since pre-Columbian times, American Indians of the southeast cooked with them, making meat sauces, pressing their oil and carrying them as snacks. Thomas Jefferson brought several of the trees to grow at Monticello. Pecans remain almost exclusively an American product, in pies, in sticky breakfast buns—and in chicken-pecan pasta.

Turkey and Pistachio Meatballs on Spaghetti with Basil Cream

Plenty for 6

20 to 40 minutes

1½ pounds spaghetti, vermicelli, or linguine

1 batch Turkey and Pistachio Meatballs (see below)
3 medium tomatoes (about ¾ pound)
6 tablespoons grated Parmesan, Romano, or aged Asiago cheese
¼ teaspoon salt
2 cups heavy cream
1½ cups thinly shredded fresh basil leaves

Bring a large pot of water to boil. Cook the pasta, drain briefly, and return to the pot.

Meanwhile, make and cook the Turkey and Pistachio Meatballs.

Just before serving, cut the tomatoes into ¼-inch dice. Add the tomatoes, cheese, salt, and cream to the spaghetti, and toss. Return the pot to low heat and cook briefly to warm the cream. Stir in ¾ cup of the basil.

To assemble the dish, spread the spaghetti on a large platter. Arrange the turkey meatballs over the noodles; sprinkle the remaining ¾ cup basil over all. Serve.

Turkey and Pistachio Meatballs

Makes about 38 walnut-size meatballs

1½ pounds ground turkey
3 medium garlic cloves
⅜ cup shelled pistachio nuts (about 1½ ounces), or ¾ cup unshelled pistachio nuts (about 3 ounces)
1 small onion (about 6 ounces)
⅜ cup grated Parmesan, Romano, or aged Asiago cheese
⅜ teaspoon salt
1 large or 2 small eggs
2 tablespoons olive oil

Place the ground turkey in a bowl. Peel the garlic and press into the turkey.

Shell the pistachio nuts if they are not already shelled. Fine chop in a food processor or with a chef's knife. Peel the onion and mince.

Add the pistachios, onion, cheese, and salt to the turkey. Break the egg into the bowl and, with your hands, mix all of the ingredients together. Using about 1 tablespoon at a time, form into meatballs.

To cook the meatballs, heat the oil in a large skillet. Add as many meatballs as will fit in a single uncrowded layer. Cook over medium-high heat 3 minutes. Turn and cook 3 minutes more. Continue with another batch until all the meatballs are cooked.

NOTES AND AFTERTHOUGHTS
1. You can make the turkey meatballs up to 2 days in advance. Cover with plastic wrap and store in the refrigerator.

2. You can find unshelled pistachios in health food stores and gourmet markets. They don't taste different, but they make for an easier job.

Spaghetti with Duck and Olives

1½ to 2 fresh ducks, backbones removed, cut into leg, thigh, and breast pieces (page 28)
Ingredients for curing duck and rabbit (page 28, optional)
Olive oil
1½ pounds spaghetti
4 tablespoons butter (½ stick)

FOR THE SAUCE:

9 ribs celery
¾ cup black olives, preferably Kalamata
6 garlic cloves
1½ cups dry red wine
¼ cup chopped celery leaves
1½ tablespoons fresh sage, tarragon, thyme, or Italian parsley
4 tablespoons butter (½ stick)
3 tablespoons chopped fresh parsley leaves

If doing the optional curing step, rub the ducks with the curing ingredients and let sit overnight or up to 2 days to cure in the refrigerator.

When ready to make the pasta, cook the duck. Rub a large nonreactive skillet with a little oil to coat it, and heat until the oil begins to smoke. Add as many of the duck pieces as will fit, skin sides down, in a single un-crowded layer. Cook over medium-high heat 10 minutes. Turn and reduce the heat to medium. Cook 10 to 15 minutes more until the juices are no longer pink. Remove the cooked duck and continue cooking the remaining pieces.

Bring a large pot of water to boil. Cook the pasta. Drain briefly, and return to the pot. Toss with 4 tablespoons of the butter. Set aside in a warm place.

While the duck and pasta cook, clean the celery. Cut the ribs crosswise into ¼-inch-thick slices. Pit the black olives. Peel the garlic.

When all the duck is cooked, use a fork and knife to remove the skin. Remove the bones from the breast pieces. Cut the breast meat crosswise into ¼-inch-thick slices. Set aside.

Pour off and discard all the liquid in the skillet, but do not scrape the bottom. Add the red wine to the skillet, and increase the heat to high. Stir well. Add the celery, celery leaves, olives, and sage. Press the garlic and add it. Bring the sauce to a boil. Cook for 10 minutes, until almost all the liquid is evaporated. Turn off the heat. Add the second 4 tablespoons butter and stir until completely melted.

To assemble the dish, spread the noodles on a large platter. Arrange the duck legs, thighs, and breast slices over the noodles. Spoon the sauce over all. Sprinkle with the parsley, and serve.

(continued)

Plenty for 6 with leftovers

20 to 40 minutes; overnight curing recommended

This recipe evolved out of our reminiscing over the first-ever Chez Panisse meal. Victoria cooked a classic French dish, duck *aux olives* with a *sauce Espagnole*. One hundred and twenty-five people were scattered about the lawn, the stairs, the porch, and leaning against the walls, waiting for their dinner, which arrived . . . rather late. *Espagnole* sauce is not on our list of things to do these days, but the combination of duck with olives is still a grand one.

1. Duck cooking time in this recipe is for just-done legs and thighs and medium rare breasts, the way we think it is best. If the thought of slightly pink duck is less than appealing, cook the pieces 5 minutes longer.

2. We give the proportions for 2 whole ducks because you can't buy a half duck or cut duck pieces. One and a half ducks is really sufficient to serve 6, so have leftovers or save half of a duck for another dish.

Pasta with Smoked Salmon, Chard, Green Beans, and *Niçoise* Olives

Plenty for 6

20 minutes or less

This dish is an example of how simple a pasta can be. Some savory morsels like a few fresh vegetables and some strips of smoked salmon tossed into the pasta with garlic and olive oil makes a meal.

¾ **pound green beans**
1½ **pounds spaghetti, vermicelli, or linguine**
1½ **pounds chard**
4 **medium garlic cloves**
Salt
Freshly ground black pepper
¾ **pound smoked salmon**
⅜ **cup *Niçoise* olives (about 1½ ounces)**
1½ **cups grated Parmesan, Romano, or aged Asiago cheese**
6 **tablespoons olive oil**

Bring a large pot of water to a boil. Trim off the stem ends from the green beans and cut the beans crosswise in half. When the water boils, drop in the beans. Cook for 2 minutes. Lift the beans out, reserving the cooking water for the pasta. Rinse the beans in cold water until cool. Pat dry with paper towels.

Bring the water back to a boil. Cook the pasta. Drain briefly, and return the pasta to the pot. Shred the chard crosswise into ¼-inch-wide strips. Rinse in plenty of cold water. Lift out and place in a large pot or sauté pan. Peel the garlic cloves and add to the chard. Lightly season the chard leaves with salt and pepper. Stir over medium heat about 3 minutes, until the leaves are thoroughly wilted. Drain.

Cut the smoked salmon into ¼-inch-wide strips or bite-size pieces.

To assemble the dish, place noodles in a large bowl. Add green beans, chard, salmon, olives, cheese, olive oil, and ½ teaspoon salt. Toss and serve.

NOTES AND AFTERTHOUGHTS

Good packaged smoked salmon has recently appeared in many supermarkets, not just delis and butcher stores. Most of it comes from Canada, has no preservatives, and is reasonably priced. This salmon is just fine for pasta. Save expensive Nova Scotia or Norwegian smoked salmon for Sunday brunch.

Pasta with Sardines, Currants, Fennel, and Pine Nuts

¾ pound fennel (sweet anise) bulb
1½ pounds spaghetti, linguine, or rigatoni
½ cup currants
⅓ cup boiling water
¼ cup pine nuts
4 whole salt-packed anchovies or 8 flat fillets
1 small onion (about ¼ pound)
6 medium tomatoes (about 1½ pounds)
8 medium garlic cloves
2 tins (3½ ounces each) sardines packed in olive oil
⅔ cup olive oil
5 tablespoons tomato paste

Bring a large pot of water to boil.

Cut the leaves off the tops of the fennel stalks. Chop and set aside. Cut the fennel bulb lengthwise in half. When the water boils, drop in the fennel bulb halves and cook 4 minutes.

Remove the fennel and save the water to cook the pasta. Rinse the fennel until cool, then squeeze out the excess water. Cut crosswise into ¼-inch-wide strips.

Bring the fennel cooking water back to a boil. Cook the pasta. Drain briefly, return it to the pot, and set aside in a warm place.

Place the currants in a small bowl. Pour the boiling water over them and set aside to soak.

Place the pine nuts in a small frying pan and stir over medium-high heat until browned, 2 to 3 minutes.

If using salt-packed anchovies, remove the bones and rinse the fillets well. Chop the anchovy fillets.

Peel the onion and cut it into ¼-inch dice. Cut the tomatoes into ¼-inch dice. Peel the garlic. Drain the sardines and cut crosswise in half.

Combine the olive oil and tomato paste in a large skillet and stir over medium heat until the oil begins to smoke. Add the anchovies and onion. Press the garlic and add to the pan. Stir over medium-high heat 5 minutes.

Add the fennel, tomatoes, currants, and pine nuts. Bring to a boil and cook 5 minutes. Remove from the heat and stir in the sardines.

To assemble the dish, spread the noodles on a large platter. Spoon the sauce over and sprinkle the reserved chopped fennel leaves over the top. Serve.

NOTES AND AFTERTHOUGHTS

1. Black raisins can be substituted for currants in this recipe. Because they are sweeter, they should be rinsed in several changes of water to remove some of the sugar.

(continued)

Plenty for 6

20 to 40 minutes

Situated in the middle of San Francisco's North Beach district lies the Cafe Sport. To say there's no other restaurant like it is an understatement. Every single square inch of the walls, ceiling, floors, and furnishings is covered with a huge continuous collage of densely arranged Italian kitsch—plastic grapes, wine bottles, antiques, pots and pans, découpage, tile mosaics, and innumerable other objects. The waiters often choose your dinner without asking what you want. One night our waiter looked us over and brought a dish of pasta with sardines and currants in a thick, Sicilian-style tomato sauce. We wouldn't have chosen it on our own, and thought the chef had run amok with his cooking as well as with his decorating. Now we always try to get the waiter to bring it to us. Sometimes he does, sometimes he doesn't.

2. If the bones in the sardines are not to your liking, remove them or use boneless sardines. We leave the bones in because they are the most nutritious part of the fish, providing a good source of calcium.

3. Fresh sardines, when available, make the dish spectacular, and more authentic. If you have them, cut off the heads, gut them, and sauté for about 1 minute, turning once. Halve crosswise and add them to the sauce when you add the fennel.

4. If you can't find fennel in your produce market, replace it with ¾ pound sliced celery and sprinkle ¼ cup chopped fresh dill over the dish before serving.

Pasta with Shrimp, Lima Beans, and Julienned Carrots

1½ pounds spaghetti, vermicelli, or linguine

4 medium carrots (about ¾ pound)
2 tablespoons butter
1 package (10 ounces) frozen baby lima beans
2 cups chicken stock
1½ cups heavy cream
¼ cup chopped fresh dill
1½ pounds medium cooked shelled shrimp

Bring a large pot of water to boil. Cook the pasta. Drain briefly, return it to the pot, and set aside in a warm place.

Peel the carrots. Cut into matchstick strips approximately 2 inches long and ⅛-inch wide.

Melt the butter in a large skillet until it begins to foam. Add the carrots and stir over medium-high heat 1 minute. Stir in the lima beans, chicken stock, cream, and dill. Remove from the heat and toss in the shrimp.

To assemble the dish, place the noodles in a large bowl. Add the shrimp mixture. Toss and serve.

NOTES AND AFTERTHOUGHTS
1. If you would like a thicker sauce, whip the cream until thickened but not stiff before adding it to the pan.

2. Fresh lima beans are sometimes available in produce markets, and, if used right away, they are delicious. You can also prepare dried lima beans for this recipe.

Plenty for 6

20 minutes or less

This recipe and the next call for chicken stock. Homemade is, of course, best, and it's very easy to keep on hand. Whenever you cook a chicken, put the wing tips, backs, neck, and gizzards into a small pot. Add water to cover by ½ inch, and simmer 45 minutes while you prepare dinner. Strain the stock and keep it in the refrigerator up to 5 days, or freeze it. The resulting light chicken stock is suitable for most cooking. To make it stronger, use stock you have already made as half the liquid for the next batch along with half water. The advantage to this procedure is that you always have your own good stock on hand. Canned stocks are too salty, over herbed, have preservatives, or are simply tasteless.

If you have a pressure cooker, chicken stock is a perfect thing to use it for. Place the parts in the pot, cover with water by 1 inch, and cook under pressure for 30 minutes.

Clams in Garlic Mayonnaise Sauce with Linguine and Black Pepper

2 cups Garlic Mayonnaise (see below)
1½ pounds linguine

4 pounds clams
4 tablespoons olive oil
1 cup chicken stock
¼ cup chopped fresh parsley leaves
2 teaspoons freshly ground black pepper

Make the Garlic Mayonnaise. Scrape it into a medium bowl and set aside at room temperature.

Bring a large pot of water to boil. Cook the linguine. Drain briefly, return it to the pot, and set aside in a warm place.

Rinse the clams in a colander. Divide the oil between 2 large skillets or pots with tight-fitting lids. Set over high heat until the oil begins to smoke. Divide the clams between the pans. Cover and cook for 2 to 5 minutes, until all of the clams open. Remove the clams with tongs, leaving the clam juices in the pans. Discard any that do not open.

Combine the clam juices in 1 pan. Add the chicken stock and parsley. Bring just to the boiling point. Pouring in a slow steady stream, stir the clam juice mixture into the Garlic Mayonnaise, blending well.

To assemble the dish, spread the linguine on a large platter. Sprinkle on the black pepper. Arrange the clams over the linguine. Pour the mayonnaise sauce over the clams and linguine and serve.

Garlic Mayonnaise

4 egg yolks
1 teaspoon lemon juice
1 teaspoon Dijon mustard
2 medium garlic cloves
1¾ cups olive oil
¼ teaspoon salt

Combine the egg yolks, lemon juice, and mustard in a medium bowl, blender, or food processor. Peel the garlic and press it in. Process until the egg yolk mixture is slightly tickened.

Slowly beat in the olive oil, starting with teaspoon amounts and working up to tablespoon amounts. Stir in the salt.

Plenty for 6

20 to 40 minutes

From ancient Greek to Medieval times, pepper was more than a spice. It was money. Coming by trade route from the Malabar coast of India, pepper was so valuable that soldiers were paid with it, land was rented with it, daughters were dowried with it, and people who married below their class were called "pepperbags." Now, next to salt, it is our most common spice. Pepper in peppercorn form will keep almost indefinitely, but once ground, it quickly loses its aromatic punch. When buying pepper to grind, look for corns of even size, black, red, green, or white. If the package has small brown ones, they are of inferior quality.

You usually can't heat a mayonnaise sauce. It curdles. But if you slowly stir hot broth into the mayonnaise, instead of the other way around, you can warm it without curdling, and create a rich and creamy white sauce that requires neither flour thickening nor cream.

Spaghetti with Mussels, Sausages, Leeks, Olives, and Bread Crumbs

Plenty for 6

20 minutes or less

1½ pounds spaghetti, vermicelli, or linguine

¼ teaspoon olive oil
½ pound spicy fresh sausage links
⅔ cup Kalamata olives (about ¼ pound)
3 pounds mussels
4 medium leeks (about ½ pound)
8 tablespoons (1 stick) butter
2 cups chicken stock
½ cup white wine
½ cup thinly shredded fresh basil leaves
¼ cup Bread Crumbs (see below)
½ cup grated Parmesan, Romano, or aged Asiago cheese (optional)

Bring a large pot of water to boil. Cook the pasta. Drain briefly, return it to the pot, and set aside in a warm place.

Coat a medium frying pan with the oil. Place the sausages in the pan and cook over medium-low heat, turning once. Timing will depend on the size of the sausages, but in general, small links take about 9 minutes and large take about 18 minutes. When sausages are done, drain on paper towels.

While the sausages cook, pit the olives. Medium chop in a food processor or with a chef's knife.

Rinse the mussels and pull off any exposed "beards."

Trim off the root ends and limp green tops from the leeks. Cut the leeks crosswise into 2-inch-long lengths. Cut each length into ⅛-inch-wide strips. Place the leek strips in a large container of water and swish them about to remove all the dirt and grit. Leave for a minute, until the water comes to rest and the dirt sinks to the bottom. Lift the leek strips out of the water into a colander. Set aside to drain.

Melt the butter in a large nonreactive skillet with a tight-fitting cover. Add the chicken stock and wine. Bring to a boil. Boil 1 minute. Add the leeks and mussels. Cover pan and cook over high heat 3 to 5 minutes, until mussels open and are slightly firm to the touch. Discard any that don't open.

To assemble the dish, toss the noodles with the olives and basil. Spread the noodles on a large platter. Arrange the mussels and leeks over the pasta. Pour the sauce over all. Cut the sausage into ¼-inch-thick rounds and scatter the rounds over the mussels. Sprinkle on the Bread Crumbs and optional cheese, and serve.

Bread Crumbs

Makes about ¾ cup

3 ounces French or Italian bread (about one 2-inch-thick piece), or 3 slices of a full loaf, or an 8-inch piece of baguette

Heat the oven to 375°F or use a toaster oven. Slice the bread. Place the bread slices in the oven and bake 5 minutes. Turn and bake 4 to 6 minutes more, until the bread is dried out all the way through. Remove and let the bread cool and harden completely.

On a cutting board, cut the bread into 1-inch squares. Crush the bread squares with a rolling pin or wine bottle. Chop any large pieces with a chef's knife until the biggest pieces are the size of peppercorns. You will have some coarse and some fine crumbs.

NOTES AND AFTERTHOUGHTS

1. Stale bread is the best to use for making bread crumbs. It dries out thoroughly, so is easiest to chop. It takes a few minutes less to toast.

2. You can make bread crumbs with a food processor, but you will wind up with less coarse and less crunchy crumbs. After cutting the toasted bread into 1-inch squares, chop in the food processor until no large pieces remain but the crumbs are not yet powdery.

Spaghetti with Poached Oysters, Leeks, Tomatoes, and Ginger

1½ pounds spaghetti, vermicelli, or linguine

3 medium leeks (about 6 ounces)
2 medium tomatoes (about ½ pound)
1 ounce ginger root (about ¼ cup sliced)
1 cup white wine
8 tablespoons (1 stick) butter
3 pints shucked oysters

3 tablespoons chopped fresh parsley leaves

Bring a large pot of water to boil. Cook the pasta. Drain briefly, return it to the pot, and set aside in a warm place.

Trim the root ends and most of the green tops off the leeks. Cut the leeks crosswise into 2-inch-long lengths. Cut each length into 18-inch-wide strips. Place the leek strips in a large container of water and swish them about to remove all the dirt and grit. Leave for a minute, until the water comes to rest and the dirt sinks to the bottom. Lift the leek strips out of the water into a colander, and set aside to drain.

Cut the tomatoes into ¼-inch dice. Peel the ginger and slice crosswise into ¹⁄₁₆-inch-thick rounds.

Combine the wine and butter in a large nonreactive skillet or sauté pan. Heat until the butter melts. Add the leeks, tomatoes, and ginger. Bring to a boil and cook over medium heat 1 minute. Add the oysters and their juices and cook 3 to 4 minutes, just until the oysters are firm.

To assemble the dish, spread the noodles on a large platter. Spoon the oysters and sauce over the noodles. Sprinkle with the parsley, and serve.

Toasted in a little butter or sprinkled on plain, homemade bread crumbs add a pleasing crunch to many dishes that need a textural counterpoint. They provide that little extra something that elevates the dish from ordinary to special. They should always be homemade, though, because the packaged ones feel, and what's worse, taste like sand. It takes little time to make your own. Turning stale leftover bread into bread crumbs also satisfies a sense of thrift.

Plenty for 6

20 minutes or less

Leeks, those obscure relatives of onions, love pasta. Shredded or chopped into the sauce, they hold their shape and texture better than an onion, and the juice they render imbues the sauce with a more oniony flavor than even onions do. Do clean them well. They're like kids from a sandbox. They come home with more grit in them than was in the garden.

If scallops weren't treat enough, adding caviar makes them truly regal. With the tarragon-infused cream, you will have a dazzling dish that lingers in your thoughts long after the actual taste has faded. The reason you rarely find live scallops still in their shells is that a scallop cannot hold its shell together out of water. If you ever do find them live, they are one of the best things you'll ever eat.

Imperial Pasta with Scallops, Caviar, and Tarragon Cream

1½ pounds vermicelli or linguine

1½ pounds bay or sea scallops
2 cups heavy cream
6 tablespoons butter
1 tablespoon lemon juice
2 teaspoons chopped fresh tarragon leaves
6 ounces black, red, or golden caviar, or flying fish roe

Bring a large pot of water to boil. Cook the pasta. Drain briefly, return it to the pot, and set aside in a warm place.

If using bay scallops, leave as is. If using sea scallops, slice into bite-size pieces.

Whip the cream until slightly thickened but not stiff.

In a large nonreactive saucepan, melt the butter until it begins to foam. Stir in the cream and lemon juice. Add the scallops and cook over medium-high heat 30 seconds. Stir in the tarragon. Remove from the heat.

To assemble the dish, spread the noodles on a large platter or divide among 6 individual plates. Spoon the scallops and cream over the noodles. Sprinkle the caviar over the top. Serve.

NOTES AND AFTERTHOUGHTS
Fresh basil leaves or snipped fresh chives make a nice substitute for the tarragon in this dish. If you have no fresh herb, don't use dried, use none at all.

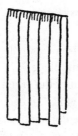

SAUCES AND DISHES FROM OTHER CHAPTERS TO USE ON SPAGHETTI OR OTHER PASTA

The list of sauces and toppings for pasta is almost endless; it doesn't stop with just pasta recipes. You can translate sauces and dishes from hors d'oeuvres, grills, or stovetop into glorious pasta dishes, too. Here are suggestions from other chapters in this book.

SAUCES:
Corsican Lasagne Sauce, page 256
Quick Lemon Garlic Butter, page 168
Red Pizza Sauce, page 61
Red Pepper Pesto, page 43
Red Pepper Sauce, page 258
Spicy Pecan Sauce, page 159
Tomato Tarragon Sauce, page 175

DISHES:
Chicken à la Corsala, page 197
Chicken Tarragon, page 199
Crab Cakes with Sage Butter Sauce, page 51
Grilled Scallop and Bacon Kebabs, page 170
Marinated Shrimp, page 49
Mom's Marinated Roasted Red and Green Peppers, page 47
Pan Kebabs with Sesame and Red Wine, page 193
Quail with Pepper and Sage, page 203
Shrimp and Mussels Sautéed with Celery and Tarragon, page 207
Trout with Pine Nuts and Smoked Salmon, page 205
Tuna Bits with Capers and Onion, page 49
Turkey Cutlets in Ginger Cream, page 202
Turkey Cutlets with Juniper and White Wine, page 203

From Barbecue
to Fish Kebabs:
GREAT GRILLING

Grilled Steaks and Chops
Steaks
  Garlic Horseradish Sauce
Lamb Chops
Pork Chops
  Papaya or Kiwi Chutney

Grilled Flank Steak in Perpetual Marinade

Grilled Burgers
Plain Hamburgers
Stuffed Hamburgers
  Brie Burgers
  Cheddar Cheese Burgers
  Blue Cheese Burgers
  Liverwurst Burgers
Turkey Burgers
Sausage Burgers

Grilled Beef Roast Rubbed in Coarse Pepper with Grilled Figs Soaked in Whiskey
Grilled Figs Soaked in Whiskey

Grilled Leg of Lamb with Spicy Pecan Sauce
Spicy Pecan Sauce

Grilled Boneless Pork Shoulder Roast with Mustard Ginger Soy Coating and Grilled Apples

Sweet and Spicy Grilled Ribs: Pork and Beef

Chicken Barbecued with Curry Yogurt Sauce
  Curry Yogurt Sauce

Game Hens Grilled with Rum Plum Sauce
  Rum Plum Sauce

Grilled Breast of Turkey

Tender Grilled Duck or Rabbit

Grilled Fish Steaks and Fish Kebabs
  Basic Fish Marinade
  Quick Lemon Garlic Butter
  Other Sauces for Grilled Fish

Grilled Scallop and Bacon Kebabs Topped with Bread Crumbs, Parsley, and Chopped Lemon Peel

Grilled Marinated Swordfish Chunks Skewered with Onion and Bay Leaf

Grilled Trout or Spanish Mackerel Marinated with Cilantro and Coated in Parmesan Cheese

Grilled Salmon with Onion Tomato Herb Salad Stuffing and Dill Cream Sauce
  Dill Cream Sauce

Grilled Oysters with Tomato Tarragon Sauce and Melted Butter
  Tomato Tarragon Sauce

Grilled Vegetables

Sauces for Grills

Grilling came into America's home cooking about 30 years ago. It started as a backyard craze of steak, chicken, and charcoal briquets. When we tasted how good the food was and saw the advantage of the quick, fresh cooking, the speed and simplicity, we took grilling to heart. Now it is one of our mainstays, an essential part of the way we cook and eat.

Over the years we have refined our grilling. No more just plain steaks, or ribs and chicken with red barbecue sauce, although we still love those. Now we grill game hens, leg of lamb, fresh vegetables, and even fruits! We use herbs. We've discovered marinades, chutneys, and a whole banquet of sauces. We've learned the different flavors imparted by different woods—the smokiness of hickory, the arid woodiness of mesquite, the herbaceousness of grape, and the latest rage, the nuttiness of pecan. These woods have all become readily available as logs, charcoal pieces, briquets, or bagged shavings to rehydrate and sprinkle on your fire. Still, grilled food is uncomplicated food, cooked without much fuss.

Although grilling is an easy cooking process, practice makes perfect. So if you are a novice, approach these recipes with a lighthearted attitude. Be prepared to put things back on the grill to finish cooking them, or for eating some things a little overdone once or twice until you get the hang of it.

PREPARING THE GRILL

The amount of time and difficulty involved in preparing the grill for cooking depends on the kind of cooker you have. Listed below are the various kinds of grills and instructions for preparing them. Be sure to allow time for the grill to heat properly. We have not included grill preparation in the recipe times, although the grill can usually heat while the dish is being prepared.

TO PREPARE A CHARCOAL GRILL
Charcoal grills—hibachis and Webers to Charboys and backyard fireplaces —are the most laborious to prepare. Their advantages are that they offer the widest range of heat control, from high to low and, without a doubt, they give the best flavor.

The amount of charcoal you need depends on the amount of food you are cooking, but in general you need 1 gallon's worth, 3½ to 4 pounds, to make an adequate fire for a meal for 6. The best charcoal is mesquite or other hardwood. The more familiar composite briquets do not burn as hot as hardwoods. Also, they often leave a petroleum taste and oily residue on the food.

To start a fire in a charcoal grill, a fire starter chimney (see Equipment for Grilling, p. 147) is almost indispensable. With one, you can rapidly and easily light the coals without noxious chemical starters. Crumple two sheets of newspaper and place them in the bottom of the chimney. Fill the chimney with charcoal, set it on the grill, and light the newspapers. Leave the charcoals in the chimney until burning brightly for 30 to 45 minutes for mesquite or other hardwood. If you are using charcoal briquets, allow an extra 10 minutes to eliminate their leaving a petroleum residue on the food. How long you let the coals burn in the chimney depends on how you will be cooking, with direct or with indirect heat.

DIRECT HEAT charcoal grilling is done uncovered with hot to medium-hot coals evenly spread over the grill bottom. This method is best for quick, hot cooking, for steaks, chops, or kebabs.

To grill with direct heat: Spread the coals out across the entire surface of the bottom for even heat. Let the coals burn until they are ash-covered and no red shows, altogether about 35 to 45 minutes depending on the size of the fire. If you want to vary the heat for different items you are grilling, heap more coals in one spot and fewer in another.

INDIRECT HEAT charcoal grilling is done with the grill covered and the coals burned down to medium-hot or low heat. This method is best for any of the meats such as chicken, rabbit, duck, game hens, or roasts that need to cook longer than a few minutes. This way, they remain moist and don't burn.

To grill with indirect heat: Let the coals burn in the chimney until they are mostly ash-covered and no flames are licking up but some red still shows through the ash, 25 to 35 minutes, depending on the size of the fire.

Once the coals are ready, they can be arranged in two ways: Either pile them in one heap in the center, or make two piles at either end with a space in the middle. The way you heap the coals depends on what you are cooking and the instructions in the recipe. In general, two piles of coals is best for a large cut of meat such as roast beef or leg of lamb. Place the meat on the grill rack between the two piles so it cooks from either side. If your grill is not large enough for two piles of coals, you can heap the coals in one pile at the side, and then place the meat next to, but not over, the coals. This arrangement requires repositioning the meat from time to time, changing the side closest to the heat to ensure even cooking all around.

For indirect grilling of smaller pieces, such as cut-up chicken, rabbit, duck, or game hen halves, pile the coals in a mound in the center of the grill and place the meat around the outside edges. Be sure to rotate the meat to change sides closest to the fire when you turn them over.

The coal arrangement for indirect heat cooking allows you to cook some things with a hot heat directly over the coals as well as some things to the side of the coals with medium or low heat.

Whether you are cooking with direct or indirect heat, when the coals are ready, place the rack on the grill and let it heat a minute or so. If it has been used previously, brush it clean with a wire grill brush before placing the food on it.

A hibachi, the favored grill of apartment dwellers, picnickers, and the casual barbecuer, is an excellent tool, but it is fashioned mainly for direct heat cooking. You can broil a fine steak or chop, or singe a great rare burger. But with no lid and not enough depth between the coals and the grill rack, you can't cook a large roast by the indirect heat method. For smaller pieces such as cut-up chicken, there is a way to fake indirect heat grilling. Burn the coals well down until thoroughly coated with ash. Place the grill rack at the highest possible distance above the coals. Turn the food often, every 2 to 4 minutes, or every 10 minutes for a small roast, so that it won't burn. This method requires more attention than if you had a fancy covered grill, but does the job just as nicely.

Any roast needs to rest before you carve it. Cutting into the meat too soon bleeds the juices out and leaves the meat tough. Always allow 20 minutes resting time, whether you are grilling the roast or cooking it in the oven.

TO PREPARE HOT ROCK AND OTHER GAS GRILLS

Gas hot rock grills are less messy then charcoal to prepare, and they heat in less time, 15 to 20 minutes. However, you can't vary the heat temperature with a hot rock grill as you can with a charcoal cooker. Good ones do attain an even medium-high heat which is fine for almost all grilling except large roasts and the like. Juices dripping onto the hot rocks create a mild smoked taste in the food, so you have a hint of the barbecue taste you get with charcoal grilling.

There are also propane and various kinds of built-in gas grills that don't use hot rocks. These get hot enough to cook meats, but they produce very little smoke. Propane gas grills can be downright dangerous unless you know exactly what you're doing.

TO PREPARE ELECTRIC GRILLS

Electric grills heat the fastest, in 10 to 15 minutes, and are the easiest to use. All you have to do is plug them in. They are, though, the most limited in their use. Vegetable or fish kebabs, thin pieces of fish, or chicken breast do best on electric grills. Beef, pork, and lamb do not cook well because the grill does not get hot enough to sear the outside of the meat. As a result juices escape during cooking and the meat turns out dry.

TO PREPARE FIREPLACE GRILLS

An indoor fireplace can make a terrific barbecue pit. There are some fireplace grills now that are designed to fit in standard-size fireplace openings (24 inches wide by 21 inches deep or larger). The best of these is the Tuscan fireplace grill, available by mail order from Cafe Fanny Imports, 1619 Fifth Street, Berkeley, California 94710, $85. With a mesquite or other hardwood fire going underneath, this grill cooks as well as the best outdoor charcoal cookers right in your living room, and you can use it in any season.

Use a fire starter chimney to start the fire as you would for an outdoor charcoal fire. The coals for a fireplace grill will take 45 minutes to burn to the right stage. Pile them at the back of the fireplace for indirect heat cooking or spread them out under the grill rack for direct heat cooking.

HINTS AND TRICKS FOR GRILLING

Here are some clues that will make your grilling easier and better.

1. Be patient in allowing the grill to heat completely and the coals to burn to the right stage for what you are grilling. Too hot a charcoal fire or too cool a gas or electric grill will burn or steam the food and dry it out.

2. Don't walk away and trust the grill to cook properly on its own. Watch the process and reposition food as necessary to achieve even cooking. A grill with at least two positions for rack height is helpful in controlling how hot the food is cooking. In general, timing for the recipes in this chapter is done with the rack positioned between 4 and 7 inches above the coals.

3. Depending on what you are cooking, you can grill covered or uncovered. Covered grilling helps maintain even cooking, particularly with the indirect heat method. If your grill does not have a cover and the directions call for covered cooking, you can devise a top with heavy aluminum foil or a double layer of regular-weight aluminum foil. Make the cover large enough to overlap the food by an inch or so. This is somewhat cumbersome to deal with, but a cover is crucial for grilling large items like roasts or a leg of lamb. Without a cover the meat won't turn out evenly browned and properly cooked through. Food grilled directly over the coals does not need to be covered.

4. Unless you have a large grill and are adept at using it, plan only two or three items for the grill in one meal. When cooking more than one thing at a time, it is easiest if you choose a meat to cook with indirect heat and vegetables to cook with direct heat, or the other way around. If you are grilling corn, whole peppers, or whole potatoes, you can put them on the fire while the flames are still licking up occasionally and then cook the other foods in a second round when the fire has burned to the right stage.

5. Remember to take large cuts of meat, such as a beef roast or leg of lamb, out of the refrigerator at least 20 minutes before cooking so that it will not be cold when you place it on the grill (or in the oven for that matter). If you forget, add 10 to 15 minutes to the cooking time given in the recipe.

EQUIPMENT FOR GRILLING

FIRE STARTER CHIMNEY: This is a must if you like to charcoal grill. With two sheets of newspaper and a match, you can start a charcoal fire using no foul-tasting chemical starters. Due to the national rage for grilling outdoors, fire starter chimneys are widely available these days. If you can't find one in a kitchen or hardware store nearby, you can mail order from Williams-Sonoma, P.O. Box 7456, San Francisco, California 94120-7456, or Brookstone, 127 Vose Farm Road, Peterborough, New Hampshire 03460.

GRILL BRUSH: There's no need to labor over cleaning the grill rack with soap and water or an oven cleaner after each use. The heat of the next fire will burn off the grease and most of the food particles remaining from the last grilling. After the coals are out of the fire starter chimney and on the bottom of the grill, place the rack on the grill and let it heat up for several minutes. Use the grill brush to scrape and clean off any charred bits remaining, then you are ready to cook.

LONG-HANDLED TONGS AND A LONG-TONGUED METAL SPATULA: Both of these tools are indispensable for turning and repositioning the food without burning yourself. A long-handled fork stabs the meat and lets the juice out, so it is best not to use one.

SKEWERS: You need either metal or disposable bamboo skewers for kebabs.

SPRAY BOTTLE: Even the most experienced grill cook has an occasional flare-up with direct heat cooking of meats. A spray bottle filled with water douses errant flames.

GRILLED STEAKS AND CHOPS

A steak done to perfection over the fire, the grill marks running across. Lamb or pork chops, nestled over the coals, the long part of one tucked in the shoulder of the other, turned, renestled, and broiled just right. With a salad and a piece of garlic bread you have a perfect meal, an American classic, simple, good, and plenty.

Steaks

Both small individual steaks and large ones work well on the grill. Three pounds of meat is plenty for six. With thin boneless steaks or bone-in steaks such as Porterhouse or T-bones, you need 1 per person. Steaks 1 inch thick or more can be shared, especially if you are serving filet mignons, markets, New Yorks, or other boneless steaks. You can also grill large steaks, such as chateaubriand, London broil, or 7 blade chuck and slice them into strips after cooking for everyone to share.

You can grill bread right along with your steaks and chops. Press or chop some garlic into some olive oil, then brush the oil onto the cut sides of French or Italian bread. Grill the bread directly over the coals for 2 or 3 minutes.

Prepare the grill for direct heat cooking (page 145).

Place the steaks on the grill rack directly over the coals. The thinner the steak the hotter the fire should be and, if possible, the closer the steak should be placed to the heat source. Thicker steaks can grill over a less hot fire and from a more elevated rack.

Grilling time depends on the steak's thickness:

Extra-thick steaks (1½ inches or more) take 30 minutes, turning once, to reach a perfect medium rare.

Thick steaks (1 inch or so) take 18 to 20 minutes to grill, turning once, to reach a perfect medium rare.

Regular steaks (about ¾ inch thick, the general supermarket thickness) take 7 to 8 minutes per side to reach medium rare.

Thin steaks (½ inch thick) take 4 to 5 minutes per side for medium rare.

For rare steaks, subtract 1 minute per side accordingly for thin steaks and 2 minutes per side for thick steaks. For well-done steaks, add 1 minute per side for thin steaks and 2 minutes per side for thick steaks.

Remove cooked steaks to a platter and allow them to rest for 5 to 15 minutes, depending on the thickness, while the juices settle before cutting.

A good steak needs no marinade, but to perk up cheaper cuts, such as chuck or flank steak, use Perpetual Marinade (page 152). For variety or added flavor, you can rub steaks with pepper or garlic before grilling, or drizzle garlic in butter or oil over the cooked side after turning.

No matter what the quality, a steak can always use a sauce. Here's our easy Garlic Horseradish Sauce.

Garlic Horseradish Sauce

30 large garlic cloves
1½ teaspoons salt
4 teaspoons grated horseradish
¼ teaspoon balsamic or red wine vinegar

Makes about 1 cup

Peel the garlic cloves. Place the garlic cloves and 1 teaspoon of the salt in a food processor or blender and process until as fine as it will become. Remove the garlic to a cutting board and sprinkle on the remaining ½ teaspoon of salt. Continue to chop the garlic together with the salt until it becomes very finely minced. Or, place the salt on a cutting board. Press the garlic and add it to the salt. Chop the garlic in the salt until very finely minced.

Place the garlic mixture in a small bowl. Stir in the horseradish and vinegar.

NOTES AND AFTERTHOUGHTS

1. Bottled horseradish is just fine for this recipe if you don't have some fresh horseradish root to grate. Most brands have the vinegar already added. If so, omit the vinegar in the recipe.

2. This sauce is also terrific with lamb.

Lamb Chops

Lamb chops—loin, rib, round bone, or blade—take to the grill in splendid style. Three rib, two loin, or one large round bone or blade chop is usually ample for one person. But if you are feeding hefty eaters, you may want more.

Prepare the grill for direct heat cooking (page 145).

Place the lamb chops on the rack directly over the coals and grill them uncovered. Grill thinner ones, such as round bone or blade chops, closer to the coals and over a hotter fire. Thicker ones, such as loin chops, can be cooked over a cooler fire and from a greater height.

The cooking time for lamb chops depends on their thickness:

Thick loin lamb chops (1 inch thick) take 6 minutes per side for medium rare.

Thin shoulder chops (½ to ¾ inch thick) take about 4 minutes per side for medium rare.

Remove the cooked chops to a platter and allow them to rest for 10 minutes for the juices to settle before cutting.

To add variety and aromatic flavors to lamb chops, grill them with sprigs of rosemary, tarragon, or oregano. Place large sprigs of fresh herbs on the top of the chop and turn with the chop. Add a second sprig to the cooked side that is now on top. Grapevine cuttings also add a marvelous flavor to lamb. If you don't live near a vineyard, you can often find packages of grape vine chips in kitchenware stores or catalogs. Just rehydrate the chips and add them to the coals of your fire.

A zesty fruit accompaniment enhances lamb chops. A pretty and unusual one is Papaya or Kiwi Chutney (see below).

Pork Chops

The smoky flavor from grilling especially enriches pork chops, if you cook them carefully so they don't dry out. Pork chops are done when they are slightly pink in the center, white curds have formed on the top, and the internal temperature is 155°F in the center. Two thin pork chops or 1 extra-thick cut is usually plenty for each person.

Prepare the grill for direct heat cooking (page 145).

Place the pork chops on the grill rack directly over the coals.

The timing depends on the thickness of the chops:

Extra-thick pork chops (about 1 inch) take 20 minutes, turning once, directly over the coals of a medium fire.

Thin pork chops (½ inch thick at most) grill in 12 to 14 minutes, turning once, directly over the coals of a medium fire.

Once cooked, pork chops must rest for at least 10 minutes before cutting into them. During this time, they continue to cook, so they should be removed from the grill before they are done all the way through or the meat will be tough.

Pork, the chameleon of meats, readily changes its flavor according to its accompaniment. To add variety and other flavors to pork chops, grill them with large sprigs of fresh sage, marjoram, or thyme. Use the same way as described above for lamb chops. Pork chops also work well with any number of marinades, and each gives it a surprisingly different taste. Try Mustard, Ginger, Soy Coating (page 161), Sweet and Spicy Coating (page 160), Marinade for Trout (page 172), or the trusty old Perpetual Marinade (page 152).

Papaya or Kiwi Chutney

½ ripe medium-size papaya, or 2 large ripe but firm kiwifruits
¼ medium red onion (about 2 ounces)
1 tablespoon fresh mint leaves or 1½ teaspoon dried
1 tablespoon lemon juice
1 tablespoon lime juice
1 tablespoon brandy
1 teaspoon sugar

Makes 1 heaping cup

For an added treat, slice the other half of the papaya into ½-inch-thick crescents without peeling. Grill the papaya along with the chops, about 3 minutes per side directly over the coals.

If using papaya, scoop out the seeds and spoon out the pulp. If using kiwis, peel and cut into 3 or 4 pieces. Place the fruit in a blender or food processor.

Rough chop the onion and add to the fruit. Add the mint, lemon and lime juices, brandy, and sugar. Process until well mashed, but not pureed. Chill until ready to use.

NOTES AND AFTERTHOUGHTS

1. Either version of this chutney goes well with lamb or pork, although we prefer the papaya with lamb chops and the kiwi with pork.

2. Like any fruit chutney or fruit salsa (Melon and Jalapeño Salsa, page 84, also goes well with chops), it loses its freshness in a day or two. The onion reacts with the fruit. With this in mind, we've written the recipe to provide just enough for one meal. If you'd like to blanket your chops, make a double amount.

Grilled Flank Steak in Perpetual Marinade

Plenty for 6

20 to 40 minutes

What is Perpetual Marinade? One that can be used over and over again and never has to be thrown away. Bring the remainder to a boil and simmer 1 minute, then refrigerate in a small sealed container after each time you use it. Every now and then, as the amount decreases, add a little more of the ingredients in the right proportion, and you can keep it going indefinitely.

You can vary the Perpetual Marinade with different flavors. We especially like adding some mustard seed or chopped fresh chilies.

FOR THE PERPETUAL MARINADE:

¼ cup soy sauce

⅔ cup red wine

1½ tablespoons chopped fresh ginger root

1½ tablespoons chopped fresh mint leaves or 1 tablespoon dried

1 tablespoon chopped or pressed garlic

2 tablespoons olive or peanut oil

1 teaspoon sesame oil (optional)

2½ pounds flank steak

Prepare the grill for direct heat cooking (page 145).

To make the Perpetual Marinade, combine the soy sauce, wine, ginger, mint, garlic, and oils in a medium bowl.

Pour the marinade into a container large enough to hold the flank steak laid out flat. Place the steak in the marinade and turn to coat on both sides. Set aside while the grill heats, turning after 10 or 15 minutes.

When the grill is ready, place the steak on the grill rack directly over the coals and cook for 3 to 4 minutes. Turn and grill 3 or 4 minutes on the other side. Remove to a platter and let rest for 10 to 15 minutes before carving.

To serve, cut diagonally across the grain into ⅛-inch-thick slices.

NOTES AND AFTERTHOUGHTS

In place of flank steak you can also use skirt steak.

GRILLED BURGERS

Have you ever tried putting the cheese on the inside of a hamburger? What an explosion of taste when you get to the center! Or have you tried turkey burgers? How about sausage burgers? Whatever version, grilled burgers are very quick to make. Half a pound per person is just the right amount.

Plain Hamburgers

3 pounds ground beef chuck or round

Plenty for 6

20 minutes or less

Prepare the grill for direct heat cooking (page 145).

Divide the meat into six ½-pound portions. Shape each into 1-inch-thick rounds or ovals. Set aside at room temperature until the grill is ready.

When the grill is hot, place the hamburgers on the rack directly over the coals. Cook 5 to 6 minutes. Turn and cook 5 to 6 minutes more. Burgers will be medium rare.

Stuffed Hamburgers

Brie Burgers

½ pound Brie cheese (about ¾ cup when the rind is removed)
3 tablespoons chopped fresh chives
1 tablespoon fresh thyme leaves or 1 teaspoon dried

3 pounds ground beef chuck or round

Plenty for 6

20 minutes or less

Burgers can be stuffed with a huge variety of cheeses, spreads, and other ingredients. Try chopped olives. Try garlic. You can also vary the herbs according to what you have around, or substitute diced peppers for the onion. And so on.

Cheddar Cheese Burgers

¼ pound sharp cheddar cheese (about ⅔ cup shredded)
3 tablespoons minced red onion
1 tablespoon Dijon mustard

3 pounds ground beef chuck or round

(continued)

Blue Cheese Burgers

5 ounces blue cheese (about ⅔ cup crumbled)
3 tablespoons chopped fresh chives
1 tablespoon chopped fresh oregano leaves or 1 teaspoon dried

3 pounds ground beef chuck or round

Liverwurst Burgers

¼ pound liverwurst (about ⅔ cup chopped)
3 fine-chopped green onions
1 tablespoon lemon juice

3 pounds ground beef chuck or round

To make stuffed hamburgers, prepare the grill for direct heat cooking (page 145).

Place the ingredients for whatever stuffing you are using in a small bowl. Mix together.

Divide the meat and shape as for plain grilled burgers. With your thumb, open a pocket in the shaped burger and place about 2 tablespoons of the stuffing inside. Pat the burger closed, covering the stuffing.

Cook as for plain grilled burgers, 5 to 6 minutes per side.

Turkey Burgers

Plenty for 6

20 to 40 minutes

3 pounds ground turkey
2 medium tomatoes (about ½ pound)
½ pound Jack cheese
½ cup grated Parmesan cheese
½ cup very thinly sliced fresh basil leaves, or a mixture of Italian parsley and celery leaves
½ teaspoon salt
1 teaspoon freshly ground black pepper

Prepare the grill for direct heat cooking (page 145).

Place the turkey in a large bowl. Peel the tomatoes and dice into ¼-inch cubes. Cut the Jack cheese into ¼-inch cubes.

Add the diced tomato and Jack cheese, the Parmesan, basil, salt, and pepper to the turkey. With your hands or a wooden spoon, mix the ingredients to blend well.

Divide the meat mixture into 6 equal portions and shape into 1-inch-thick rounds or ovals.

When the grill is hot, place the burgers on the grill rack directly over the coals. Cook 8 minutes per side, turning once.

Sausage Burgers

¾ pound fresh spinach (about 1 bunch)
2 tablespoons butter
¾ pound boneless skinless chicken breast
1½ pounds ground pork
⅛ teaspoon ground allspice
⅛ teaspoon freshly grated nutmeg
¾ teaspoon freshly grated black pepper
⅛ teaspoon cayenne pepper
1½ teaspoons salt

Plenty for 6

20 to 40 minutes

A sausage doesn't have to be a hot dog, it can also be a hamburger. Here is a delicious and unusual combination of chicken and pork with spinach that Victoria developed when she operated her delicatessen.

Prepare the grill for direct heat cooking (page 145).

Cut the spinach leaves crosswise into ¼-inch-wide strips, discarding the stems. Wash the spinach shreds well, then place in a colander to drain briefly. In a medium nonreactive skillet, melt the butter until it foams. Add the moist spinach and stir over medium heat until completely wilted. Remove to a bowl and set aside to cool.

Fine chop the chicken breast with a knife or food processor. Place the chicken in a large bowl and add the pork, allspice, nutmeg, black pepper, cayenne, and salt. Lift the cooled spinach out of the bowl, leaving the juices behind but without squeezing dry, and add to the other ingredients. With your hands or a wooden spoon, mix well.

Form the sausage into 6 patties, ½ to ¾ inch thick. (Thicker patties will dry out on the outside before they cook through.) Cover and refrigerate until ready to cook.

When the grill is hot, place the sausage burgers on the rack directly over the coals of a medium-low fire or around the edges of the coals of a medium-hot fire. Cook 15 minutes. Turn and cook 15 more. Have a spray bottle handy to douse any flames that flare up from dripping fat and juices.

Grilled Beef Roast Rubbed in Coarse Pepper with Grilled Figs Soaked in Whiskey

Plenty for 6

1½ hours

On the road that follows the curving border between Albania and Yugoslavia, every little village is lined with roadside barbecues grilling the abundance of local meat raised on the hilly terrain. Veal chops as thick as your wrist, smoky kebabs, sausage, lamb shanks, goat. By the time you round through Titograd and arrive above the coast you come to the figs. Figs and brandy for breakfast. Figs and eggs for lunch. Figs and fish. Figs and grilled roast. Here we have repeated the smoky Croatian flavors with grilled beef and figs soaked not in fiery grappa but in American whiskey.

You can easily use any large cut of beefsteak, such as chateaubriand, instead of a roast. In order to ensure even cooking, the roast or steak should be of fairly even diameter all over and no more than 3 inches thick. Since a large steak is generally thinner than a roast, reduce the cooking time accordingly, still using the 130°F. internal temperature guideline.

3 pounds boneless beef roast
¼ cup coarse-ground black pepper

Prepare the grill for indirect heat cooking with the coals mounded in 2 piles at either end or 1 pile to one side (page 145).

Pat the beef roast dry with paper towels. Rub the pepper over the entire surface of the meat. Set aside at room temperature while the grill heats.

When the grill is hot, place the roast on the rack between the 2 piles of coals. Cover the roast with the grill top or foil and cook 30 minutes. Turn the roast and grill another 30 minutes, or until the internal temperature is 130°F. If the coals are in 1 pile to the side, place the roast on the grill rack at the edge of the coals and cover. Every 15 minutes, rotate the roast a quarter turn so a new side faces the coals. Turn the whole roast over after 30 minutes as above.

While the roast grills, marinate the figs (see below).

When the roast is done, remove to a platter. Let rest 20 minutes before carving. While the roast rests, grill the figs.

When ready to serve, arrange the grilled figs around the roast on the platter. Cut the roast across the grain into ⅛-inch-thick slices.

NOTES AND AFTERTHOUGHTS

1. The black pepper for this recipe should be freshly ground and coarse. Preground, fine pepper is not aromatic enough and feels sandy in the mouth. If you don't have a way to freshly grind peppercorns on a coarse setting, crack them with a mallet or hammer. For the maximum punch from the pepper, refrigerate the roast with the pepper coating overnight.

2. Grilled artichokes make a wonderful accompaniment to this dish.

Grilled Figs Soaked in Whiskey

12 whole sun-dried figs
⅓ cup whiskey
1 small onion
3 tablespoons balsamic or red wine vinegar

Plenty for 6

20 to 40 minutes

Place the figs in a small bowl, and pour the whiskey over them. Set aside to marinate 20 to 30 minutes at room temperature.

Peel the onion and cut it in half. Cut each half into wedges about 1 inch wide. Separate each wedge into 2 or 3 pieces and place in another small bowl. Pour the vinegar over the onion wedges. Set aside to marinate 20 to 30 minutes at room temperature.

When the figs and onions have marinated, thread them on a skewer, starting with an onion wedge, then a fig, and so on. Place the skewers on the grill rack directly over the coals and cook 10 to 12 minutes, turning once.

Grilled Leg of Lamb with Spicy Pecan Sauce

Plenty for 6 with leftovers

1½ hours

1 bone-in leg of lamb, whole or short cut (4½ to 6½ pounds, depending on the cut)
6 large or 8 medium garlic cloves

2 cups Spicy Pecan Sauce (page 159)

Prepare the grill for indirect heat cooking with the coals mounded in 2 piles at either end or 1 pile to one side (page 145).

Trim the fat off the outside of the leg of lamb without cutting into the meat underneath.

Peel the garlic cloves and cut them into slivers. Stuff the garlic slivers into all of the spaces in the leg of lamb that can easily be opened with your fingers. Set aside at room temperature while the grill heats.

When the grill is ready, place the lamb on the grill rack between the 2 piles of coals. Cover with the grill top or foil and cook 30 minutes. Turn, cover again, and cook 30 minutes more, or until the internal temperature is 140°F. If the coals are in 1 pile to the side, place the lamb on the grill rack at the edge of the coals and cover. Every 15 minutes, rotate the lamb a quarter turn so a new side faces the coals. Turn the whole leg over after 30 minutes as above.

While the lamb cooks, make the Spicy Pecan Sauce.

When the lamb is done, remove it to a platter and let rest 20 minutes for the juices to settle before carving.

When ready to serve, cut the meat perpendicular to the large leg bone, making slices as thick as you like. Accompany with a bowl of Spicy Pecan Sauce.

NOTES AND AFTERTHOUGHTS

Leg of lamb is as good leftover cold as it is hot off the grill. If there's any Spicy Pecan Sauce left, serve it with the cold lamb. Or you might make a light mustard sauce. Mix 2 tablespoons Dijon mustard with 2 tablespoons mayonnaise. Whisk in ½ cup olive oil and some chopped fresh herbs such as dill, thyme, or chervil.

Spicy Pecan Sauce

8 ounces shelled pecan pieces (about 2 cups)
4 medium garlic cloves
2 or 3 jalapeño or serrano chili peppers
1 cup walnut or peanut oil
⅛ teaspoon cayenne pepper
⅛ teaspoon salt
2 teaspoons balsamic or red wine vinegar

Fine chop the pecans in a blender or food processor or with a chef's knife.

Peel the garlic cloves. Remove the stems from the chilies.

If using a blender or food processor, cut the garlic and chilies into pieces. Add the garlic and chili pieces to the pecans and process until the mixture is finely minced. Add the oil, cayenne, salt, and vinegar and process until well blended. Remove to a bowl.

If making the sauce by hand, place the chopped pecans in a bowl. Press the garlic and add to the pecans. Mince the chilies. Add to the pecans, along with the oil, cayenne, salt, and vinegar. Mix with a fork or wire whisk to blend well.

Makes 2 cups

In the midst of writing this chapter, we tried out our new Spicy Pecan Sauce on 120 unsuspecting guests who arrived for Susanna's children's double bar and bat mitzvah. Intending it merely as a garnish for the thin slices of rare roast beef we served, we made 12 times the recipe. It was gone in 1 hour—15 pounds of roast beef too soon. People ate gobs. They liked it so much, some put it on their pizza, others their salad. We had to cut the cakes early.

Sweet and Spicy Grilled Ribs: Pork and Beef

Plenty for 6

40 to 60 minutes plus overnight marinating

2 cups packed brown sugar
2 tablespoons tomato paste
6 tablespoons soy sauce
1 tablespoon dried red chili flakes
2 tablespoons chopped fresh oregano leaves or 2 teaspoons dried
1 tablespoon salt
2 slabs pork spareribs, 2 slabs beef ribs, or 9 beef shortribs

Cilantro or watercress sprigs, for garnish (optional)

The day before grilling the ribs, mix together the brown sugar, tomato paste, soy sauce, chili flakes, oregano, and salt in a nonreactive container large enough to hold the ribs in 2 layers. Rub the entire surfaces of the ribs with the marinade and place in the container. Cut the pork rib slabs into sections if they don't fit. If beef ribs are in a slab, cut into individual ribs. Refrigerate overnight or up to 3 days, turning occasionally to coat the top surfaces.

When you are ready to cook the ribs, prepare the grill for direct heat grilling (page 145). Remove the ribs from the refrigerator to come to room temperature.

When the grill is hot, place the ribs on the rack directly over the coals. Cook 15 minutes for pork spareribs, 9 minutes for beef ribs, or 17 minutes for beef short ribs. Turn and cook the same amount of time on the other side.

Remove the ribs to a platter. If grilling pork spareribs, cut the ribs apart as soon as they are cool enough to handle. Decorate the platter with the cilantro or watercress sprigs and serve.

NOTES AND AFTERTHOUGHTS

1. The ribs need to sit overnight for the coating to fully permeate the meat with its hot, sweet, and spicy flavors. If you don't have time to prepare the ribs the day before, a few hours in the coating mixture will still add flavor to the meat. Pork ribs grill better in at least partial slabs, but beef ribs grill better as individual ribs.

2. You can make these ribs in the oven—use the same timing at 375°F— and they are still divine. Be prepared for a hard clean-up job because the brown sugar caramelizes on the bottom of the baking pan.

Grilled Boneless Pork Shoulder Roast with Mustard Ginger Soy Coating and Grilled Apples

FOR THE COATING:

2 tablespoons Dijon mustard
1 tablespoon soy sauce
1 teaspoon grated ginger root
1 teaspoon freshly ground black pepper

3 to 3½ pounds boneless pork shoulder roast

4 large or 5 medium firm apples (about 1½ pounds)

Prepare the grill for indirect heat cooking with the coals mounded in 2 piles at either end or 1 pile to one side (page 145).

In a nonreactive baking pan or casserole, combine the mustard, soy sauce, ginger, and pepper. Place the roast in the mustard mixture and turn to coat all over.

When the grill is hot, center the pork roast on the rack between the 2 piles of coals. Cover with the grill top or foil. Cook 1 hour, or until the internal temperature is 150°F. in the center and 165°F. on the ends. If the coals are in 1 pile to the side, place the roast on the grill rack at the edge of the coals and cover. Every 15 minutes rotate the roast a quarter turn so a new side faces the coals.

When the roast is done, remove it to a platter. Let rest 20 minutes to allow the juices to settle before carving.

While the roast rests, add a few more coals to the fire if it has burned too low to cook the apples. Cut the apples into ¾-inch-thick slices. Place them on the grill rack directly over the coals. Cook 8 minutes. Turn and cook 7 or 8 minutes more. Remove the apples to the platter with the roast.

To serve, carve the roast across the grain into ¼-inch-thick slices.

Plenty for 6

40 to 60 minutes

When the grilling fad hit around 1956, it spread through every town like wildfire. Some afternoons a thin spiral of smoke could be seen rising from almost every yard in the neighborhood, signaling the end of a hot summer day, dusk, and dinner.

Chicken Barbecued with Curry Yogurt Sauce

2 chickens (3½ pounds each)
3 cups Curry Yogurt Sauce (see below)

Prepare the grill for indirect heat cooking with the coals mounded in 1 pile in the center (page 145).

Cut the chickens into quarters and remove any excess fat.

Make the Curry Yogurt Sauce. Place in a container that is large enough to hold the chicken pieces. Add the chicken and turn to coat the pieces on all sides. Set aside at room temperature.

When the grill is hot, lift the chicken quarters out of the sauce. Place them, skin side up, on the grill rack around the perimeter of the coals. Cover with the grill top or foil and cook 30 to 35 minutes, turning once.

While the chicken cooks, place the remaining sauce in a small saucepan. Bring to a boil, reduce the heat to medium, and cook 5 minutes, until thickened slightly.

When the chicken is done, remove it to a platter. Spread the extra sauce over the chicken and serve.

NOTES AND AFTERTHOUGHTS

1. On a cold or rainy day when firing up the outdoor grill is out of the question, this chicken dish can be cooked with equal success in the oven. Place the chicken quarters, skin side up, in a baking dish. Pour the Curry Yogurt Sauce over the chicken. Bake at 400°F 20 minutes. Turn the chicken pieces over. Reduce the heat to 350° F and bake 20 minutes more. Turn the pieces again. Increase the heat to 400°F and finish cooking 15 minutes more.

2. For fewer calories and less cholesterol, you can skin the chicken pieces completely. It will be just as good.

Curry Yogurt Sauce

3 cups plain yogurt
3 teaspoons ground turmeric
3 teaspoons curry powder
1 teaspoon salt

Makes 3 cups

This is an unusual barbecue sauce, and its color is downright fun. Turmeric tints the sauce a blazing yellow reminiscent of hot dog mustard. Curry powder makes the flavor mildly Indian.

In a medium bowl, mix the yogurt, turmeric, curry powder, and salt.

If using as a barbecue sauce, coat whatever meat you are cooking. Place the remaining sauce in a saucepan. Bring to a boil. Reduce the heat, and cook 5 minutes, until thickened slightly.

If using as a sauce to accompany meat, place in a saucepan and bring to a boil. Reduce the heat, and cook 15 minutes, until thickened slightly.

Curry Yogurt Sauce also makes a wonderful dip, especially for vegetables. No cooking is required, simply chill it.

Game Hens Grilled with Rum Plum Sauce

4 game hens
2½ cups Rum Plum Sauce (page 164)
2 tablespoons thinly sliced fresh basil leaves, chopped chives, or a mixture

Plenty for 6

20 to 40 minutes

Fresh, not frozen, game hens taste like tender young chicken and cook in less time. The delicate flavor of these small birds goes especially well with fruit sauces. One game hen is enough for one and a half servings, so for 6 you will need 4 game hens to make a plentiful meal.

Prepare the grill for indirect heat cooking with the coals heaped in 1 pile in the center (page 145).

Cut the game hens in half, splitting them first down the backbone and then through the breast.

Make the Rum Plum Sauce, but do not cook it yet. Pour the uncooked sauce into a dish large enough to hold the game hen halves in a single layer. Place the game hen halves in the sauce. Turn to coat on both sides. Set aside at room temperature.

When the grill is hot, place the game hen halves, skin side down, around the perimeter of the coals. Cover and cook 12 minutes. Turn the pieces over, making sure to rotate them so that a new edge is closer to the coals. Cook 12 minutes more.

While the game hens are grilling, pour the remaining sauce into a small nonreactive saucepan. Simmer for 10 minutes on the stove or grill, until the alcohol evaporates and the sauce thickens slightly.

When the game hens are cooked, remove the pieces to a platter. Pour the sauce over them. Sprinkle on the fresh basil, chives, or both.

NOTES AND AFTERTHOUGHTS

1. When using Rum Plum Sauce to coat poultry, we skip the step of cooking and reducing the sauce until after the meat has been dipped in it. The sauce on the meat will cook over the grill and the sauce remaining needs to be boiled briefly after the dipping to ensure that the poultry juices are cooked.

2. If you are grilling on a hibachi, see the note on page 145 for how to simulate indirect heat cooking.

3. This dish cries out for a Sauce Sopper (page 218) to soak up the wonderful sauce. Any of them—Saffron Rice, Armenian Pilaf, or Herbed Polenta—would be delicious.

Rum Plum Sauce

Makes 2½ cups

16 whole fresh plums (about 2 pounds), or 16 canned plums in syrup
   (about two 17-ounce cans)
½ cup rum
¼ cup granulated sugar mixed with ¼ cup water, or ½ cup plum syrup from the can
2 tablespoons lemon juice
2 teaspoons chopped or coarse-grated lemon peel

Pit the fresh plums or drain and pit the canned plums, reserving the syrup.

In a food processor or blender, process the plums until well mashed but not pureed smooth. Or chop plums with a chef's knife and then mash them with a fork. Add the rum, sugar and water or plum syrup, lemon juice, and lemon peel. Mix to blend well.

Place the sauce in a small nonreactive sauce pan. Bring to a boil. Cook over medium heat 10 minutes, until the alcohol evaporates and the sauce thickens slightly.

Grilled Breast of Turkey

2 garlic cloves
1 whole bone-in turkey breast (4½ to 5 pounds)
1 teaspoon chopped fresh sage leaves or ½ teaspoon dried rubbed sage

Prepare the grill for indirect heat cooking with the coals mounded in 2 piles at either end or 1 pile to one side (page 145).

Peel the garlic and cut into slivers. With a paring knife and your fingers, gently lift the turkey skin away from the meat without separating it completely. Spread the garlic slivers and sage over the top of the turkey breast, underneath the skin.

When the grill is hot, place the turkey breast skin up on the grill rack between the 2 piles of coals. Cover with the grill top or foil. Cook 2 hours, or until the internal temperature is 160 to 165°F in the thickest part. If the coals are in 1 pile to the side, place the turkey breast on the grill rack at the edge of the coals and cover. Every 15 minutes, rotate the turkey a quarter turn so a new side faces the coals.

Remove the turkey breast to a platter. Let rest 15 minutes or so to allow the juices to settle before carving.

NOTES AND AFTERTHOUGHTS

1. If you have the time, cure the turkey breast overnight as recommended for duck or rabbit, page 28.

2. Half a turkey breast serves only 4 hearty dinner diners, so to feed 6 we give this recipe for a whole turkey breast and count on lots of leftovers. If half a turkey breast suits your purpose, though, it takes 1½ hours to cook.

3. For a fresh and different taste combination, serve cold grilled turkey breast with the Dill Cream Sauce (page 174), or with Melon and Jalapeño Pepper Salsa (page 84).

Plenty for 6 with leftovers

2 hours

The supply-and-demand principle has been at work on the price of turkey. What used to be an economical as well as an out-of-the-ordinary dish is no longer a bargain. Still, it's very low in fat and calories, and in terms of taste, it's worth the elevated price.

Be sure to purchase turkey breast with the bone still in. As with any meat, poultry, or fish, the bone adds immeasurably to the flavor.

Curing turkey breast, like duck and rabbit (page 28), works like magic to keep the meat tender, firm, and juicy. Curing also adds a pleasing rosy hue to the turkey meat.

*40 to 60 minutes
plus overnight curing*

We always recommend briefly curing duck and rabbit no matter how you are preparing them. For grilling, it is essential. The only way to have moist barbecued duck or rabbit that is not tough or dried out is to tenderize and firm the meat by rubbing it with salt and herbs and letting it cure overnight. This involves no more bother than planning one day in advance, and the taste cannot be duplicated any other way. What's more, the aromatic seasoning and intricate, ham-like flavor that this particular cure imparts eliminate the need for a sauce. Your work is done simply with the quick and easy step of curing.

Tender Grilled Duck or Rabbit

**2 ducks or 2 rabbits, cut into quarters (see Note below)
Ingredients for curing duck and rabbit (page 28)**

The day before grilling, cure the duck or rabbit following the instructions on page 28.

When you are ready to cook the duck or rabbit, prepare the grill for indirect heat cooking with the coals mounded in 1 pile in the center (page 145).

Use paper towels to brush the salt off the meat, leaving behind any bits of herbs and spices that cling to the meat.

When the grill is hot, place the duck or rabbit pieces, meaty side down, on the rack around the perimeter of the coals. Cover with the grill top or foil and cook 15 minutes. Turn the pieces over and reposition them with the uncooked side toward the fire. Cover again. Grill 12 minutes more for rabbit, 15 to 18 minutes more for duck.

NOTES AND AFTERTHOUGHTS

1. If you are grilling the duck or rabbit on a hibachi, see the note on page 145 for how to simulate indirect heat cooking.

2. In this recipe, we don't use the duck wings because they don't cook enough to be crisp or even chewable. Use them for stock. We remove the backbones because this is the neatest way to open the duck for quartering and no meat is sacrificed.

3. Leftover duck can be put to good use in the Spaghetti with Duck and Olives (page 131). Briefly reheat the duck in a lightly oiled sauté pan, then proceed with the recipe.

Grilled Fish Steaks and Fish Kebabs

Pink salmon, red tuna, ivory swordfish, variegated shrimps, and speckled squid, whether in steaks or strung on kebabs—the light smoke flavor of direct heat grilling enhances almost any fish to mouthwatering perfection. If you are grilling steaks, purchase them ¾ to 1 inch thick. If you are grilling kebabs, buy the delicious, bargain basement–priced chunks, or cut thick steaks or fillets into 1½-inch squares. Leave shrimp in their shells. We think most kinds of fish benefit from a pre-grill bath in a pungent marinade, so we give an unfussy, versatile one.

¾ cup Basic Fish Marinade (page 168)
2½ pounds tuna, shark, salmon, sturgeon, or other meaty fish in steaks, fillets, or chunks, or 2½ pounds shrimp
1½ cups Quick Lemon Garlic Butter (page 168, optional)

Prepare the grill for direct heat cooking (page 145).

Make the Basic Fish Marinade.

Place the fish steaks, chunks, shrimp, or squid in the marinade and turn to coat well. Cover and refrigerate at least 20 minutes.

Make the Quick Lemon Garlic Butter if you are using it.

When the grill is hot, lift the fish out of the marinade. If grilling fish steaks, place them on the rack directly over the coals. Cook about 6 minutes per side for ¾-inch-thick steaks, about 4 minutes per side for thinner steaks. If grilling kebabs, thread the chunks on skewers. Place the kebabs on the rack directly over the coals. Cook about 4 minutes per side, turning once. If grilling shrimp, thread them on skewers for easier handling and turning. Place the skewers on the rack directly over the coals. Cook 4 to 5 minutes, depending on the size. Turn and cook 4 to 5 minutes more. Serve with Quick Lemon Garlic Butter, if desired.

NOTES AND AFTERTHOUGHTS

1. If grilling thinner steaks or kebabs, you need to reduce the cooking time. Half-inch-thick steaks take about 4 minutes per side. Kebabs with ½-inch-thick chunks take about 3 minutes per side. If the steaks or fillets are thinner than ½ inch, forgo grilling and sauté them instead (see the recipe for Sole Sautéed with Lemon, Capers, and Olives, page 206).

2. If you want to prepare the fish in advance, you can marinate it up to 2 hours. Not much longer, though, or it will pickle and become mushy.

3. If the shrimp have a black sand vein running along the back, make a cut through the shell and remove it.

(continued)

Plenty for 6

20 to 40 minutes

Grilled fish is ready to remove from the fire when it is medium rare— that is, when it is firm but not hard to the touch, when the juices rising from the inside form white curds on the surface, and when the internal temperature is 115°F. Like meat, fish continues to cook after it is removed from the grill. Also like meat, it tastes better if the juices are allowed to settle for a few minutes before eating.

Basic Fish Marinade

Makes ¾ cup

⅔ cup olive oil
½ tablespoon balsamic or red wine vinegar
1 tablespoon Dijon mustard
⅛ teaspoon salt
1 tablespoon chopped fresh herbs, such as oregano, thyme, bay, marjoram,
    tarragon, cilantro, dill, Italian parsley, or chives, or 1 teaspoon dried herbs

Mix together the olive oil, vinegar, mustard, salt, and herbs in a nonreactive container.

NOTES AND AFTERTHOUGHTS

The marinade for Grilled Swordfish (page 171) is also a fine, basic fish marinade. It is especially desirable if you don't care for the pungency of mustard.

Quick Lemon Garlic Butter

Makes 1½ cups

3 large or 5 medium garlic cloves
⅓ cup olive oil
1 tablespoon lemon juice
¼ teaspoon salt
⅛ teaspoon white pepper
1 cup (2 sticks) butter
1 tablespoon chopped fresh herbs such as oregano, thyme, bay, marjoram,
    tarragon, cilantro, dill, Italian parsley, chives, basil or watercress
1 tablespoon capers (optional)

Peel the garlic. Press into a small nonreactive saucepan, and add the oil, lemon juice, salt, and white pepper. Set over medium heat and bring to a boil. Stir in the butter, 4 tablespoons at a time, until well blended. Stir in the herbs and capers.

Set aside in a warm place until ready to serve.

OTHER SAUCES FOR GRILLED FISH

It's not too much to use both a marinade and a sauce on fish. In fact, to be at their best, blander fish need both. Other sauces in this book suitable for grilled fish are:

Ancho Chili Sauce, page 85
Chive Salsa, page 83
Corn and Red Bell Pepper Salsa, page 84
Dill Cream Sauce, page 174
Garlic Pine Nut Paste, page 247
Greek Sour Cream or Yogurt Sauce, page 70
Lemon, Caper, and Olive Sauce, page 206
Melon and Jalapeño Salsa, page 84
Papaya or Kiwi Chutney, page 151
Polynesian Mango Sauce, page 207
Tomato Salsa, page 82
Tomatillo Sauce, page 85
Spicy Pecan Sauce, page 159
Tomato Tarragon Sauce, page 175
Zesty Garlic Mayonnaise, page 209

Grilled Scallop and Bacon Kebabs Topped with Bread Crumbs, Parsley and Chopped Lemon Peel

Plenty for 6

20 minutes or less

FOR THE TOPPING:
Peel of 3 large lemons
½ cup chopped fresh parsley leaves
⅔ cup Bread Crumbs (page 136)
3 tablespoons fresh lemon juice

5 strips thin sliced bacon (about 5 ounces)
2⅓ pounds medium or large sea scallops

Prepare the grill (page 145) for direct heat cooking.

Make the topping first. Mince the lemon peel. Add the parsley and lemon peel to the bread crumbs and mix. Have the lemon juice ready and set both aside.

Cut the bacon slices crosswise into 1½-inch-wide pieces. If the scallops are more than 1 inch thick, cut them crosswise into 2 thin disks.

Starting with a piece of bacon and then a scallop, thread 6 skewers, finishing with bacon.

When the grill is hot, place the kebabs on the rack directly over the coals. Cook 5 minutes, turning once. Remove to a platter.

To serve, mix the lemon juice into the bread crumb mixture. Sprinkle over the scallops.

Grilled Marinated Swordfish Chunks Skewered with Onion and Bay Leaf

2½ pounds swordfish, in chunks or ¾-inch-thick steaks

FOR THE MARINADE:

1½ medium onions (10 to 12 ounces)
8 to 10 whole bay leaves
⅓ cup olive oil
⅓ cup lemon juice
1 teaspoon salt

Plenty for 6

20 to 40 minutes

Swordfish chunks, as well as being less expensive, are often the most delicious pieces. They usually come from the particularly succulent collar or belly parts that can't be sliced into steaks.

Cut the ends off the onions. Cut the onions in half and peel them. Cut each half into 4 or 5 wedges and separate the layers. Place the onion pieces in a large bowl. Cut the bay leaves crosswise into 1-inch pieces. Add the bay leaf pieces to the bowl. Stir in the olive oil, lemon juice, and salt. Mix together.

Cut swordfish steaks into 1½-inch squares. Place the swordfish pieces or chunks in the marinade and turn to coat. Cover and marinate at least 30 minutes at room temperature, or up to 2 hours refrigerated, turning once or twice to make sure all the chunks are well covered with the marinade.

Prepare the grill for direct heat cooking (page 145).

When the grill is hot, thread 6 skewers, starting with an onion section, then a bay leaf, then a chunk of swordfish, and so on, ending with a piece of onion. Place the skewers on the rack and cook for 8 minutes, turning once.

NOTES AND AFTERTHOUGHTS

1. The bay leaves are for seasoning and not consumption. Set them aside as you unstring the kebabs. Don't ingest them. They've been known to catch in the throat.

2. If you care for a sauce as well as a marinade on your swordfish, without hesitation our sauce of choice is Garlic Pine Nut Paste (page 247). Also good are Tomato Tarragon Sauce (page 175), Spicy Pecan Sauce (page 159), or any of the salsas (pages 82 to 84).

3. Swordfish overcooks and dries out very quickly. If the swordfish is thinner than ¾ inch, reduce the cooking time accordingly.

4. The more marinating time, up to 2 hours, the better with swordfish. After that the flesh begins to break down and tastes too pickled.

Grilled Trout or Spanish Mackerel Marinated with Cilantro and Coated with Parmesan Cheese

6 whole trout or Spanish mackerel (about ½ pound each)

FOR THE MARINADE:

½ cup lemon juice
⅓ cup olive oil
⅓ cup whole cilantro leaves
¼ cup chopped fresh parsley leaves
¼ teaspoon salt

⅔ cup grated Parmesan cheese
1 lemon, cut into 6 wedges
12 whole cilantro sprigs (optional)

In a nonreactive dish large enough to hold the fish in a single layer, combine the lemon juice, oil, cilantro leaves, parsley, and salt. Place the fish in the dish. Turn to coat with the marinade. Cover, and refrigerate at least 20 minutes or up to 2 hours, turning once or twice.

Prepare the grill for direct heat cooking (page 145).

When the grill is hot, lift the fish out of the marinade. Without drying them, coat them inside and out with the grated cheese. Take the cilantro leaves out of the marinade and stuff them into the fish cavities. Put the fish on the rack directly over the coals. Cook 6 minutes. Turn and cook 6 minutes more.

While the fish grill, pour the remaining marinade into a small nonreactive saucepan. On the stove or grill, boil the marinade until reduced by half, about 5 minutes.

When the fish are done, remove to a platter. Moisten with a little of the reduced marinade. Arrange the lemon wedges and cilantro sprigs all around and serve.

NOTES AND AFTERTHOUGHTS

1. If you are one who avoids fish because of the bones or bother, try this recipe with boneless trout. Marinate and coat the already boned trout as described in the recipe. Place them, opened out and skin side down, on the grill rack and cook 8 minutes without turning. Remove the trout with a metal spatula (their skins will probably be left behind). The fish will be slightly underdone in the thick part, but they will continue cooking completely as you bring them to the table.

2. Spanish mackerel is also called Jack mackerel or Pacific Jack. If you find it in your fish market, grilling is an uncomplicated way to tone down and mellow out its somewhat strong flavor. Contrariwise, the marinade and grated cheese jazz up the rather mild taste of trout.

Grilled Salmon with Onion Tomato Herb Salad Stuffing and Dill Cream Sauce

1½ cups Dill Cream Sauce (page 174)
1 medium onion (about 7 ounces)
1 medium tomato (about 4 ounces)
8 large sprigs fresh basil, dill, or tarragon
4- to 6-pound whole or half salmon, cleaned and scaled
8 thin slices bacon (about ½ pound)

Plenty for 8 to 12

40 to 60 minutes

Stuffing and wrapping a large piece of salmon not only adds flavor and helps prevent the fish from sticking to the grill, it is also a good way to keep the fish flesh moist while it cooks.

Prepare the grill for direct heat cooking (page 145).

While the grill heats, make the Dill Cream Sauce.

Peel and slice the onion into ⅛-inch-thick rounds. Slice the tomato into ⅛-inch-thick rounds. Arrange the onion rounds, tomato slices, and herb sprigs inside the cavity of the salmon. Close the salmon cavity with toothpicks. Wrap the bacon slices around the salmon at 2-inch intervals, securing them with toothpicks.

When the grill is hot, place the salmon on the rack directly over the coals. Position it so that the thickest part is over the hottest part of the fire. Cook 20 minutes. With a metal spatula, carefully loosen the fish from the grill. Then, using 2 long spatulas (or 3 short spatulas and some help), turn the fish over. Cook for 20 minutes more, or until an instant-reading thermometer registers 115°F in the middle.

Remove the salmon to a large platter. Let rest 20 minutes to allow the meat to firm before serving.

Just before serving, remove the skin, saving any pieces of bacon you can. The onion, tomato, and herb become the salmon's own salad. Remove them from the fish cavity and arrange them, along with the bacon, to the side of the fish. Spoon a little Dill Cream Sauce over the top of the salmon. Serve the remaining sauce on the side.

NOTES AND AFTERTHOUGHTS

Four to 6 pounds of salmon is a lot of fish. When it comes to turning it over on the grill in one piece and later removing it to a platter, you need 2 snow shovel-size spatulas or a few extra hands to help.

(continued)

Makes 1½ cups

By integrating the lemon with the oil, heating it, then adding the cream slowly, we solved the curdling that inevitably occurs when you add lemon to heated cream. The outcome is a quick-to-make, smooth Dill Cream Sauce that goes well with fish, poultry, and many vegetables.

Dill Cream Sauce

2 tablespoons sour cream
1 cup heavy cream
¼ cup olive oil
1 tablespoon lemon juice
⅛ teaspoon salt
3 tablespoons chopped fresh dill leaves or 2 teaspoons dried

Place the sour cream in a small bowl and stir until smooth. Stir in the heavy cream and set aside.

Combine the oil, lemon juice, salt, and dill in a small nonreactive saucepan. Bring to a boil. Reduce the heat to low, and slowly drizzle in the cream mixture, whisking constantly. Continue stirring over low heat for 2 minutes. Remove to a small bowl.

Chill the sauce at least 30 minutes to thicken it. When ready to use it, whisk to smooth it out.

NOTES AND AFTERTHOUGHTS

Don't worry if the Dill Cream Sauce turns out thin because you add the cream too rapidly. It will set up in the refrigerator if you chill it thoroughly. On the other hand, if the sauce thickens too much when it is chilled, add a few drops more olive oil to thin it. Dill Cream Sauce can be made the day before or hours in advance of grilling and kept in the refrigerator.

Grilled Oysters with Tomato Tarragon Sauce and Melted Butter

2 cups Tomato Tarragon Sauce (see below)
¼ pound (1 stick) butter
30 large oysters

Prepare the grill for direct heat cooking (page 145).

While the grill is heating, make the Tomato Tarragon Sauce.

In a small saucepan, melt the butter. Set the butter and the sauce aside in a warm place.

Rinse and scrub the oysters.

When the grill is hot, place the oysters on the rack directly over the coals. Cover with the grill top or foil and cook 12 to 15 minutes, until the oysters open. Using a mitt or towel to protect your hand, remove the oysters, taking care not to spill their juices.

Pry the oysters the rest of the way open with an oyster knife, paring knife, or screwdriver. Sever the muscle that connects the shells, leaving the oyster on the half shell. Place on a serving platter.

Dot each oyster with about ½ tablespoon of the Tomato Tarragon Sauce. Drizzle melted butter over the tops, and serve.

NOTES AND AFTERTHOUGHTS
Chinese markets are a good source for large oysters.

Tomato Tarragon Sauce

½ medium onion (about 4 ounces)
3 tablespoons butter
2 tablespoons chopped fresh parsley leaves
2 teaspoons chopped fresh tarragon leaves or ½ teaspoon dried
1 tablespoon white wine vinegar
1 cup crushed tomatoes in puree

Peel the onion and fine chop it in a food processor or with a chef's knife.

In a small nonreactive saucepan, melt the butter. Add the onion, parsley, and tarragon. Cook over low heat 5 minutes.

Increase the heat to medium and stir in the vinegar. Add the tomatoes. Bring to a boil and remove from the heat right away.

Set aside in a warm place, or refrigerate and reheat when ready to use.

Plenty for 6

40 to 60 minutes

Grilling is a great way to prepare large oysters that aren't the most appealing raw on the half shell. It's also an easy way to make them open. Grilling in the shell does not work with small oysters, though, because they shrivel up before they open.

To grill smaller oysters, shuck them or buy them in the jar already shucked, and thread them on skewers. Place the skewers on the rack directly over hot coals and cook 8 to 10 minutes, turning once. Serve with the melted butter and the Tomato Tarragon Sauce on the side.

Makes 2 cups

GRILLED VEGETABLES

Grilled vegetables are tasty beyond compare. Besides, grilling the vegetables means you can cook your whole meal on the barbecue. You don't have to scurry between kitchen and yard tending two fires. Not all vegetables take to the grate, but most, adult and "baby" alike, do. Below are directions for grilling those legumes, gourds, nightshades, roots, and thistles that turn out particularly well.

Artichokes

Artichokes benefit from the smoky flavor of grilling, but they require pre-cooking and a light oil coating to come out well. Grilling them straightaway dries them out and results in a leathery texture.

To grill baby artichokes, leave them whole but trim the leaves down to the light green part. Parboil 5 minutes. Drain, and rinse under cold water to cool. Set aside to drip dry, or gently squeeze out excess water and pat dry with paper towels. Toss them with olive oil flavored with a little pressed garlic and some herb. Place the artichokes on the rack over the coals and cook 5 or 10 minutes, depending on the heat of the fire. Turn once.

To grill large artichokes, halve medium ones or quarter large ones. Parboil 10 minutes. Drain and cool. Coat with oil as above. Place them on the rack over the coals and cook 10 to 15 minutes, depending on the heat of the fire. Turn once.

Brussels Sprouts

Even people who usually turn up a nose at Brussels sprouts often like them grilled. However, like artichokes; they must be precooked. Parboil 5 minutes. Rinse in cool water to stop the cooking. Skewer and grill directly over the coals of a medium-hot fire 5 to 6 minutes, until browned but not charred all around. When done, toss the grilled Brussels sprouts with butter or olive oil and grated Parmesan, Romano, or other hard cheese.

Corn

The easiest and best way to grill corn—and grilling is by far the best way to cook corn—is in the husk. Soak the ears of corn in water to cover about 10 minutes. Place on the grill rack directly over the coals of a medium-hot fire or to the side of the coals of a hot fire. Cook, covered or uncovered, for about 20 minutes, until the kernels are just tender. Reposition occasionally to keep the husks from burning through.

Eggplant

Eggplants of any variety grill superbly, either whole, sliced, or cubed on kebabs.

To grill eggplants whole, pierce them with a knife to allow steam to escape and prevent bursting. Place on the rack and cook, uncovered, over direct heat or covered over indirect heat, turning once. Large ones take 40 to 50 minutes; small ones take 20 to 25 minutes. Whole eggplants are done when they are puffed out and a finger poke will leave a depression. Slit open and drizzle on olive oil or melted butter flavored with a little pressed garlic. Sprinkle with salt and pepper.

For cut-up eggplants, slice the eggplant into ¾-inch-thick rounds or ovals. Brush both sides with oil. Place the slices on the rack to the side of the coals and grill 10 minutes. Turn and reposition directly over the coals. Cook 10 minutes more, or until soft in the centers.

Or cut eggplants into 1½-inch cubes. Toss the cubes with oil to coat. Skewer and cook over medium-hot coals about 10 minutes, until soft.

Garlic

Grilled garlic is sweet, not pungent or sharp at all. The pulp becomes soft and spreadable, a perfect condiment in itself for meat, poultry, or fish.

To grill garlic, remove the dry peel from the outer layer of whole heads without separating the cloves. Place the whole heads on the grill rack around the edges of the coals. Cover and cook 25 to 30 minutes.

Or remove the dry peel from the outer layer, then wrap the whole heads in foil with a sprig or pinch of thyme and a pat of butter. Place the packages on the rack directly over the coals of a hot fire or to the side of coals of a medium-hot fire. Cook 25 to 30 minutes, turning once.

Separate the garlic cloves and squeeze out the soft pulp.

Mushrooms

Grilling particularly enhances the flavor of ordinary mushrooms that usually are bland.

To grill mushrooms, clean them, and trim the ends. Toss with a little oil seasoned with some herbs or garlic if you like. Skewer the mushrooms through the centers.

Place the skewers on the rack directly over the coals of a medium-hot fire or around the edges of the coals of a hot fire. Cook, covered, 15 to 20 minutes in indirect heat, or, uncovered, 6 to 7 minutes directly over the coals. Turn once or twice.

Onions

All kinds of onions grill very successfully because the heat of grilling cooks their sugars, releases their sweetness, and eliminates the acrid taste. Also, they contain enough water to remain moist and firm when grilled.

Large and medium onions can be grilled whole, but they are usually cut up for quicker cooking. Peel them and cut into ¾- to 1-inch thick rounds. Place on the rack directly over the coals of a medium-hot fire or around the edges of a hot fire. Cook 20 minutes, turning and repositioning once.

Alternatively, peel large or medium onions and cut them into 1-inch-wide wedges. Skewer the wedges, and place them on the rack. Cook as for rounds, about 10 minutes.

Small boiling or tiny pearl onions should be grilled whole on kebabs. Peel and skewer them. Place on the rack directly over the coals of a hot fire or around the edges of a medium-hot fire. Boiling onions take about 20 minutes; pearl onions take 5 to 10 minutes depending on the size. Turn often.

Whole shallots grill nicely. Treat them the same way as skewered boiling onions.

For green onions, trim away the root ends and limp parts of green tops. Place on the rack over the coals and cook 3 to 5 minutes, turning once, depending on their thickness.

Leeks are almost impossible to grill unless they are tender and young. Older ones have so much dirt between their leaves that you must cut them open to clean them and then they fall apart. To grill tender, young leeks, wash off the outside dirt. Trim off the tough part of the green tops. Place the leeks on the rack around the edges of the coals. Cook 15 to 20 minutes, turning once, until soft. When the leeks are done, toss with olive oil or melted butter and perhaps a twist of lemon juice.

Peppers

Fresh peppers, from green to red, yellow, and purple, and from sweet to hot, are delicious grilled.

To grill whole peppers, place them on the rack directly over the coals of a hot fire and cook until charred all around, turning and repositioning frequently to avoid burning the pulp below the skin. Large sweet peppers take 20 to 25 minutes. Smaller chili peppers such as pasillas and Anaheims take 12 to 15 minutes. When the skins are blistered and charred, remove the peppers to a bowl of cold water or a paper bag. Set aside for 10 to 20 minutes. Remove the peppers from the bowl or bag, and peel with your fingers or a paring knife.

If you don't care to peel the peppers, you can cut them and grill on kebabs. To grill kebabs, cut the peppers in half. Remove the seeds and core. Cut the halves into 1½-inch squares. Skewer the squares. Place on the rack directly over or around the edges of the coals, and cook 10 to 12 minutes, turning occasionally.

Small hot peppers—chilies—are usually not grilled, but if your taste runs to hot and spicy, you can grill them most easily on kebabs. Skewer them and place the skewers on the rack directly over the coals of a hot fire. Turn frequently for 5 minutes. For a cooling treat on a hot day, try grilled red or green jalapeño chilies served with grilled flour or corn tortillas and a bowl of well chilled yogurt lightly seasoned with salt and marjoram.

Potatoes

Of the commonly available potatoes, russets—with their mealy texture— roast the best whether in the oven or on the grill. Red or white potatoes also grill nicely, as do yams and sweet potatoes. Potatoes grilled whole come out soft, much the same way as oven roasted. Sliced potatoes form a nice crunchy crust on the cut sides, and they cook faster. Neither needs precooking, but sliced potatoes need an oil coating

To roast potatoes whole, wash and wrap them in foil. Place directly in the coals or on a rack directly over the coals of a medium-hot fire. If the fire is hot, place the potatoes around the edges of the coals. Medium and large russet, red, or white potatoes take 45 minutes to 1 hour, depending on the size. Yams and sweet potatoes take 1½ hours. Tiny red or white potatoes, often called creamers, roast in about 30 minutes. Alternatively, you can parboil creamers for 10 minutes, skewer them, and grill 15 minutes to finish cooking.

Whatever potatoes you are cooking, reposition them every 15 minutes to ensure even cooking. To test for doneness, pinch lightly between thumb and forefinger. If the potatoes give all the way to the centers, they are done. Also, potatoes are done when a skewer slides easily into the center.

To grill potatoes in slices, wash and cut into ¾-inch-thick rounds. Crush a little garlic and rosemary into a few tablespoons of oil. Toss the potato slices in the oil mixture to coat well. Place the slices on the rack directly over the coals of a medium-hot fire or around the edges of a hot fire. Cook 15 minutes, turning once.

Summer Squash

Summer squash—crooknecks, zucchini, and patty pans—grill exquisitely if they are not too large. Large ones with well-developed seeds and sugars turn out mushy.

To grill summer squashes, cut crooknecks and zucchini lengthwise in half. Cut patty pans crosswise through their centers. Leave baby squashes whole. Place on the rack directly over the coals of a medium-hot fire or around the edges of the coals of a hot fire. Cook for 12 to 15 minutes, turning once.

Tomatoes

Tomatoes are a perfect vegetable for grilling. Their flavor combines well with most other grilled foods, and they also provide an element of moisture to other drier grilled vegetables and unsauced meats. Indeed, when they are at their best in high summer and early fall, they are so flavorful grilled that they make a sauce by themselves.

To grill tomatoes, cut large or medium ones crosswise in half, or thread small or cherry tomatoes on skewers. Place tomato halves, cut side up, on the rack directly over the coals of a medium-hot fire or around the edges of a hot fire. Cook 15 minutes without turning. Position skewered tomatoes on the rack the same way. Cook 10 minutes for small tomatoes and 5 minutes for cherry tomatoes. Turn and reposition the skewers once or twice.

Tomato halves are especially good drizzled with a little olive oil and sprinkled with some chopped fresh herb such as thyme or oregano before grilling.

Winter Squashes

Of the winter squashes, acorn squash and small pumpkins grill particularly well. In fact, if you've never thought of pumpkin except as a large gourd for pies or a jack o' lantern, you will be pleasantly surprised by the delicious taste and smooth texture of grilled small pumpkins.

To grill acorn squash or small pumpkins, cut them in half and remove the seeds. Cut the halves into half rounds or wedges about 1½ inches thick. Place the pieces on the rack around the edges of the coals. Cook 15 minutes, turning once. Reposition the pieces directly over the coals, and cook another 10 minutes, turning once. Remove to a platter and garnish with melted butter, pepper, and minced fresh chives or green onion tops.

SAUCES FOR GRILLS

The true delight and adventure of grilling is that you can sauce the food in any number of ways according to whatever edible you are barbecuing, the caprice that overtakes you, and whatever you find in your cupboard at the time. If you like a sauce from any recipe in this or another chapter, chances are you can find other uses for it in your grilling repertoire. Following is a list of sauces we like to dollop on our grilled food and suggestions of what they best suit.

Ancho Chili Sauce: use with everything, page 85

Chick Pea Paste: use with lamb or pork, page 45

Chive Salsa: use with everything, page 83

Corn and Red Bell Pepper Salsa: use with everything, page 84

Curry Yogurt Sauce: use with chicken, game hens, turkey breast, rabbit, lamb, vegetables, page 162

Dill Cream Sauce: use with turkey burgers, chicken, game hens, turkey breast, rabbit, any grilled fish, shrimp, vegetables, page 174

Garlic Horseradish Sauce: use with steaks, chops, hamburgers, beef, lamb, pork roasts, ribs, chicken, duck, shark, swordfish, tuna, scallops, shrimp, oysters, bread, page 149

Garlic Pine Nut Paste: use with pork chops or roasts, chicken, game hens, duck, quail, turkey burgers, turkey breast, rabbit, shark, tuna, swordfish, trout, vegetables, bread, page 247

Greek Sour Cream or Yogurt Sauce: use with almost any grilled meat, poultry, fish (except scallops or oysters), vegetables, or bread, page 70

Kiwi Chutney: use with pork chops, turkey breast, chicken livers, shark, swordfish, page 151

Lemon, Caper, and Olive Sauce: use with pork chops, sausage or turkey burgers, chicken, game hens, turkey breast, rabbit, any grilled fish, shellfish, vegetables, page 206

Melon and Jalapeño Salsa: use with lamb, pork, poultry, or fish, page 84

Mock Hoisin Sauce: use with pork, chicken, game hens, duck, rabbit, page 106

Orange Onion Marmalade: use with almost any meat or poultry or chicken livers, page 192

Papaya Chutney: use with chops, sausage or turkey burgers, lamb or pork roast, ribs, chicken, game hens, duck, quail, turkey breast, rabbit, shark, shrimp, page 151

Polynesian Mango Sauce: use with lamb, pork, fish, shrimp, chicken livers, page 207

Quick Lemon Garlic Butter: use with any grilled fish, shellfish, vegetables, page 168

Red Pepper Pesto: use with beef, lamb, pork, chicken, game hens, rabbit, or vegetables, page 43

Red Pizza Sauce: use with hamburgers, turkey burgers, sausage burgers, or beef or pork ribs, page 61

Rum Plum Sauce: use with pork chops and roasts, chicken, game hens, duck, quail, turkey breast, rabbit, chicken livers, page 164

Sour Cream Sauce: use with fish or fish kebabs, especially salmon, page 71

Spicy Pecan Sauce: use with steaks, chops, beef, lamb, pork roasts, ribs, chicken, game hens, duck, quail, turkey breast, rabbit, chicken livers, shark, swordfish, scallops, page 159

Tomatillo Sauce: use with everything, especially fish and poultry, page 85

Tomato Salsa: use with everything, page 82

Tomato Tarragon Sauce: use with steaks, pork chops, beef and pork roasts, burgers, ribs, chicken, game hens, turkey breast, rabbit, any grilled fish or shellfish, vegetables, bread, page 175

Yogurt and Feta Cheese Dip: use with lamb or vegetables, page 46

Zesty Garlic Mayonnaise: use with steaks, chops, beef, lamb, pork roasts, burgers, ribs, turkey breast, rabbit, shark, swordfish, tuna, scallops, oysters, trout, salmon, vegetables, page 209

Fast from the Stovetop:
SAUTÉ, QUICK FRY, AND STEAM

Pan-Fried Steaks and Chops
  Basic Wine Sauce for Pan-Fried Steaks and Chops
  Variations
  Pickled Pan-Grilled Onions

Pine Nut-Coated Pork Chops with Mushrooms, Onions, and Sherry

Pork Chops with Orange and Onion Marmalade
  Orange and Onion Marmalade

Pan Kebabs
  Chicken, Anchovy, and Asparagus Kebabs
  Beef, Eggplant, Red Pepper, and Garlic Kebabs

Desperation Chicken
  Variations
  Chicken à la Corsala
  Desperation Game Hens

Reduced-Calorie Southern Fried Chicken

Chicken Tarragon

Quick-Fry Bourbon Chicken

Turkey Cutlets
  Basic Sautéed Turkey Cutlets
  Turkey Cutlets with Ginger Cream
  Turkey Cutlets with Juniper and White Wine

Quail with Pepper, Sage, and Pan-Fried Cheese Corn Bread
  Pan-Fried Cheese Corn Bread

Trout with Pine Nuts and Smoked Salmon

Sole Sautéed with Lemon, Capers, and Olives

Halibut in Cornmeal Crust with Polynesian Mango Sauce
  Polynesian Mango Sauce

Shrimp and Mussels Sautéed with Celery and Tarragon

Steamed Fish Extravaganza with Zesty Garlic Mayonnaise
  Zesty Garlic Mayonnaise

Stovetop Vegetables
  Sautéed Vegetables
    Sesame Sautéed Vegetables
  Vegetables Simmered in Broth, Wine, or Water

Sauce Soppers to Go with Stovetop Dishes
  Saffron Rice
  Armenian Pilaf
  Herbed Polenta

The stovetop. From a 2-ring electric burner in a walk-up apartment to a 6-burner restaurant range, we use the stovetop more than any other cooking device. From it we have instant heat, no coals to start, no oven to warm. Thirty years ago, the oven took precedence over or was used at least as much as the stovetop. Now it seems we rarely have time to throw a chicken in the oven or bake a pot pie, and stovetop cooking has become increasingly important to us.

And happily so, because the stovetop allows us to cook in a remarkably diverse number of ways and provides us with an incredible variety of dishes. On the stovetop we can boil, fry, simmer, and steam. We can use wine, bread the food, combine nuts, vegetables, capers, olives, or apples all together with the meat, fish, or fowl.

Along with the trend away from long-cooked dishes as our daily fare, we have departed from the ritual of stewing and deep frying on the stovetop. Now we mostly sauté. Sautéing is rapid frying in a very little oil over brisk heat. In sautéing, food does not absorb much oil because it is cooked quickly. We use butter sometimes, but we have replaced the lards and other fats of yesteryear with more healthful vegetable and nut oils.

Sautéing has another advantage. It permits us to make a sauce from the meat-flavored juices right in the pan. This often involves the addition of wine. The alcohol evaporates when the wine is cooked, and you are left with the wine flavor, an essential ingredient for most fine sauté sauces. For pan wine sauces, almost any white or red wine will do. Even a good jug or leftover is fine for cooking. The choice of wine should be based on what you have around and what flavor you want to add to your dish. A hearty red will add a deep, robust, earthy flavor; a dry white will add a crisp, slightly tart flavor; a dry sherry will add a light and musty flavor; a Marsala will add a dark, sweet flavor. Avoid the very inexpensive, large jug wines because they often have ill-tasting stabilizers added.

In addition to sautéing, this chapter includes other stovetop cooking methods. We fry steaks and chops with no oil at all, steam an extravagant array of fresh seafood, and simmer fresh vegetables in a little broth, wine, or water.

Most of our stovetop recipes call for 2 frying pans because to cook properly on the stovetop, meats need room. When cooking for 6, you usually need 2 skillets. If the food cooks very rapidly, as do turkey cutlets, or you are cooking lesser amounts for fewer people, you can use 1 pan and cook in batches. We have noted which dishes cook rapidly enough in the recipes.

EQUIPMENT

The equipment you need for stovetop cooking includes a metal spatula; a stainless steel, pointed-tip basting spoon; hot pads; and 1 or 2 good frying pans or skillets. A real sauté pan, called a *sauteuse* in French, is best. Sauté

America has discovered olive oil, and generally the recipes in this book—especially the sauté recipes—call for it. Olive oil goes well with many foods and many cooking styles. It is a viscous and not watery oil, which means it fries, sealing in juices, and doesn't steam. It cooks hotter and faster than other vegetable oils. Also, it is supposed to be good for you.

The reason leftover wine "goes off" is that it reacts with the oxygen that replaces the liquid you've poured out of the bottle. If you want to save leftover wine for drinking later, transfer it to a jar or bottle just large enough for the amount of liquid to fill it and seal tightly. Or, to avoid this bother, use the wine in cooking. Even days old, leftover wine makes a terrific pan sauce.

The stovetop is so versatile that many of the recipes from the other chapters of this book—especially the grills—can be translated into sautés. For example, Game Hens in Rum Plum Sauce or the Flank Steak in Perpetual Marinade translate perfectly to stovetop cooking.

Kosher salt won't do for pan frying. The crystals are too small and will dissolve into the meat much as table salt would, leaving a very salty steak or chop. *Gros sel* is preferable in taste, but if you can't find any, get the rock salt out of your garage. It's useful for more than melting snow.

pans have high, straight—rather than sloped—sides. The best are made of very heavy-gauge metal that allows for even heat distribution in fast cooking. They are available in good kitchenware shops. You should avoid using thin-gauge aluminum pans which react with wine, tomato, and other acidic ingredients to leave a bitter taste in the food. Another option is an old-fashioned American cast-iron skillet. They are inexpensive and, if well seasoned and treated with care, they are excellent for many stovetop dishes—except those with long-cooked wine or tomato sauces—and will last a lifetime or more. ■

PAN-FRIED STEAKS AND CHOPS

Pan frying is one of the quickest, simplest ways to make a delicious dinner. The following method of pan frying steaks or chops over hot rock salt or *gros sel* is not only fat free, it turns the meat out perfectly seasoned. The large salt crystals provide an insulated layer between the meat and the pan so you can cook with high heat to seal in juices without sticking or burning. In addition, salt absorption is minimized because the rock salt doesn't dissolve into the meat as smaller crystals of table salt would.

It is important to use a heavy skillet, one which can be heated quite hot without developing hot spots. Nothing beats the familiar, old-fashioned cast-iron skillets for pan frying with the rock salt method. An 8- to 10-inch-diameter skillet needs ¼ teaspoon rock salt; a standard-size large skillet, 11 to 12 inches in diameter, requires ½ teaspoon rock salt; and a very large, 13- to 14-inch-diameter skillet needs ¾ teaspoon.

The Basic Wine Sauce is very quick and can be made in the same skillets you used to fry the steaks or chops. As an alternative, you can make the Pickled Pan-Grilled Onions also in the same pan.

Pan Frying Meats over Rock Salt

Rock salt or *gros sel* for the bottom of the skillet (see above)
3 or 4 sprigs fresh herbs or ½ teaspoon dried, per 12-inch skillet

Sprinkle the salt evenly over the bottom of the skillet. Place the pan over medium-high heat until it begins to smoke. Add the meat.

Cook until half done. Turn and add the herbs. Finish cooking on the second side.

Steaks

Any steak will do for pan frying. Plan on ½ pound boneless or ¾ pound bone-in steak per person.

Large cuts such as chateaubriand or London broil (more than 1 inch thick) take 20 minutes, turning once, for medium rare.

Thick individual steaks (about 1 inch thick) take 8 minutes, turning once, for medium rare.

Thin steaks (½ inch thick or less) will cook to medium rare in 4 minutes, turning once.

Chops

Any chop will also do for pan frying. Plan on 3 small loin or rib lamb chops, 2 round bone or blade lamb chops, 2 regular pork chops, or 1 very thick pork chop per person.

Thick lamb chops (¾ inch or more) take 10 to 12 minutes, turning once, for medium rare.

Thin lamb chops (½ inch thick) take 8 minutes, turning once, for medium rare.

Thick pork chops (¾ inch or more) take 16 minutes to fry to medium well, that is, cooked through but not dried out.

Thin pork chops (½ inch thick or less) take 8 minutes, turning once, for medium well.

The clue to getting tender, succulent pork chops—of any cut or thickness, no matter how you cook them, grilled, pan-fried, or even in a sauce—is to let the meat rest a few minutes after cooking and before serving.

Normally we recommend
against reducing wine or
vinegar in a cast-iron pan.
However, if your cast-
iron skillet is well
seasoned, the quantity of
wine here is so small and
it remains in the pan so
briefly that it does not
have time to corrode
through the pan's
seasoning.

Basic Wine Sauce for Pan-Fried Steaks and Chops

4 tablespoons butter
4 to 5 large shallots or ½ medium yellow onion
⅔ cup hearty red wine

You can make this sauce in a separate pan or the same one in which you fried the steak or chops. If using the same pan, remove the meat. Use a paper towel to brush out the salt and herbs remaining in the pan.

Melt 2 tablespoons of the butter over medium-high heat. Peel and mince the shallots or onion. Add to the pan and stir for 1 minute. Add the wine and boil until reduced by half, about 2 minutes. Add the remaining 2 tablespoons butter and stir until completely melted.

Immediately spoon the sauce over the steaks or chops.

VARIATIONS

For pork chops, a dry white wine in place of the hearty red also works.

For a more piquant sauce, stir in 1 tablespoon Dijon mustard after cooking the shallots.

For mushroom lovers, add ¼ pound thin-sliced mushrooms along with the shallots. Cook 1 to 2 minutes longer than directed above, until the mushrooms are well wilted.

NOTES AND AFTERTHOUGHTS

Be sure to serve the Basic Wine Sauce in any variation as soon as it is done. If you leave it in the pan for any length of time, it will separate and react with the iron and make the sauce bitter.

Pickled Pan-Grilled Onions

2 large or 3 medium onions (about 1½ pounds)
¼ cup red wine
2 tablespoons balsamic, sherry, or red wine vinegar

Peel the onions and slice them into ¼-inch-thick rounds. After removing the steaks or chops from the pans, use a paper towel to wipe out the rock salt. Add the onions to the pans. Pour in the wine and vinegar. Stir and cook over medium-high heat for about 5 minutes, until the onions are soft but still crunchy in the centers.

Heap on top of the meat and serve.

NOTES AND AFTERTHOUGHTS

You can pan grill and pickle onions even if you are not cooking steaks or chops in the pan first. Melt 2 tablespoons butter in a heavy skillet, then proceed with the recipe.

Pine Nut-Coated Pork Chops with Mushrooms, Onions, and Sherry

1 cup pine nuts (about 5 ounces)
½ teaspoon salt
12 regular or 6 extra-thick pork chops (about 4 pounds)

½ pound mushrooms
1 large onion (about 9 ounces)
4 tablespoons peanut oil
½ cup dry sherry
1 teaspoon chopped fresh thyme leaves or ⅓ teaspoon dried
⅛ teaspoon freshly ground black pepper
1½ teaspoons sherry vinegar

Place the pine nuts and salt in a food processor, blender, or grinder and fine chop. Spread the nuts out on a plate or waxed paper. Press both sides of each pork chop with the nuts to coat. Set aside.

Clean and trim the mushrooms. Cut into ¼-inch-thick slices. Peel the onion, quarter it, and cut each quarter crosswise into ⅛-inch-thick slices. Set the mushrooms and onions aside.

Divide the oil between 2 large heavy skillets and heat until the oil begins to smoke. Add the pork chops to the pans along with any of the chopped nuts remaining on the plate. Fry over medium-high heat, 4 minutes for regular chops or 8 minutes for extra-thick chops. Turn and cook the same amount of time on the other side, reducing the heat to medium for the last 2 or 3 minutes. Remove the chops to a platter.

Add ¼ cup of the sherry to the skillet and stir. Immediately add the mushrooms, onions, thyme, pepper, and vinegar. Stir for 2 to 3 minutes, until the mushrooms and onions are wilted. Add the remaining ¼ cup sherry and stir 1 minute more.

Spoon over the pork chops on the platter and serve.

NOTES AND AFTERTHOUGHTS

1. Pine nuts make this dish particularly rich and delicious, but chopped peanuts or blanched almonds also make delectable and subtly different coatings. If you are using peanuts for the coating and they are already salted, omit the additional salt.

2. With peanuts as the coating, pitted and chopped olives, preferably Kalamata, make a zesty substitute for the mushrooms.

(continued)

Plenty for 6

20 to 40 minutes

We both grew up in the West where pine nuts were a real treat. They had been a basic food of the mountain-dwelling Ute and Shoshone Indians, causing them to wander much, for pine nuts are an unpredictable crop. As kids we got them in a stiff, crinkly cellophane bag, still encased in their very hard shells. It would take a day to crack open a bag full with your teeth. Now you can buy them shelled by the pound in almost any grocery store and speedily grind up a pork chop coating. Of course, in some ways they were better then, savored one by one.

Unfortunately you can't make up a batch of ground nuts for coating ahead and store it. The nut oils released by grinding quickly become rancid and turn sour out of the refrigerator. In the refrigerator the chopped nuts absorb too much moisture to stick to the chops.

3. Another winner with nut-coated pork chops is Polynesian Mango Sauce (page 207). In this case, just fry the pork chops with their nut coating. Omit mushrooms and onions, and make the mango sauce to accompany the chops.

Pork Chops with Orange and Onion Marmalade

Plenty for 6

20 minutes or less

The word "marmalade" comes from the Greek for fruit and honey. Cooking fruit with sugar was a way of preserving the fruit for winter, and with such a special treat as an orange, even the peel was included. People developed a taste for it as a bittersweet condiment and served it often with meats, poultry, and game long before it became associated with English muffins.

2 cups Orange and Onion Marmalade (see below)
Rock salt or *gros sel* to cover the bottom of the frying pan (page 188)
12 regular or 6 extra-thick pork chops (about 4 pounds)
3 tablespoons chopped fresh chives or green onion tops

Make the Orange and Onion Marmalade.

To cook the pork chops, sprinkle the salt evenly over the bottom of 2 large skillets and heat the pans until they begin to smoke. Add as many pork chops as will fit in a single uncrowded layer. Cook over medium to medium-high heat 4 minutes for thin chops, 8 minutes for extra-thick chops. Turn and cook the same amount of time on the other side.

Remove to a platter. Let rest for 10 minutes to allow the juices to settle.

Spread the marmalade over the pork chops. Sprinkle with the chives, and serve.

Orange and Onion Marmalade

Makes 2 cups

1 whole large orange
2 medium onions (about 14 ounces)
Peel of ½ orange
2 tablespoons olive oil
2 teaspoons soy sauce
2 tablespoons white wine vinegar
1 tablespoon brown sugar or honey
1 cup white wine

Cut the orange, peel and all, lengthwise into 8 sections. Cut each section crosswise into ¼-inch-thick pieces. Peel and cut the onions the same way. Fine chop the additional orange peel.

In a large nonreactive saucepan or skillet, heat the olive oil until it smokes. Add the orange, onions, orange peel, soy sauce, vinegar, brown sugar, and ⅓ cup of the wine. Cook 15 minutes over medium heat.

Add ⅓ cup more wine. Cook 15 minutes more.

Add the remaining ⅓ cup wine. Cook 15 minutes more.

NOTES AND AFTERTHOUGHTS

The Orange and Onion Marmalade is delicious cold, too. It will keep in the refrigerator at least 1 week and can be reheated or served cold with other meats or omelets.

PAN KEBABS

For pan kebabs you will need metal or bamboo skewers short enough to fit inside whatever skillet you are using. If you use bamboo skewers, thread the skewers and bend up the ends so they fit in the skillet. The bent ends become handy handles to turn the kebabs.

Chicken, Anchovy, and Asparagus Kebabs

2½ to 3 pounds boneless chicken thighs or drumsticks
12 asparagus spears
24 anchovy fillets, preferably salt-packed
24 small fresh sage leaves
¼ cup sesame seed
4 tablespoons olive or peanut oil
Salt
Freshly ground black pepper
½ cup red wine
2 tablespoons butter

If the boneless chicken thigh or drumstick pieces are folded over, leave them folded. If the pieces are unfolded, double them over. Cut the folded pieces into 1½-inch squares.

Rinse the asparagus spears. Snap off and discard the tough bottom parts. Cut the spears into 3 or 4 pieces about 1½ inches in length.

Halve the anchovy fillets crosswise. Thread each of 6 skewers with alternating rounds of chicken, asparagus, and then anchovy, using 4 pieces of each ingredient. Tuck in 2 sage leaves per skewer.

Spread the sesame seeds on a plate. Roll each skewer in the seeds to coat.

Divide the oil between 2 large skillets and heat until the oil begins to smoke. Add as many skewers to each pan as will fit in a single uncrowded layer. Lightly sprinkle the kebabs with salt and pepper. Cook 16 minutes over medium to medium-high heat, turning one quarter turn every 4 minutes.

Remove the skewers to a platter. Continue with another round until all the kebabs are cooked.

Immediately divide the red wine between the 2 pans. Increase the heat to high and reduce the wine for 2 minutes. Add 1 tablespoon of the butter to each pan. Stir, blending in any sesame seeds that cling to the bottom.

Pour the sauce with the sesame seeds over the kebabs and serve.

(continued)

Plenty for 6

20 minutes or less

Our epiphany for pan kebabs came from Marcella Hazan. The glory of pan kebabs over grilled ones is that you can whip up a quick sauce in the same pan and take advantage of the meat juices released during cooking. Marcella, who says she got her inspiration from the Italian method of pan cooking little birds strung on skewers, alternates chicken with sausage on the skewers, but the variations are legion. In the following two recipes, for instance, you can use chicken in the beef version and beef in the chicken version with equally fine results. You can also be adventuresome in your choice of vegetables. Remember to cut whatever you are using small enough to cook in the same amount of time required for the meat.

NOTES AND AFTERTHOUGHTS

Chicken breast also works well in this recipe. You can use the thick side of the breast in one layer, but the thin end should be doubled over like the thighs and drumsticks, otherwise the meat will dry out. Skewering thinner pieces and reducing the cooking time doesn't work because the asparagus doesn't get done.

Beef, Eggplant, Red Pepper, and Garlic Kebabs

Plenty for 6

20 minutes or less

2½ pounds beef sirloin or top round steak
½ medium eggplant (about ½ pound)
2 medium red bell peppers (about ¾ pound)
4 large garlic cloves
3 large or 4 medium bay leaves
¼ cup sesame seed
4 tablespoons olive or peanut oil
Salt
Freshly ground black pepper
½ cup red wine
2 tablespoons butter

Cut the beef into 1½-inch cubes.

Cut the eggplant lengthwise into ¼-inch-thick slices. Cut the slices into 1½-inch squares.

Remove the seeds and core from the bell peppers. Cut the peppers into 1-inch squares.

Peel the garlic and cut into very thin slivers. Thread 6 skewers with alternating rounds of beef, eggplant, pepper, and garlic, using 4 pieces of each ingredient. Tuck 2 pieces of bay leaf into each skewer.

Spread the sesame seeds on a plate. Roll each skewer in the seeds to coat.

Divide the oil between 2 large frying pans and heat until the oil begins to smoke. Add as many kebabs to each pan as will fit in a single uncrowded layer. Lightly sprinkle the kebabs with salt and pepper. Cook 3 minutes over medium-high heat. Turn and cook 3 minutes more. Remove the skewers to a platter and continue with another round until all the kebabs are cooked.

Immediately divide the red wine between the 2 pans. Increase the heat to high and reduce the wine for 2 minutes. Add 1 tablespoon butter to each pan. Stir, blending in any sesame seeds that cling to the bottom.

Pour the sauce with the sesame seeds over the kebabs and serve.

NOTES AND AFTERTHOUGHTS

The eggplant slices should be at least the same size, or a little longer, than the beef cubes so that they touch the pan. Otherwise, they won't cook through.

Desperation Chicken

Chicken is one of the quintessential quick foods. You can roast it whole in an hour, stew the pieces even faster, or quick fry small pieces fastest of all, depending on just how speedily you want your dinner. One 3½-pound chicken will serve 3 generously. You can stretch this to 4 if your people aren't big meat eaters and you add plenty of vegetables.

Desperation Chicken is one of the fastest ways to handle chicken. It is simply cooked in olive oil with lots and lots of garlic. It takes about 25 minutes, goes with anything you can find in your larder, and serves for desperation family fare (when you get in at 6:26 and the kids are hungry) or a desperation quick company delight (when you have only half an hour to prepare for guests, expected or unexpected).

1½ chickens, or 5 pounds cut-up chicken pieces
6 tablespoons olive oil
Salt
Freshly ground black pepper
4 to 20 garlic cloves

If whole, cut the chickens into leg, thigh, ½ breast, and wing pieces. (You can cook the back, neck, and giblets or reserve them for stock if you wish.) Remove as much skin as you can.

Divide the olive oil between 2 large skillets and heat until the oil begins to smoke. Place the chicken pieces in the pans. Lightly season with salt and pepper.

As soon as you have put the chicken in the skillets, peel as many garlic cloves as you care to use. Cut into slivers or press and add to the pan.

Cook the chicken over medium to medium-high heat 20 to 25 minutes, turning once. The breast and wing pieces take 20 minutes to cook, turning once, and the leg and thigh pieces take about 5 minutes more.

While the chicken and garlic cook, you have time to search out whatever else you have in the way of sauces, garnishes, and veggies. Since almost anything goes with chicken, you can concoct an accompaniment for your meal while the chicken cooks.

VARIATIONS

BREAD THE CHICKEN: Coat the chicken pieces with flour, cornmeal, bread crumbs or fine chopped nuts.

ADD HERBS: Almost any herb will do. Use 1 tablespoon of fresh or 1 teaspoon of dried at any point in the cooking. The exceptions are fresh parsley, cilantro, and fresh basil, which don't dook well and should be added at the end.

ADD SPICES: Paprika, sesame seeds, and caraway seeds are especially good.

(continued)

In our urban lives we think of chickens as ever available. But it wasn't always that way. Left to their own devices, chickens are seasonal.

In the tiny Greek village where Susanna lived for four years, the chicken season would start in the fall, when people would save out one or two hens and a rooster to keep all winter. From those two hens and one rooster, the eggs would start in January, and the first batches were kept aside to raise new chickens. From the next supply, a few of the eggs were carefully doled out, but care was taken to keep most for the spring festivals. They gave real meaning to the idea of the Easter egg. The chickens themselves weren't eaten until they stopped laying in September or so. One by one, they met the stewpot until about November, when two hens and a rooster were once again spared to start the process over.

Now we have chickens all the time, but the reason is, chickens no longer know what season it is.

In a serious time pinch, you don't have to peel the garlic for Desperation Chicken at all. Separate the cloves of a whole head and toss them into the pan to cook along with the chicken. Or cut a whole head of garlic in half through the middle to make 2 half spheres and plunk each half, cut side down, into the skillet. You can easily squeeze out the cooked garlic from the cloves or half spheres at the table. In fact, it doesn't have to be for Desperation Chicken that you deal with garlic in this desperate way. It works for roasts and other vegetable and meat dishes as well, as long as the cooking time is 20 minutes or more. If you're doubly seriously in a time bind, you can pound the unpeeled garlic to mash the cloves, and then they take only 10 minutes to cook.

ADD WINE: Five minutes after turning the chicken pieces and lightly browning the second side, add ½ cup of red or white wine. You can also add wine along with almost any herb or other ingredient but not when you are using liquors.

OTHER THINGS YOU CAN ADD WHEN YOU TURN THE PIECES:
artichoke hearts
bacon or ham
bell peppers, any color
capers
ginger
hearts of palm
leeks
lemon slices
mushrooms
olives
onions
shallots

AT THE VERY END YOU CAN ADD:
cream
sour cream

OTHER LIQUORS INSTEAD OF WINE: at the very end you can add
Bourbon
brandy
Marsala
Scotch
sherry

SAUCES

After the chicken is cooked, you can also add almost any sauce.

Quick Tomato and Bacon *Amatriciana* Sauce, page 121

Barbecue Sauce, any you like, page 118

Basic Red Zucchini Tomato Sauce, page 116

Basic Meat Sauce Bolognese, page 118

Corsican Lasagne Sauce, page 256

Garlic Pine Nut paste, page 247

Greek Sour Cream or Yogurt Sauce, page 70

Holiday Cranberry Cumberland Sauce, page 248

Hot Peanut Sesame Sauce, page 127

Pesto Sauce, green or red, page 43

Red Pepper Sauce, page 258

Spicy Pecan Sauce, page 159

Tomato Tarragon Sauce, page 175

Rum Plum Sauce, page 164

Taco Salsas and Sauces, any of them (pages 82 to 85)

Chicken à la Corsala

One of our favorite variations of Desperation Chicken is something we rummaged from the freezer stock one night in desperation for a last-minute, Italian dinner event. We've repeated it, on purpose, ever since. "Chicken à la Corsala" seemed like a good name because the lush combination of sauces bid forth images of Corsica, that sun-drenched sea-washed island where the people grow basil in pots by the front door, make gutsy sauces from vine-ripened tomatoes, and spawn romantic errant heroes like Napoleon. And the name stuck.

Just as the chicken finishes cooking, stir in 1½ cups Basic Meat Sauce Bolognese (page 118) and ½ cup pesto sauce, or if you don't have pesto, heaps of basil, ground pine nuts, and grated Parmesan cheese. Add the two sauces to the pan and blend well, covering all the chicken pieces. Cook 1 or 2 minutes, until the sauces are heated through. Provide big napkins.

Desperation Game Hens

Anything you can do with chicken, you can also do with game hens. Cut into halves or quarters, game hen pieces take the same time as chicken. It takes 2 game hens to serve 3 generously, or they can be stretched the same way chicken can.

Here's a way to enjoy the fried chicken we all love with far fewer calories and cholesterol than usual. Thanks to the flour and cornmeal batter, this chicken comes out as crispy as if it had skin. (Just see how you'll still nibble at the crust.)

The timing for cooking chicken pieces is not as complicated as it might seem. Basically, breasts, backs, and wings cook in 15 minutes, 10 minutes on the meaty side, 5 on the other. Legs and thighs take 20 minutes, 10 on each side. That's it, whether you deep fry, sauté, grill, or bake the pieces.

The trick to pulling the skin off the leg pieces is to grasp the skin with a paper towel and pull down. The paper towel allows you to get a firm hold of the skin and pull it off the leg without its slipping out of your hand.

Reduced-Calorie Southern Fried Chicken

2 chickens (3½ pounds each), cut-up
3 or 6 cups vegetable oil
1½ cups unbleached all-purpose flour
¾ cup cornmeal
4 teaspoons cayenne pepper
3 teaspoons salt
1 bottle (12 ounces) beer
4 teaspoons dry mustard or 2 tablespoons prepared

Skin the chicken pieces, except for the wings, which are too hard to skin, and cut off any extra fat as you go.

Pour 3 cups oil into a heavy skillet. Set over high heat until a pinch of flour dropped into the oil rises immediately to the top. (To hasten the cooking, use 2 pans and a total of 6 cups of oil.)

While the oil heats, combine the flour, cornmeal, cayenne, and salt together in a paper or plastic bag. Pour the beer into a bowl. If you are using dry mustard, add it to the flour mixture. If you are using prepared mustard, stir it into the beer.

When the oil is properly heated, dip as many pieces of chicken as will fit in the pan in a single uncrowded layer into the beer. Then, drop them into the bag. Close and shake the bag until the pieces are thoroughly coated. Place the pieces, meaty sides down, in the skillet. Reduce the heat to medium-high and cook 10 minutes. Turn and cook 5 to 10 minutes more, depending on the piece. The breasts, backs, and wings will finish cooking first, in 15 minutes. The legs and thighs will take 5 minutes more. As the pieces are done, remove them to drain on paper towels.

When there is room in the pan, increase the heat to bring the oil temperature up. Dip and coat the remaining pieces and add them to the pan. Continue cooking until all the pieces are done.

NOTES AND AFTERTHOUGHTS

1. In spite of the amount of cayenne in the batter, this is not at all a hot or spicy dish. It is flavorful enough, however, to be as good cold as hot. You could serve it for a picnic or a buffet dinner.

2. Usually, 1½ chickens is enough for 6, but with Southern Fried Chicken, people eat more, so this recipe calls for 2 chickens.

Chicken Tarragon

9 half-breasts of chicken
½ cup olive oil
6 garlic cloves
1½ cups white wine
1 tablespoon fresh tarragon or 1 tablespoon dried
1 teaspoon salt
½ teaspoon freshly ground black pepper

Divide each split chicken breast crosswise in half to make 18 pieces.

Divide the oil between 2 large nonreactive skillets. Peel and press the garlic. Divide it between the pans. Set over high heat. Stir the garlic around to distribute it in the pan.

When the oil begins to smoke, place the chicken pieces, skin side down, in the pans. Reduce the heat to medium-high. Cook the chicken 10 to 12 minutes, or until the skin is well browned.

Turn the pieces over. Divide the wine between the pans. Sprinkle the tarragon, salt, and pepper over the chicken. Cook 10 minutes, basting the pieces with the liquid in the pan every 2 to 3 minutes and coating the tops well.

Remove the chicken to a platter. Increase the heat to high and cook 3 or 4 minutes to reduce the sauce. The sauce is ready when it turns clear and bubbles rise from the bottom.

NOTES AND AFTERTHOUGHTS

Tradition calls for using white wine in chicken tarragon, and the flavor is more delicate that way. But on a cold and wintery day, or if you have an open bottle handy, you can use red wine for a heartier version.

Plenty for 6

20 minutes or less

The trick to reducing a sauté-pan sauce without drying out the meat is to keep the top of the meat moist with frequent basting. Use an oval-shaped spoon with a pointed tip (to scoop from around the edges of the frying pan) and drizzle a little liquid over the meat each time you walk by the stove.

Plenty for 6

20 to 40 minutes

Quick-Fry Bourbon Chicken

1½ chickens or 5 pounds cut-up chicken pieces
4 tablespoons peanut oil
1 cup unsalted peanuts
¼ teaspoon cayenne pepper
Salt
Freshly ground black pepper
2 large bunches green onions
½ cup bourbon

If you have purchased whole chickens, cut them into pieces.

Divide the oil between 2 large skillets. Set 1 skillet over medium heat. Add the peanuts, cayenne, and salt and sauté, stirring constantly, 3 minutes, until the peanuts are browned. Remove them and set aside.

Set both skillets over medium-high heat. Divide the chicken pieces, skin side down, between the 2 pans. Sprinkle the chicken with pepper. Cook on one side 10 minutes.

While the chicken cooks, trim the root ends and limp tops off the green onions. Cut the onions diagonally into 1 to 1½-inch pieces.

Turn the chicken and cook 5 minutes on the second side. Remove the breasts and wings to a platter, leaving the legs and thighs. Add the green onions. Cook 5 minutes more.

Return the chicken breasts and thighs to the skillets. Add the peanuts and the bourbon. Stir 2 to 3 minutes, until the alcohol evaporates. Serve at once.

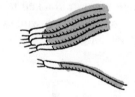

TURKEY CUTLETS

In 1858 in Paris, truffled turkey was the thing to have for special occasions. Here in America, until recently our own native bird remained roasted whole and more or less limited to a holiday centerpiece. All that has changed. Turkey is truly the meat of modern times.

The reason for turkey's new popularity stems from a lucky confluence of two factors. First, we, the consumers, became more health conscious and started to demand turkey for its low calories, low cholesterol, and tasty meat. At the same time, the turkey industry, realizing the treasure trove they had, began to market turkey in new ways, as pieces, parts, ground pounds, and slices. Undoubtedly we influenced the turkey industry to give us the new variety of cuts, and they influenced us to use them.

To make turkey cutlets, purchase either breast slices already cut, tenderloins, or whole breasts to cut into cutlets. Whatever you start with, turkey cutlets should be pounded. The difference between unpounded and pounded turkey cutlets is the difference between divine and sublime. Unpounded, they tend to be dry. When pounded, they melt in your mouth and taste as good as the finest veal cutlet.

Depending on the cut you started with, you will have 12 to 16 cutlets to cook for 6 people, pounded or unpounded. So, it is most efficient to use 2 pans and do several batches. Pounded cutlets take up more room in the pan, so you will have to cook them in more batches than unpounded cutlets. But since they take only 2 minutes, the extra few minutes are worth it.

Basic Sautéed Turkey Cutlets

2 pounds turkey breast, tenderloins, or cutlets
½ cup unbleached all-purpose flour
4 tablespoons peanut oil
Salt

Plenty for 6

20 minutes or less

If you are using turkey breast, remove the skin and the breastbone. Slice the breast into cutlets as you would if you were carving cooked turkey breast. For tenderloins, cut them in half to get two ½-inch-thick cutlets. Or use already cut cutlets.

Place 1 cutlet between 2 sheets of plastic wrap or waxed paper. Pound with a wooden mallet or rolling pin until they are ¹⁄₁₆ inch thick.

Spread the flour over a large plate. Place the turkey cutlets on the flour, and turn to coat both sides; shake off any excess.

Divide the oil between 2 large heavy skillets, and heat until the oil begins to smoke. Add as many turkey cutlets as will fit in the pans in a single uncrowded layer. Sprinkle lightly with salt. Cook over medium-high heat 1

(continued)

minute. Turn and sprinkle salt on the other side. Reduce the heat to medium, and cook 1 minute more.

Remove the cutlets to a platter and set aside. Continue with another round until all the turkey is cooked.

NOTES AND AFTERTHOUGHTS

If you skip the pounding step, cook the cutlets 2½ minutes per side. You can also skip the flouring, if you want to. The cutlets won't be as brown, but they will be just as tasty.

Turkey Cutlets with Ginger Cream

Basic Sautéed Turkey Cutlets (page 201)
3 cups heavy cream
3 tablespoons grated ginger root (about 6 ounces)
2 tablespoons chopped lemon peel
¼ cup very thin sliced fresh mint leaves
¼ teaspoon freshly ground black pepper

Plenty for 6

20 minutes or less

Sauce lovers might want to double the amount of the luscious sauce to have some for noodles, too.

Follow the Basic Sautéed Turkey Cutlet recipe to prepare and cook the cutlets.

When the turkey cutlets are cooked and removed to a platter, and while the pans are still hot, divide the cream, ginger, lemon peel, mint, and pepper between the pans. Stir to mix well. Bring to a boil. Cook 1 or 2 minutes, until thickened.

Remove the pans from the heat and let the sauce rest for 1 or 2 minutes to allow the flavors to blend.

Pour the sauce over the turkey cutlets on the platter. Serve with buttered noodles.

NOTES AND AFTERTHOUGHTS

You can replace the mint in this dish with lemon thyme, if you have some growing in the garden, or lemon grass, if you have some from an Oriental market.

Turkey Cutlets with Juniper and White Wine

Basic Sautéed Turkey Cutlets (page 201)
16 juniper berries
3 medium garlic cloves
¼ teaspoon freshly ground black pepper
¾ cup white wine
¼ cup lemon juice
6 tablespoons butter
3 tablespoons chopped fresh parsley

Follow the Basic Sautéed Turkey Cutlet recipe to prepare and cook the cutlets.

When the turkey cutlets are cooked and removed to a platter, turn off the heat under one of the pans. Make the sauce in the other.

Crush or smash the juniper berries with a mallet or hammer. Peel the garlic. While the pan is still hot, press in the garlic, then add the juniper berries, pepper, and wine. Bring to a boil. Remove from the heat, and stir in the lemon juice, butter, and parsley.

Spoon the sauce over the turkey cutlets on the platter. Serve.

Plenty for 6

20 minutes or less

Juniper berries are not only for gin. Their fresh, pungent taste gives a pleasing aromatic lift to almost any meat. The Italians, wise in the ways of flavor, have long recognized this. They stew shredded pork with juniper berries.

Quail with Pepper, Sage, and Pan-Fried Cheese Corn Bread

Pan-Fried Cheese Corn Bread (page 204)

4 tablespoons olive oil
12 quail
2 teaspoons freshly ground black pepper
3 tablespoons chopped fresh sage leaves or 3 teaspoons dried rubbed sage

Make the Pan-Fried Cheese Corn Bread.

When the cornbread is half cooked, divide the olive oil between 2 large heavy skillets. Set over high heat until the oil begins to smoke. Place 6 quail in each pan and sprinkle on the pepper and sage. Cook 2 minutes, turning frequently.

Reduce the heat to medium high and continue cooking, turning often, 10 minutes more.

Remove to a platter and let rest 5 minutes to allow the juices to settle.

Serve surrounded by squares of cheese corn bread.

(continued)

Plenty for 6

20 to 40 minutes

Quail is delicious grilled or roasted, but by far the most succulent way to cook quail, or for that matter, halved squab, is quick pan-frying over high heat. Seared in hot oil, their juices are sealed in and their delicate meat stays moist and tender.

Pan-Fried Cheese Cornbread

1 cup yellow cornmeal
½ cup unbleached all-purpose flour
2 teaspoons baking powder
1 egg
½ cup milk
¼ cup water
¼ cup grated Parmesan, aged Asiago, or Romano cheese
⅛ teaspoon salt
¼ cup peanut oil
2 tablespoons butter

In a bowl, mix the cornmeal, flour, baking powder, egg, milk, water, cheese, and salt until well blended.

Pour the oil into a 9- to 10-inch skillet or omelet pan. Pour in the corn-meal mixture and spread to cover the bottom evenly. Tightly cover the pan. Cook over high heat 5 minutes. Reduce the heat to low and cook 20 minutes more. Uncover the pan and spread the butter over the top of the corn bread. Using a large metal spatula, turn the cornbread over so the top is now on the bottom. Cover, increase the heat to medium high, and cook 5 minutes more.

Turn out onto a plate. Cut into squares or wedges.

NOTES AND AFTERTHOUGHTS
Cheese corn bread can be baked in the oven. It doesn't turn out as browned, but it is still crunchy. Bake, uncovered, at 350°F for 20 minutes. Butter the top as above, turn, and cook 10 minutes more.

Trout with Pine Nuts and Smoked Salmon

4 tablespoons peanut oil
⅔ cup pine nuts
6 whole trout
4 ounces smoked salmon
⅔ cup white wine

1 lime

Divide the oil between 2 large frying pans. Heat 1 pan until the oil begins to smoke. Add the pine nuts. Stir until browned, just 2 or 3 minutes. Remove the nuts and set aside.

Place both skillets over medium-high heat until the oil begins to smoke. Place 3 trout in each pan and cook 7 minutes.

Meanwhile, cut the salmon into ¼-inch squares or strips.

Turn the trout and cook 3 minutes.

Divide the pine nuts, salmon, and wine between the pans. Cook 4 minutes.

Remove the trout to a platter, scooping the pine nuts and salmon pieces onto the top.

Cut the lime into 6 wedges. Arrange them around the trout and serve.

NOTES AND AFTERTHOUGHTS

1. You can use bone-in or filleted trout, but for flavor and firmness of flesh, trout with the bone is preferable. The cooking time is the same.

2. For a fancier version of this dish, remove the trout from the pans, leaving the pine nuts and salmon pieces behind. Divide 1 cup heavy cream between the pans. Bring to a boil and reduce 1 minute to make a sauce. Pour the sauce with the pine nuts and salmon over the trout. Arrange the lime wedges all around.

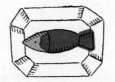

Plenty for 6

20 minutes or less

Using a stronger fish flavor to enhance a milder fish flavor is one of our favorite tricks. Here we do it with rich smoked salmon on milder trout. This is also a good way to use bits and pieces of smoked fish, which you can sometimes buy less expensively. Caviar, smoked tuna, or smoked sturgeon will also do the trick. If you don't have any of these around, prosciutto or lightly smoked ham pieces provide a similar touch.

Sole Sautéed with Lemon, Capers, and Olives

FOR THE SAUCE:

18 black olives, preferably Kalamata
Peel of 2 medium lemons, about 3 tablespoons chopped
4 to 6 tablespoons olive oil
3 tablespoons capers
6 tablespoons lemon juice

2 to 2½ pounds sole fillets

Pit the olives and chop into small pieces about the size of the capers. Rough chop the lemon peel or, for a nicer look, cut into tiny slivers.

Place 2 tablespoons of the oil in a large, nonreactive skillet and heat until the oil begins to smoke. Add as many sole fillets as will fit in a single uncrowded layer. Cook over medium-high heat 30 seconds. Turn the fillets and cook 30 seconds more.

Remove the fillets to a warm platter. Add a little more olive oil and continue with another batch until all the sole is cooked.

While the pan is still hot, stir in the olives, lemon peel, capers and lemon juice. Immediately pour over the sole fillets and serve.

NOTES AND AFTERTHOUGHTS

Thirty seconds per side really is enough to cook boneless sole. Any more, and the delicate fillets will fall apart.

Halibut in Cornmeal Crust with Polynesian Mango Sauce

2 cups Polynesian Mango Sauce (page 207)

1 cup cornmeal
6 halibut steaks (6 to 7 ounces each), or 2½ pounds halibut fillets, about ¾ inch thick
4 tablespoons olive or peanut oil

Make the Polynesian Mango Sauce.

Spread the cornmeal on a plate. Place the halibut in the cornmeal and coat both sides.

Divide the oil between 2 large heavy skillets and heat until the oil begins to smoke. Divide the halibut between the pans. Cook 5 minutes, adjusting the heat between medium and high to maintain very hot pans without burning the fish. Turn the fish over and cook 5 minutes more for ¾-inch-thick steaks or fillets, or 6 minutes more for 1-inch-thick fish.

Serve with the sauce on the side.

Plenty for 6

20 minutes or less

A potato peeler not only peels potatoes and carrots, it also easily and cleanly removes the peel from lemons without taking any of the bitter white part along. Once removed, you can chop, julienne, or leave the peel in wide strips, depending on the recipe and the look you want. Be sure to peel the lemons *before* halving and squeezing them or you won't be able to get a good grip.

Plenty for 6

20 to 40 minutes

NOTES AND AFTERTHOUGHTS

The cornmeal crust on the fish adds a nice crunchy texture to go along with the soft pureed fruit sauce. Red snapper or rock cod fillets work as well as halibut for this recipe.

Polynesian Mango Sauce

1 ripe mango
½ ripe papaya
½ to 1 jalapeño chili pepper, depending on taste
1 teaspoon soy sauce
1½ tablespoons lemon juice
1 tablespoon chopped fresh chives or green onion tops

Makes 2 cups

Cut the mango in half. Remove all of the pulp from the seed and the peel. Remove the seeds from the papaya, and scoop out the pulp. Rough chop the fruit pulp. Place in a bowl.

Mince the jalapeño pepper and add to the bowl. Stir in the soy sauce, lemon juice, and chives. Stir to blend and chill until ready to use.

NOTES AND AFTERTHOUGHTS

It's tempting to use a food processor for this sauce, but it doesn't work. You lose all the flavored chunks that make it so gustable.

Shrimp and Mussels Sautéed with Celery and Tarragon

1½ pounds medium uncooked shrimp
3 pounds mussels
4 to 6 celery ribs (2½ cups when cut)
1 large red bell pepper (about 8 ounces)
5 garlic cloves
4 tablespoons olive oil
3 tablespoons chopped fresh tarragon leaves or 1 tablespoon dried

Plenty for 6

20 to 40 minutes

The subtle, sweet flavor, rich with the sea, certainly does not justify the lowly reputation of mussels as the country cousin of the more elegant oysters and clams. We love to use them in all kinds of dishes, from this quick sauté to soups and pastas.

If the shrimp have a sand vein running down the back, remove it by cutting along the line through the shell meat with a sharp paring knife. Rinse the shrimp. Refrigerate until ready to cook.

Pull off any exposed beards from the mussels. Rinse the mussels in a colander. Refrigerate until ready to cook.

Remove the celery strings with a vegetable peeler. Cut the celery diagonally into ⅛-inch-wide slivers. Quarter the bell peppers and remove the core and seeds. Slice each quarter lengthwise into ⅛-inch-wide slivers. Peel the garlic and cut into slivers.

(continued)

Use 1 large skillet with a cover and cook the shellfish in 2 rounds, or divide the ingredients between 2 large covered skillets.

Heat the oil. Add the celery, bell pepper, and garlic. Stir over medium heat 4 to 5 minutes, until the vegetables are wilted but not cooked through.

Add the mussels and shrimp. Cover and cook 4 mintues.

Add the tarragon. Increase the heat to high. Cover and cook 1 minute more.

NOTES AND AFTERTHOUGHTS

1. Mussels go naturally with Saffron Rice, page 218.
2. We prefer to cook shrimp with the shells on because, like bones, they add flavor to the dish.

Steamed Fish Extravaganza with Zesty Garlic Mayonnaise

Arriving company, poking around the kitchen, wondering what delicacy we were serving them that evening, were invited to open the steamer and have a peek. Much to their dismay, they saw boiling bricks. One was quick enough to ask, "How do you know when they're done?"

For this recipe, a variation of Robert Capon's inspired Steamed Fish Platter, you will need to contrive a steamer with a large roasting pan and two bricks, coffee cups, or other heatproof objects.

2½ cups Zesty Garlic Mayonnaise (page 209)

8 large red potatoes (about 2½ pounds)
12 baby or 6 medium carrots
8 large or 16 small scallops
24 mussels (about 3 pounds)
16 medium clams (about 1¾ pounds)
8 slices prosciutto, not paper thin
6 to 8 sole fillets (about 1⅓ pounds)
16 shucked oysters with their juices

Bring 2 medium pots of water to a boil.

Make the Zesty Garlic Mayonnaise.

Wash the potatoes. Cut the potato flesh into balls using a melon baller or a paring knife. Drop the potato balls into one of the pots of boiling water and parboil 6 minutes. Drain in a colander. Rinse with cold water and set aside to drain.

While the potatoes are cooking, trim the tops off the carrots. If using baby carrots, wash and then quarter lengthwise. If using medium carrots, peel and then cut into ⅛-inch-thick rounds. Drop the carrots into the second pot of boiling water. Cook 4 minutes. Drain in a colander. Rinse with cold water and set aside to drain.

Plenty for 6

40 to 60 minutes

When shellfish are in season and at their best, from late September until April, Steamed Fish Extravaganza is one of our favorite dinners for company. Since the dish includes oysters, clams, mussels, and scallops, it is indeed somewhat of an extravaganza in terms of money but not in terms of time. Most of the work can be done beforehand. You can prep the vegetables and make the sauce anytime the day of the party. Then all you have to do is arrange the morsels on their platters and pop them into their steam bath 10 minutes before sitting down to eat.

If the scallops are large, 1 inch thick or more, cut them in half to make 2 thinner scallops.

Rinse the mussels and clams. Remove any exposed beards from the mussels with your fingers or a paring knife.

Use a tiered steamer or a makeshift steamer made from a roasting pan with cups or bricks used as a pedestal.

Choose 2 heatproof platters small enough to fit into the steamer one at a time. Layer the prosciutto over the bottom of the platters. Top with the sole fillets, then the potato balls, raw clams, and scallops. Scatter the carrots over the top.

To cook the dish, fill the steamer with 1½ inches of water. Bring the water to a rapid boil. Set 1 platter in the steamer and cover tightly. Steam 5 minutes. (If you have a tiered steamer, you can cook both platters at one time.)

Lift the cover carefully. Add the mussels and shucked oysters. Cover and steam 4 minutes more, or until the mussels open. Remove the first platter and set aside in a warm place. Cook the second platter in the same way.

Serve on cooking platters and accompany with Zesty Garlic Mayonnaise.

NOTES AND AFTERTHOUGHTS

1. You can cook this dish right away or refrigerate the prepared platters for up to several hours.

2. Other sauces that go well with this dish are Chive Salsa (page 83) and Corn and Red Bell Pepper Salsa (page 84).

Zesty Garlic Mayonnaise

4 large egg yolks
2 teaspoons Dijon mustard
2 teaspoons lemon juice
¼ teaspoon salt
2 cups olive or peanut oil, or a mixture
4 teaspoons very hot water
10 medium garlic cloves
¼ cup minced fresh chives
6 tablespoons fresh parsley leaves
¼ cup dried red chili flakes

Makes about 2½ cups

With a wire whisk, an electric beater, or in a blender or food processor, beat the egg yolks until thickened. Blend in the mustard, lemon juice, and salt. Slowly add the oil, starting with a few drops and working up to tablespoon amounts. Blend thoroughly as you add the oil. Beat in the hot water. Set aside.

Mince the garlic, chives, parsley, and chili flakes. Stir into the mayonnaise. Chill until ready to serve.

STOVETOP VEGETABLES

Properly done, boiling or steaming produces vegetables that are healthful and tasty, it's true. But thank heavens we've expanded our horizons beyond the long-standing method of cooking the life and sugar out of our vegetables. We've discovered sautéing and simmering. Sautéing and simmering both bring out the natural vegetable flavors. They also allow you to combine vegetables with herbs or other enhancing flavors while cooking.

The amount of vegetables you need for any meal depends on what the main dish is, how many vegetables you are serving, and how much vegetable you like to eat. As a rule of thumb, you can plan on ¼ pound or so per serving when you are having only one vegetable.

Sautéed Vegetables

As with meats, sautéing vegetables means to cook them quickly over a brisk fire in a small amount of oil. The vegetables become lightly glazed, never greasy. The oil glaze brightens the colors, making the vegetables appealingly lustrous.

Sautéing in olive oil, or better still, olive oil and garlic, is one of the tastiest and quickest ways to prepare vegetables. You can successfuly cook almost any vegetable this way. For a 12-inch skillet and vegetables for 6, you will need 2 tablespoons of oil, just enough to coat the bottom of the pan. For smaller amounts in a smaller pan, reduce the oil measure accordingly.

Below is a list of vegetables that come out particularly well when sautéed in olive oil.

Beets

Practically everyone boils beets, and they think beets take a long time. But while beets are good boiled, they are absolutely superb sautéed in oil, and they take only 12 minutes to cook.

Cut the tops off the beets. Peel the beets with a potato peeler or paring knife. Cut small beets in half or quarter larger beets. Cut the halves or quarters into ¼-inch-thick slices. Heat 1 to 2 tablespoons olive oil, depending on the size of the skillet. Add the beets and 2 to 4 pressed garlic cloves. Lightly season with salt and pepper. Stir and cook over medium heat 12 minutes.

For an added treat, wash and then slice the beet greens into very thin, ⅛-inch-thick shreds. Add the greens at the last moment and stir in. Add some chopped fresh dill or a pinch of dried dill and a splash of vinegar. Stir and serve hot or cold.

To brown all the pieces of sautéed vegetables and cook them evenly, it's best to cut them more or less the same size.

Chard

The Italian way with chard will make you an avid eater of this leafy green. Sautéed in olive oil with bacon, garlic, and vinegar, there's nothing better. And the chard makes a substantial side dish for almost any meat or poultry.

For 1 pound red or green chard, cut ¼ pound bacon crosswise into ¼-inch-wide pieces. Heat 1 tablespoon olive oil in a large nonreactive pan. Add the bacon. Cook over medium heat 4 to 5 minutes while preparing the chard.

Cut the chard crosswise, stems and all, into very thin ⅛-inch-wide strips. Wash in plenty of cold water and lift into a colander to drain. When the bacon has cooked 4 or 5 minutes, add the chard and 2 to 4 pressed garlic cloves. Season with salt and pepper. Stir 2 or 3 minutes, until the chard is wilted a bit. Cook 20 to 25 minutes over medium-low heat, until the stem pieces are quite tender. Stir in 1 tablespoon balsamic or red wine vinegar and serve. Makes enough for 4 servings.

Eggplant

Eggplant is a renowned "oil eater," so it takes a bit more oil than other sautéed vegetables. It is also a natural pair with garlic.

Cut the green top off the eggplant. Cut lengthwise into whole oval slices, ¼ or ½ inch thick, depending on whether you want the cooked eggplant crisper or softer. Press or slice 2 to 4 cloves of garlic.

Start with ¼ cup olive oil for one layer of slices in the skillet. Heat the oil in a large skillet. Place the eggplant and garlic in one layer on the bottom of the skillet and salt the pieces lightly. After about 2 minutes, add another tablespoon of oil. Slices ¼ inch thick take 7 minutes, turning once. Slices ½ inch thick take 9 minutes, turning once.

Remove the cooked eggplant, and continue with another layer until all the slices are cooked. When done, they should be browned on the outside, soft and pulpy in the middle. You might add oregano or thyme to accentuate the Mediterranean taste.

Mushrooms

All sorts of exotic mushrooms are appearing on the market these days. They all sauté beautifully and benefit from the garlic and olive oil treatment. Ordinary commercial mushrooms, which pale in comparison to the exotic varieties, can be further perked up with some tarragon and lemon juice.

Clean the mushrooms, trim off the ends, and slice about ¼ inch thick. Heat 2 tablespoons olive oil in a large skillet. Add the mushrooms and stir. Add 4 to 6 pressed garlic cloves, 1 tablespoon chopped fresh tarragon or 1½ teaspoons dried, and a generous sprinkling of salt and pepper. Cook 3 minutes over high heat, stirring all the while. Stir in 2 tablespoons lemon juice, correct seasoning to taste, and serve.

Onions

Slightly crunchy sautéed onions, their sweetness tempered with a splash of vinegar, make a wonderful vegetable accompaniment for most meats and poultry. Peel the onions and cut them into ¼-inch-thick strips, half rounds, or quarter rounds. Heat 1 to 2 tablespoons olive or peanut oil, depending on the size of the skillet. Add the onions, and stir 1 to 2 minutes, until they begin to wilt. Cook 10 minutes over high heat. Add 2 or 3 tablespoons balsamic or sherry vinegar and stir another minute or two, until the vinegar is blended in. For pan frying onions with garlic, see the Fried Onion and Garlic Pizza recipe, page 66, or the Pickled Pan-Grilled Onions for steaks and chops, page 190, for a version with red wine and no oil.

Peas

Quick sautéing—a mere 2 minutes—is not a way we usually think of cooking sweet peas. Yet, this method brings them to the peak of their sweetness and prevents them from getting waterlogged and overcooked, which can so easily happen when you boil them. Sautéing also allows you to combine them with other vegetables or herb tidbits to enhance their flavor. Peas are especially delicious sautéed with onion.

Shell the peas. Chop red onion into about ⅓-inch dice, using about 2 tablespoons for every 1 cup of peas. Heat 1 to 2 tablespoons olive or peanut oil, depending on the size of the skillet. Add the onion and cook 1 minute. Add the peas and pepper them lightly. Don't add any salt. Salt counteracts the sweetness of the peas. Cook 2 minutes more. In the last moment, stir in some chopped fresh mint, and serve.

For variation, you might try peas garnished with crumbled bacon. For an herb variation, try chervil or thyme.

Snow, or Chinese, peas also sauté crisp, sweet, and delicious. Snap off the stem ends, toss them into the pan with garlic and olive oil, and pull them out the instant they turn bright green, about 2 minutes.

Peppers

There's nothing quite as good as sautéed sweet red bell peppers, with or without garlic (but with garlic is best!).

Remove the stems and core from the peppers. Cut the peppers lengthwise into long slices, about ¼ inch thick. Heat 1 to 2 tablespoons olive oil, depending on the size of the skillet. Add the pepper slices, pressed or chopped garlic to taste, and a pinch of salt and pepper. Cook 6 to 7 minutes, stirring occasionally. The oil in the bottom of the pan will turn red and be flavored from the pepper juices. Use it to pour over meat, rice, or noodles, or save it as a flavored cooking oil. Green and yellow bell peppers are delicious sautéed, too.

Potatoes

Really divine mashed potatoes, which you can also do on the stovetop, need lots of butter and cream. French fries take too much oil for guilt-free consumption. Besides, for perfect French fries you need to double fry them, which takes too much time. Hash browns are the solution. You can have a totally satisfying potato feast with little oil or trouble.

Russet potatoes work best for hash browns. Peel the potatoes. Grate in a food processor or through the large holes of a hand grater. Heat 1 to 2 tablespoons oil, depending on the size of the skillet. If the potatoes rendered a lot of moisture when grated, squeeze out the excess liquid. Spread the grated potato over the bottom of the pan as if making a large pancake, no more than ¼ inch thick. Salt lightly. Cook over medium heat 15 minutes. Turn with a metal spatula and cook 10 minutes more. Increase the heat for the last 5 minutes to brown and crisp the second side.

For another version of stovetop fried potatoes, see Taco Toppings, page 86.

For good, crispy hash browns, you need to allow time for the moisture to evaporate during cooking, so don't be tempted to rush the process by raising the heat.

Hash browns invite embellishment. Try minced onion, chopped or pressed garlic, grated cheese, or herbs sprinkled on while they are cooking. Or garnish with anchovies, sun-dried tomatoes, salsa, or sour cream and caviar.

String Beans

Even though most string beans no longer have strings, the name remains. Both green string beans and yellow wax beans are excellent sautéed.

Cut off the stem ends and either leave the beans whole or cut them into 2 or 3 sections. Heat 1 to 2 tablespoons olive oil, depending on the size of the skillet. Add the beans and 2 to 4 cloves pressed garlic. Lightly salt and pepper the beans. Cook 5 minutes, stirring occasionally. In the last moment add a dash of lemon juice to bring up their flavor.

Zucchini and Crookneck Squash

Summer squash, especially zucchini, is another natural with garlic and oil. For zucchini, remove the ends and slice into ¼-inch-thick rounds, or halve crosswise, then slice the halves lengthwise into 8 thick spears. Cut crooknecks into rounds or lengthwise slices.

For each squash, or a combination of all three, heat 1 to 2 tablespoons olive oil, depending on the size of the skillet. Add 2 to 4 pressed garlic cloves and the squash. Cook, stirring occasionally, for 3 to 4 minutes.

Other Vegetables

Asparagus, broccoli, carrots, and green onions are all good sautéed in garlic and olive oil. Cut asparagus into 1½ inch pieces down to the fibrous part. Cut broccoli into florets and diagonal slices of stem. Cut carrots into thin rounds or strips. Cut green onion into 1 inch slices up to where the greens get limp.

Vegetable Medleys

A medley of sautéed vegetables is a good way to create a vegetable dish of varying colors, textures, and flavors as well as a way to use up small amounts that aren't enough for a whole dish. For example, combine asparagus, broccoli, snow peas, zucchini, and green onion. For color you can add red pepper, wax beans, or carrots.

Here is another delightful miscellany with an Oriental dash:

Sesame Sautéed Vegetables

6 asparagus spears
¾ pound broccoli
¼ pound snow peas
4 green onions
4 to 6 garlic cloves
¼ cup olive or peanut oil
2 tablespoons sesame seed
1 tablespoon grated fresh gingerroot (about 1½ ounces)

Snap off the tough ends of asparagus at the breaking point. Cut the spears into 1½-inch-long pieces. Cut the florets off the broccoli stalks. Cut the florets into bite-size pieces, and cut the stems diagonally into ½-inch-wide pieces. Trim the stem ends off the snow peas. Trim off the root ends and limp green tops from the green onions. Cut the onions into 1-inch-long pieces. Peel the garlic.

Heat the olive oil in a large heavy skillet. Over medium-high heat stir in the sesame seed and the ginger. Press the garlic into the oil. Add the asparagus, broccoli, and green onion. Stir 2 minutes over medium-high heat. Add the snow peas and continue stirring 2 minutes more. Serve right away.

Asparagus will break naturally at the point where the spear becomes fibrous and no longer chewable. Bend a spear between your hands and the end will snap right off.

Plenty for 6

20 minutes or less

Vegetables Simmered in Broth, Wine, or Water

If you have any of the vegetable broth, water, or wine left over from simmering in liquid, save it in your refrigerator or freezer. You can use it as a base for the mussel pasta (page 136), in other pasta dishes, in taco fillings, or to sauté more vegetables.

Almost any vegetable that can be boiled can be simmered in broth, wine, or water. Carrots, celery, crookneck squash, and leeks take particularly well to simmering this way.

For a 12-inch skillet, you will need 2 tablespoons butter and 1½ cups liquid.

Carrots

Peel the carrots if they are large, or leave small, baby carrots unpeeled. Cut large carrots into julienne strips about 3 inches long and ¼ inch wide. Leave baby carrots whole. Melt the butter until it foams. Add the carrots and water or chicken stock. Cook over medium to medium-high heat 8 or 10 minutes, until the carrots are limp and cooked through but still slightly crunchy. Sprinkle with fresh chopped herbs such as chervil, tarragon, parsley, chives, or green onion tops.

Celery

Remove the tough outer ribs from the celery stalk, then wash the stalks. Cut the stalks lengthwise in half; cut each half lengthwise into quarters. Melt the butter in a large skillet until the butter foams. Add the celery, water or chicken stock, and a pinch of caraway seed. Cook over medium heat about 16 minutes, until the celery is limp and cooked through but still crunchy.

Crookneck Squash

Cut crookneck squash lengthwise in half taking care to follow the natural curve. Cook as for carrots and celery, using wine or broth for the liquid. Crooknecks take 4 to 6 minutes, depending on their size. Sprinkle with chopped fresh dill or oregano.

Leeks

To prepare leeks, trim off the root ends and upper part of the green tops, leaving about 4 inches of the green leaves. Cut the leeks lengthwise in half, then into long shreds about ¼ inch wide. Wash the leeks in plenty of cold water—2 or 3 rinsings is usually necessary to remove all the dirt from the inside leaves.

Place 2 tablespoons olive oil and 2 cups water, chicken broth, wine, or a combination of the three in a large skillet or sauté pan. Bring the liquid to a boil. Add the leeks and cook 2 or 3 minutes. Lift the leeks out of the liquid, and sprinkle with chopped fresh parsley and a pinch of dried red chili flakes. Serve with lemon or lime wedges.

Simmered Vegetable Medley

For an unusual vegetable medley using no oil or butter at all and having a cilantro touch, make the Vegetables Stewed with White Wine filling for tacos, page 103, as a vegetable side dish. It's particularly delicious with plain meats and unsauced dishes, such as steaks, chops, and Desperation Chicken.

SAUCE SOPPERS TO GO WITH STOVETOP DISHES

Exquisite stovetop sauces, infused with pan essences, cry out for sauce soppers so you can enjoy every last drop. Here are three marvelous sauce absorbers. For a fourth, see the Pan-Fried Cheese Corn Bread, page 204.

Saffron Rice

1½ cups white rice
3 cups chicken stock
¼ teaspoon saffron threads or 2 teaspoons saffron powder

Combine the rice, chicken stock, and saffron in a 1-quart saucepan with a tight-fitting lid. Bring to a boil over medium heat. Cover and reduce the heat to low. Cook 16 minutes. Turn off the heat but leave the rice on the burner 5 minutes more to steam dry.

NOTES AND AFTERTHOUGHTS

1. It is important to use the right size pot for the amount of rice you are cooking. The pot has to be small enough so that the liquid covers the uncooked rice by about ½ inch or else the liquid will evaporate before the rice is cooked. To make more, or less, follow the basic proportion of 1 part uncooked rice to 2 parts liquid, and choose your pot accordingly.

2. Rice needs to steam slowly over low, even heat. If your pot is not heavy or your burner won't turn very low, use a metal stovetop trivet, sometimes called a heat spreader or Flame-Tamer, under the pot.

Armenian Pilaf

4 tablespoons butter
½ cup vermicelli broken into ½-inch-long pieces
1½ cups white rice
3 cups chicken or light beef stock
Freshly ground black pepper

In a 1-quart saucepan with a tight-fitting lid, heat the butter over medium heat until it foams. Add the vermicelli to the pan and stir until browned, about 2 minutes. Add the rice, stir to coat with the butter, and cook 1 to 2 minutes more, until the rice is translucent.

Add the stock. Cover and reduce the heat to low. Cook 20 minutes.

Turn off heat, lift lid, and sprinkle the pilaf with plenty of freshly ground black pepper. Cover pot again and set aside 15 minutes to steam dry.

Fold the pepper into the rice with a fork, fluffing up the grains at the same time. Serve right away, or cover and set aside in a warm place up to 30 minutes.

Plenty for 6

20 minutes or less

Making real rice is just as fast and certainly a lot better than making processed rice. Just pop the raw rice and water in the pan, slap on the lid, and go away for 16 minutes. Once you know the correct pan for the amount you make, you don't even have to measure. Just judge by eye the amount of rice you need and put it in the pan. Cover with water or broth until the liquid is ½ inch over the rice.

Plenty for 6

20 to 40 minutes

Victoria learned this recipe from her non-Armenian mother, who learned it from her husband's Armenian mother. The trick is to let the pot sit for 15 minutes after the pilaf is cooked so that the flavors marry.

NOTES AND AFTERTHOUGHTS

1. You can make Armenian pilaf with water instead of chicken or beef stock. If using water, add a little salt when browning the vermicelli.

2. You can make pilaf in advance and reheat it in a low oven or on the stovetop. If you are reheating by the stovetop method, add a tablespoon or so of water or butter to the pan to prevent burning and heat it slowly.

Herbed Polenta

1 tablespoon butter
3¼ cups lukewarm water
1 cup yellow cornmeal or polenta
1 teaspoon salt
1 teaspoon chopped fresh thyme, rosemary, sage, or marjoram leaves or ¼ teaspoon dried
⅓ cup grated Parmesan, aged Asiago, Romano, Cheddar, or other grated sharp cheese, or crumbled Gorgonzola or Blue (optional)

Plenty for 6

40 to 60 minutes

If there was ever an unappreciated dish in American cuisine—though the ingredient is more American than apple pie—it's cornmeal mush. To some extent that's what polenta is. Rather than mushy, it's more like the creamiest mashed potatoes. It can be blended with almost any herb or cheese and provides a perfect element for sauces.

Preheat the oven to 350°F.

In a 10-by-6-inch rectangular or 8-inch square baking pan, melt the butter in the lukewarm water. Stir in the cornmeal, salt, herbs and cheese. Blend well.

Bake for 1 hour, stirring every 15 minutes.

Remove from the oven. Fluff with a fork and serve.

NOTES AND AFTERTHOUGHTS

1. Yellow cornmeal can be bought under the names yellow cornmeal, polenta, and *masa harina*.

2. Polenta can be made faster on the stovetop, but to do so requires using a double boiler and cooking for 40 minutes, or pouring it slowly into boiling water and stirring for 20 minutes. The oven method is an easy way, but should you choose to make it on the stovetop, the amounts are the same.

DELICIOUS STOVETOP DISHES THAT GO ESPECIALLY WELL WITH SAFFRON RICE, ARMENIAN PILAF, OR HERBED POLENTA:

Pan-Fried Steaks and Chops with Basic Wine Sauce, pages 188–190
Chicken Tarragon, page 199
Turkey Cutlets with Ginger Cream, page 202
Turkey Cutlets with Juniper and White Wine, page 203
Sole Sautéed with Capers and Olives, page 206

EASY
ELEGANCE
FROM
THE OVEN

Perfect Roast Beef
Pan Juice and Red Wine Sauce
Other Sauces to Accompany Perfect Roast Beef

Beef Rib Roast with Onions, Walnuts, and Mushrooms

Dos Equis Oven Beef Stew with Bread Toasts

Braised Beef and Rabbit Greek Style

Perfect Roast Lamb
Pan Juice, Tequila, and Mint Sauce
Other Sauces to Accompany Perfect Roast Lamb

Provençal-Style Roast Leg of Lamb with Baked Tomatoes and Vinegar-Deglazed Onions
Baked Tomatoes
Vinegar-Deglazed Onions

Perfect Roast Pork
Pan Juice, Tarragon, White Wine, and Mustard Sauce
Other Sauces to Accompany Perfect Roast Pork

Roast Pork Loin with Apricot, Lemon Peel, Almond Stuffing, and New Potatoes

Perfect Roast Chicken
Variations
Sauces to Accompany Perfect Roast Chicken

Festive Stuffed Chicken

Oven Chicken with Lemons, Capers, and Shallots

Sherry-Steeped Chicken in Paprika Mayonnaise Sauce

Game Hens Stuffed with Currants, Red Pepper, and Rice

Roast Turkey with Garlic Pine Nut Paste and Holiday Cranberry Cumberland Sauce
Garlic Pine Nut Paste
Holiday Cranberry Cumberland Sauce

Duck with Honey Mustard Sesame Rum Glaze on a Bed of Braised Red Cabbage
Braised Red Cabbage

Basic Baked Fish Steaks or Fillets with Sesame Spinach Garnish
Variations
Sesame Spinach Garnish
Sauces to Accompany Basic Baked Fish

Oven-Steamed Trout Chinese Style

Corsican Lasagne with Corsican Lasagne Sauce

Lasagne with Chard, Turnips, Pine Nuts, Ricotta, and Fontina
Corsican Lasagne Sauce

Two Meatloaves
Beef and Pork Meatloaf with Red Pepper Sauce
Red Pepper Sauce
Spicy Ground Beef Meatloaf with Hard-Boiled Eggs, Jalapeño, Sherry, and Cilantro

Poor Man's Stuffed Eggplant

Quick Upside Down or Right-Side-Up One-Crust Pot Pies
Chicken, Mushroom, and Cream Pot Pie Filling
Beef, Potato, and Saffron Pot Pie Filling
Filling Variations
Quick Pastry Dough

Oven Vegetables
Oven Fries

The heat source beckons us to the kitchen. Anticipation builds with each developing aroma. Then the meal, always a special one even if it's an ordinary day. Whole roasts of meat, birds browned to perfection, succulent meatloaves, pot pies, plump potatoes, steamy onions, bubbling oven stews.

The oven is an important focus of our cooking. We use it frequently. Not perhaps as much as we did in the past, but still often. We carry the sense that an oven meal is somehow more filling, warmer, more special. From oven cooking comes our idea of what is "good" and what is "plenty," the simple, satisfying, filling, and abundant foods we think of as the heart of our home cooking.

To this day, we precede an oven meal with a special "watch," not just for the food to finish cooking, but for the last family member or guest to arrive. And though our lives are crisscrossed in many directions now, and we often eat at separate times or on the run, we feel we should be together. And when we are, we like to roast something in the oven.

Oven cooking has benefits we often forget. With a dish in the oven, you can walk away, free to do other things. You don't have to stand over a hot flame, attending every moment. You can take a shower, have a glass of wine. You can put everything you want to eat in the oven together. Oven cooking is faster than you might think. You can use a higher temperature and less cooking time than people used to. Doing so prevents roasts from overcooking and drying out, and even a turkey or baked fish can be on the table by the time you've finished relaxing.

In the oven, as with stovetop dishes, you can add wine, stock, spices, or beer and let their flavors meld into a savory richness. In the heat-surrounded cooking of an oven the elements become still more steeped in the mixture of flavors than they do in a stovetop pot. Foods turn out more evenly done, with less chance of burning should a ringing phone or crashing vase distract you for a moment.

That newest of ovens, the microwave, can speed up the cooking time for some baked dishes, but very few. Microwave ovens "cook" by steaming the food from within. This causes more fluid loss than in conventional cooking methods. In addition, the rapid cooking time does not allow many flavors in food, like natural sugars, to develop. This leaves the food blander yet. Microwaves cook unevenly, so parts of the food may get quite done while other parts remain uncooked. You can stop the oven, turn the food, wrap, stir, and rewrap a dish to make it cook evenly, but with all that fuss, what's the gain? And microwave cooking often saves no time. It seems that those dishes that actually do well in a microwave take almost as long to cook as in a regular oven. For these reasons, we do not recommend microwave ovens as a substitute for standard ovens. Those dishes that do turn out well in a microwave oven we have marked with the symbol ≈.

One or two of the recipes in this chapter can also be cooked on the stovetop or in a pressure cooker. We have noted them, marking those for the pressure cooker with the symbol ≡.

HINTS AND TRICKS FOR OVEN COOKING

1. Allow 15 to 20 minutes for the oven to heat before putting the food in. Putting food in an oven that is not yet the correct temperature throws off the timing.

2. Roasts and other large pieces of poultry or meat should be at room temperature when placed in the oven. If the meat or bird is introduced into the oven cold from the refrigerator, it must first come up to oven temperature before it starts cooking, and this throws the timing off.

3. When roasting large cuts of meat and whole birds, start with a high oven temperature for 10 to 15 minutes to seal in the juices and begin the cooking process rapidly so the meat doesn't steam.

4. In general we recommend roasting large cuts of meat and whole birds at a higher temperature than that called for in many other recipes. A higher temperature browns the poultry or meat better and cooks it faster. Instructions for cooking at moderate temperatures come from when food was customarily cooked more well done. Even to roast foods well done, we prefer a higher temperature and shorter cooking time. Food cooked in the oven a long time at a low temperature steams more than it roasts.

5. When oven cooking a roast or whole bird, it is important that you allow time for the juices to settle after it is done. This makes the meat tender and more moist. Composed dishes like the oven stews and lasagne also need a few moments' rest for the flavors to reach their peak.

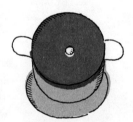

EQUIPMENT

To stew or roast oven dishes, you need a large, nonreactive roasting pan or dish. Occasionally an oven dish requires a lid. If your baking pan does not have one, you can devise a cover with aluminum foil.

A roasting rack is more than useful for roasting turkey, whole ducks, or chickens over 5 pounds, it's essential. A rack lifts the bird out of the fat that is rendered during cooking and allows the skin to brown all around.

If you like to cook oven stews or casseroles, an unglazed pottery dish is wonderful. Unglazed pottery allows an exchange between moist air generated in the pot and dry air from the oven. This works magically in long-cooking dishes to produce succulent meats and vegetables and rich sauce.

Römertopf is a widely available brand of unglazed pottery and works marvels with any oven dish that cooks with liquid. The Alsatian Kitchen also makes unglazed pottery oven dishes that are even dishwasher safe and don't have to be soaked (to mail order: The Alsatian Kitchen, 1590 Jackson Street, San Francisco, California 94109, 415-775-7960).

And don't forget your instant-reading meat thermometer. ∎

Perfect Roast Beef

3 pounds beef roast, sirloin tip, top round, or cross rib
1 whole head garlic
Salt
Freshly ground black pepper

18 Little Toasts (page 38)

Plenty for 6

1 to 2 hours

Heat the oven to 475°F.

Place the beef roast in a baking pan. Liberally season the top and sides of the meat with salt and pepper. Cut the head of garlic crosswise in half. Place the halves face down on top of the roast.

Roast in the oven 15 minutes.

Reduce the oven temperature to 350°F. Continue roasting until the meat is the desired doneness:

Rare: 35 to 40 minutes more, or until a meat thermometer registers 120 to 125°F in the center, 50 to 55 minutes total cooking time, about 17 minutes per pound

Medium: 50 to 55 minutes more, or until a meat thermometer registers 130 to 135°F in the center, 65 to 70 minutes total cooking time, about 22 minutes per pound

Well done: 60 to 65 minutes more, or until an instant meat thermometer registers 155 to 160°F in the center, 75 to 80 minutes total cooking time, about 26 minutes per pound

Remove from the oven. Let rest for 20 minutes to allow the juices to settle before carving.

To serve, carve the roast across the grain into ⅛-inch-thick slices. Accompany with the baked garlic halves and Little Toasts. Squeeze the garlic cloves out of their skins onto the toasts or potatoes.

Pan Juice and Red Wine Sauce

Pan juices from the beef roast
½ cup red wine

Add the red wine to the juices in the baking pan the last 20 minutes of cooking. Be sure to use a nonreactive pan if you are making this sauce.

OTHER SAUCES TO ACCOMPANY PERFECT ROAST BEEF

Ancho Chili Sauce, page 85

Chive Salsa, page 83

Corn and Red Bell Pepper Salsa, page 84

Garlic Horseradish Sauce, page 149

Garlic Pine Nut Paste, page 247

Orange and Onion Marmalade, page 192

Red Pepper Pesto, page 43

Red Pepper Sauce, page 258

Spicy Pecan Sauce, page 159

Tomato Tarragon Sauce, page 175

Makes about ¾ cup

Although many beef roasts—often with marvelously inventive names—appear in grocers' and butchers' cases, we think only a few cuts make a "perfect" roast beef. They are cross rib, top sirloin, and top round. Rump roasts and bottom round are too tough for roasting and should be saved for braised dishes and stews. Seven-bone chuck roast straddles the line. It makes a modest oven roast, but is better grilled or used for Dos Equis Oven Beef Stew (p. 229).

Besides the cut, the grade of the beef and how it is aged makes a significant difference in the flavor of a beef roast or steak. The best quality is Prime beef, followed by Choice and then Good. Grocery store beef is generally "no roll" beef—that is, inspected but not graded. If graded, "no roll" would be Good beef, one grade below Choice. Most butchers still carry only Prime and Choice quality beef.

As for aging, hanging beef in carcasses remains the best way to age it but causes shrinkage and therefore less product to sell. As a result, most grocery store meat is cut off the carcass immediately at the processing plant and "aged" in vacuum packages where it can't shrink as it travels to the retail market. It is then cut further and repackaged in the ways you see it. Better butchers still hang the beef carcasses in their cold rooms for a certain length of time before cutting.

In Denver—once a rich gold-rush city and a terminus for many of the old cattle drive trails—prime beef is revered. Susanna grew up in that city, and her family's big once-a-month treat was an outing to the Ship's Tavern room of the elegant Brown Palace Hotel, where they served only prime rib and fresh-caught Rocky Mountain rainbow trout. The beef roasts are still as big as a barrel. You can get a cut from either end or the middle—well done for Dad, medium for Mom, rare for the kids. Restaurants like the Ship's Tavern buy up most of the Prime beef these days, but a Choice-grade standing rib is no mean substitute.

This roast beef with wine-steeped walnuts, mushrooms, and onions is as rich and elegant as the Brown Palace Hotel. It makes a luxurious company dinner and an easy one, since roasting a joint of meat is far simpler than composing a dish. For a less extravagant occasion, sirloin tip, top round, or cross rib beef roast can be substituted for the rib roast.

Beef Rib Roast with Onions, Walnuts, and Mushrooms

2 garlic cloves
1 4-pound rib roast (2 ribs' worth)
Salt
Freshly ground black pepper
26 to 30 pearl onions (about 10 ounces)
1 teaspoon oil
1 cup walnut halves (about 4 ounces)
24 medium or 12 large mushrooms (about 1 pound)
1 cup red wine
½ teaspoon fresh thyme leaves or ⅛ teaspoon dried

Heat the oven to 475° F.

Cut the garlic into slivers. With your fingers, push the garlic slivers into all the natural crevices of the roast.

Liberally season the meat with salt and pepper. Set the roast ribs down in a roasting pan. Place in the oven and roast 10 minutes.

Reduce the heat to 350°F and continue cooking 40 minutes more.

While the roast cooks, bring a medium pot of water to boil. Drop in the pearl onions and blanch 2 minutes. Drain and rinse to cool. Peel the onions.

Heat the oil in a small skillet. Add the walnut halves and toast over medium heat 3 to 4 minutes, until browned.

Clean the mushrooms and trim the stem ends.

When the roast has cooked 40 minutes at 350°F, scatter the onions, mushrooms, and walnuts around the roast. Roast 20 minutes more.

Add the red wine and roast 15 minutes, or until a meat thermometer registers 112°F in the center and 120°F at the ends of the roast for rare meat (see Note 1 for medium and well-done meat timings).

Remove the roast to a platter. Let rest to allow the juices to settle.

Place the roasting pan with the onions, mushrooms, and walnuts on the stovetop. Add ¼ teaspoon salt and the thyme. Cook over medium heat for 10 to 12 minutes, until almost all the liquid evaporates.

Arrange the onions, mushrooms, and walnuts around the roast.

To carve the roast, cut the meat free from the ribs, then slice about ⅛ inch thick.

NOTES AND AFTERTHOUGHTS

1. For medium-cooked roast beef, add 15 minutes to cooking time, until a meat thermometer registers 135°F. For well done, add 30 minutes to cooking time, until a meat thermometer registers 160°F.

2. Be sure to count on 20 minutes resting time for the roast after it is out of the oven. With an elegant and expensive cut of beef like a rib roast, it would be a pity to serve it at less than its succulent best. Don't worry if it's not piping hot when you serve it. Steaming hot is for stews and soups. In roasts, it is best to opt for full flavor and tender juiciness in each slice.

Dos Equis Oven Beef Stew with Bread Toasts

6 medium onions (about 2½ pounds)
8 tablespoons (1 stick) butter
5 pounds bone-in chuck roast, or about 3½ pounds cubed chuck
2 bottles Dos Equis beer
3 garlic cloves
2 tablespoons balsamic or red wine vinegar
1 bay leaf
¼ teaspoon dried thyme
1¼ teaspoons salt
½ teaspoon freshly ground black pepper
6 slices French or Italian bread
4 tablespoons butter

Heat the oven to 400°F.

Peel the onions and cut them in half. Slice the halves into ¼-inch-thick half rounds.

Melt 4 tablespoons of the butter in a large roasting pan or casserole. Add the onions and cook over medium-low heat 20 minutes, until thoroughly wilted.

While the onions cook, remove the meat from the bones of the chuck roast. Cut the meat into 2-inch cubes, trimming off any large chunks of fat. Reserve the bones.

Melt 4 tablespoons of the butter in a large heavy skillet. Add half the meat and half the bones to the skillet. Brown the meat and bones on all sides over medium-high heat for 8 minutes, turning once. Remove the meat and add it to the onions in the roasting pan. Brown the remaining meat and bones in the same way.

When the second round of meat is browned, add the beer to the skillet. Stir to loosen and scrape up any bits of meat that are stuck to the pan. Transfer the mixture to the roasting pan.

Peel the garlic and press it into the roasting pan. Add the vinegar, bay leaf, thyme, salt, and pepper.

Cover the roasting pan and place in the oven. Cook for 1½ hours.

Just before serving, melt the final 4 tablespoons butter in a small saucepan. Brush melted butter over both sides of each slice of bread. Place the bread slices on a baking sheet. Put in the oven and toast 3 minutes. Turn and toast 3 minutes more.

When the stew is cooked, spoon the meat and sauce onto a large deep serving platter. Surround with the bread toasts and serve.

NOTES AND AFTERTHOUGHTS

1. We brown the meat in two separate pans to save time in getting the stew put together. If time is not of the essence and you wish to save on pot washing, you can brown the meat in one pan.

Plenty for 6

1 to 2 hours

We call for that Mexican thirst quencher regular Dos Equis beer in this divine stew because the sauce requires a malt roasted to an amber brew, which gives the beer more character and a distinctly sweet taste. Should you find the shelves empty of Dos Equis, you can use some other amber beer, but *not* a light lager or very dark beer.

2. Dos Equis Oven Beef Stew becomes even better if you let it rest for a few minutes before serving. The sauce melds and clarifies once it is no longer bubbling.

3. This dish can be cooked on the stovetop as well as in the oven. The timing is the same. We find oven roasting makes the sauce richer and the dish less trouble since you don't have to stir it.

≡ Pressure cooking is another way to make this dish. The timing is about one-third the oven or stove time. You will need only 1½ bottles of beer.

Braised Beef and Rabbit Greek Style

1 pound small red or white pearl or boiling onions
1 pound shallots
6 garlic cloves
1¾ pounds bone-in beef chuck roast, or about 1¼ pounds cubed chuck
1 rabbit (about 2¼ pounds)
¾ cup olive oil
2 tablespoons tomato paste
1 cup red wine
½ cup balsamic or red wine vinegar
2 bay leaves
1 3- to 3½-inch piece of a thin cinnamon stick
1/16 teaspoon ground cumin
3 whole cloves
½ teaspoon salt
¼ teaspoon freshly ground black pepper

Heat the oven to 400°F.

Bring a small pot of water to a boil. Drop in the onions and parboil 2 minutes. Remove to a colander and rinse to cool.

Peel the onions, shallots, and garlic. Cut the garlic in half.

With a sharp kinfe, remove the meat from the bones of the chuck roast. Cut the meat into 1-inch cubes, trimming off any large chunks of fat. Reserve the bones.

If the rabbit is whole or in quarters, cut it into pieces following the instructions on page 28, using a chef's knife.

Heat the oil in a nonreactive roasting pan or pot. Add the beef, rabbit, and beef bones. Brown the meat over medium-high heat 5 minutes, turning once. Add the onions, shallots, garlic, tomato paste, wine, vinegar, bay leaves, cinnamon stick, cumin, cloves, salt, and pepper. Stir together.

Cover the pan. Place in the oven and cook 1½ hours.

To serve, remove the bay leaves, cinnamon stick, and bones. Transfer the stew to a serving dish or platter. Accompany with Herbed Polenta (page 219) or warm French or Italian bread.

Plenty for 6

1 to 2 hours

By the time of vulgar Latin this dish, or something similar, was familiar all around the Mediterranean. The area lay so near the spice routes, cinnamon and cloves were already favored aromatics. Bay or laurel—Daphne in Greek name and myth—was a native tree. The name as it developed in all its versions around the Mediterranean, *estufado, stufata,* and so on, stems from the Greek *typhos,* meaning steam, from which we also get the name of the fever typhus. Beef and veal are typical for this heady, saucy concoction, but more common is wild hare. Best of all, we think, is our version combining the bovine with the coney.

If you decide to serve this stew as they do in the Mediterranean, with good bread, you should heat the bread. To warm French or Italian bread, sprinkle a few drops of water on the top of the loaf and place in a 375 to 475°F oven for 4 to 6 minutes, until the crust is crisp. This is not only the way to heat fresh bread, it is the way to refresh day-old bread.

NOTES AND AFTERTHOUGHTS

1. This dish improves if you have a chance to cure the rabbit (page 28).

2. Rabbit cannot be reheated with success. It becomes bitter and gamy. Should you have leftovers, eat them cold, with a salad or bread.

3. Parboiling the onions for a few minutes loosens the skins so that they peel easily.

≡ Braised Beef and Rabbit Greek Style, like Dos Equis Oven Beef Stew, can also be done on the stovetop or in a pressure cooker. The timing is the same for the stovetop version and about 30 minutes under pressure.

Perfect Roast Lamb

4 medium garlic cloves
3½ pounds boneless lamb shoulder roast
3 small sprigs fresh rosemary or ½ teaspoon dried
Salt
Freshly ground black pepper

Heat the oven to 475°F.

Peel the garlic and cut into slivers. With your fingers, push the garlic slivers into all the natural openings in the lamb roast. If using fresh rosemary sprigs, push them into the opening in the center of the roast. If using dried rosemary, sprinkle it on top of the roast. Liberally season the outside of the roast with salt and pepper.

Place the roast in a baking pan. Roast for 10 minutes.

Reduce the oven heat to 350°F. Roast until the meat has reached the desired doneness:

Medium-rare: 1 hour and 20 minutes more, or until a meat thermometer registers 145 to 150°F in the center, 1 hour and 30 minutes total cooking time, about 26 minutes per pound

Well done: 1 hour and 40 minutes more, or until a meat thermometer registers 170 or 175°F in the center, 1 hour and 50 minutes total cooking time, about 30 minutes per pound

When the roast is cooked, remove it from the oven. Let rest for 20 minutes to allow the juices to settle.

To serve, carve the roast across the grain into ⅛-inch-thick slices. Serve with Pan Juice, Tequila, and Mint Sauce (see below) or one of the other suggested sauces.

(continued)

Plenty for 6

1 to 2 hours

Where has all the mutton gone? Turned to lamb, every one. It used to be you could get lamb in the spring, hence the appellation, spring lamb. You could tell practically the day the lamb turned to mutton—it had given up milk, was eating entirely grass, and was approaching one year old —by the smell and taste it had cooking. Now farmers breed sheep year-round, and 90 days after each breeding, we get lamb again. Technically, in America a spring lamb is 90 to 120 days old. Then it becomes just lamb, and finally mutton at 1 year. The roasting parts of lamb, all excellent, are the shoulder, leg, and rack (called the saddle when it is double).

NOTES AND AFTERTHOUGHTS
We think lamb is best medium-rare, done on the outside but with plenty of pink in the center.

Pan Juice, Tequila, and Mint Sauce

Makes about ¾ cup

We love the customary combination of lamb with mint, but shudder at the traditional glob of mint jelly on the plate. Having cold lamb with margaritas one day gave us the inspiration for a new mint sauce made with tequila and lime juice. Instead of a jellied sugar, we substitute the lamb's own savory juices.

Tequila is a distilled liquor made from the *agave* cactus. There are two kinds, aged and unaged. In the aged category, there are three variations, regular gold, aged one year; *anejo*, aged 6 to 8 years; and *Centenario*, saved for every sixth year to celebrate the inauguration of a new Mexican president. For mixed drinks or "paregoric use," the unaged will do. But for straight drinking Mexican style, with just a little fresh lime and a lick of salt or a glass of spicy Sangrita to soften the kick, use the aged kind. The smoother, aged tequila is best for our elegant Pan Juice, Tequila, and Mint Sauce.

Pan juices from the roast lamb
¼ cup tequila
2 tablespoons lime juice
½ cup whole fresh mint leaves or 1 tablespoon dried
3 tablespoons butter
1 tablespoon chopped fresh chives or green onion tops
1 tablespoon very thinly shredded fresh mint leaves (optional)

When the lamb roast is done, pour the roasting juices into a cup. Set aside for a few minutes, until the fat rises to the top.

While the juices settle, combine the tequila, lime juice, and mint in a small nonreactive saucepan. Bring to a boil. Cook 1 minute to burn off the alcohol. Add the butter to the saucepan and turn off the heat.

Spoon off as much of the fat from the top of the pan juices in the cup as you easily can. Pour the juices from the bottom of the cup and any more that have collected under the resting lamb roast into the saucepan.

Strain the sauce and discard the mint leaves. Stir in the chives and shredded mint, if you are using it.

OTHER SAUCES TO ACCOMPANY PERFECT ROAST LAMB

Provençal-Style Roast Leg of Lamb with Baked Tomatoes and Vinegar-Deglazed Onions

Plenty for 6

1 to 2 hours

If it seems like we have garlic on every roast, you're right. We've tried to do without for different reasons—for variety, for those who don't care for it, to eliminate the chore of peeling it. But the garlic always returns. A roast of beef, lamb, or pork without its garlic is just not worth its salt.

6 medium garlic cloves
1 leg of lamb (6 to 7 pounds)
1 tablespoon olive oil
2 teaspoons fresh thyme leaves or ½ teaspoon dried, or ½ teaspoon dried
    herbes de Provence
Salt
Freshly ground black pepper

Baked Tomatoes (page 235)
Vinegar-Deglazed Onions (page 235)

Heat the oven to 475°F.

Peel the garlic and cut into slivers. With your fingers, push the garlic slivers into all the natural openings in the leg of lamb. Rub the olive oil and then the thyme over the outside of the lamb. Season liberally with salt and pepper on all sides.

Place the lamb in a roasting pan. Put in the oven and roast 15 minutes.

Reduce the oven temperature to 350°F. Roast 1 hour, or until a meat thermometer registers 145°F in the center of the leg, for medium-rare. (See Note 2 below for well-done timing.)

While the lamb roasts, prepare the Baked Tomatoes and Vinegar-Deglazed Onions.

When the lamb is done, remove from the oven. Let rest 20 minutes to allow the juices to settle.

To serve, place the lamb on a large platter. Surround with the tomatoes and onions.

To carve the lamb, cut perpendicular to the large leg bone, making slices as thick as you like.

NOTES AND AFTERTHOUGHTS

1. A 6- to 7-pound leg of lamb will feed six big meat eaters generously. For daintier appetites, you can stretch it to feed eight. If you are cooking a smaller leg of lamb to serve fewer people—a "short cut" or half a leg—you can calculate the cooking time following the guideline of 10 minutes per pound for medium-rare and 13 minutes per pound for well done.

2. For well-done meat, cook the leg of lamb 1 hour and 15 minutes after reducing the oven to 350°F, or until a meat thermometer registers 160°F.

3. Provençal-style is also a good way to cook and garnish a rack of lamb. Calculate 12 minutes per pound total cooking time for medium-rare, and 15 minutes per pound for well done.

Baked Tomatoes

2 garlic cloves
¾ cup coarse Bread Crumbs (page 136)
2 tablespoons chopped fresh basil leaves or 1 teaspoon dried, or 2 bay leaves,
    minced
¼ teaspoon salt
⅛ teaspoon freshly ground black pepper
¾ cup olive oil
6 medium tomatoes (about 1½ pounds)

Makes 12 halves

Heat the oven to 350°F.

Peel the garlic and press into a small bowl. Add the bread crumbs, herbs, salt, pepper, and oil. Mix together.

Cut the tomatoes crosswise in half. Arrange the tomato halves, cut sides up, in a baking dish. Spread about 1 tablespoon of the bread crumb mixture over the top of each half.

Bake 12 to 15 minutes, until the tomatoes give slightly when the edges are squeezed together between thumb and forefinger.

Remove and serve hot or cold.

Vinegar-Deglazed Onions

3 medium onions (about 6 ounces each)
3 tablespoons butter
Salt
Freshly ground black pepper
3 tablespoons balsamic vinegar

Makes 6 halves

Heat the oven to 350°F.

Cut the unpeeled onions crosswise in half. Cut a small slice off each end so the halves will sit flat in a baking pan. With a sharp knife, make 3 or 4 ½-inch-deep slashes in the top of each onion half.

Set the onion halves, cut sides up, in a baking dish. Put ½ tablespoon butter on top of each half. Season lightly with salt and pepper.

Bake 45 minutes, until the onions give slightly when the edges are squeezed together between your thumb and forefinger.

Sprinkle the balsamic vinegar over the onions. Bake 5 minutes more.

Remove the onions from the oven. Serve hot or cold.

Plenty for 6

1 to 2 hours

From spits to pits to ovens, dank jungle to urban canyon, roasted pork is a worldwide favorite. After all, the pig was probably the second domesticated animal, following the faithful dog.

To roast pork in home-size ovens, the best cuts are the loin—including the center rib—the tenderloin, and the shoulder roast, sometimes called Boston butt. Blade roasts come from the fattest part of the pork loin and, despite the lean look their ends sometimes display, you pay for far more fat than meat. Arm roasts are gristly, with sections held together by connective tissue rather than a solid piece of meat. The leg, called the ham, is usually cured, although for special occasions you can order one fresh to grill or roast.

Pork is graded differently from beef, into categories called U.S. 1, 2, 3, and 4. The grading is based on the same principles—the conformation of the animal, the quality of the meat (tenderness, juiciness, and flavor), and the cutability (the amount of usable meat).

Perfect Roast Pork

3 medium garlic cloves
3 pounds boneless pork shoulder, called butt or Boston butt
Salt
Freshly ground black pepper

Heat the oven to 450°F.

Peel the garlic and cut into slivers. With your fingers, push the garlic slivers into all the natural openings in the roast and over the top. Sprinkle generously with salt and pepper.

Put the roast in a baking pan. Place in the oven and roast 15 minutes.

Reduce the oven temperature to 350°F. Continue cooking until the roast is the desired doneness.

Medium well: 1 hour and 25 to 30 minutes more, or until a meat thermometer registers 162°F in the center, 1 hour and 40 to 45 minutes total cooking time, 35 minutes per pound

Well done: 1 hour and 40 to 50 minutes more, or until a meat thermometer registers 170 to 175°F in the center, 1 hour and 55 to 65 minutes total cooking time, about 45 minutes per pound

When the roast is done, remove it from the oven. Let rest 20 minutes to allow the juices to settle before carving.

To serve, carve the roast across the grain into ¼-inch-thick slices.

NOTES AND AFTERTHOUGHTS

1. For larger or smaller boneless pork roasts, follow the same procedure of starting the cooking at 450°F for 15 minutes, then reducing the heat to 350°F for the remainder of the cooking time. Calculate 35 minutes per pound altogether for medium well, or 40 minutes per pound for well done.

2. For bone-in pork roasts, such as Boston butt, center rib, or loin cuts, cook the roast 5 minutes per pound less than for boneless roasts. That makes about 30 minutes per pound for medium-well, or 35 minutes per pound for well-done pork.

3. Medium-well in reference to pork roast means that the meat is cooked to just done, barely past the pink stage, with the juices running yellow-pink. Medium-well pork is still juicy, not dried out, and perfectly safe to eat.

4. For a more elaborate pork roast, and a sweeter one, glaze the top and sides of the meat with the Honey Mustard Sesame Rum Glaze (page 248) 30 minutes before the roast is done.

Pan Juice, Tarragon, White Wine, and Mustard Sauce

Pan juices from the pork roast
2 tablespoons Dijon mustard
½ cup white wine
1 tablespoon chopped fresh tarragon or 1 teaspoon dried

Makes about ¾ cup

When the roast is done, pour the juices from the bottom of the baking pan into a cup. Set aside 10 minutes, until the fat rises to the top.

Spoon off the fat and pour the cooking juices into a small nonreactive saucepan. Stir in the mustard and wine. Bring to a boil. Cook over high heat 10 minutes.

Remove from the heat and stir in the tarragon.

OTHER SAUCES TO ACCOMPANY PERFECT ROAST PORK

Ancho Chili Sauce, page 85
Chick Pea Paste, page 45
Chive Salsa, page 83
Corn and Red Bell Pepper Salsa, page 84
Corsican Lasagne Sauce, page 255
Garlic Horseradish Sauce, page 149
Garlic Pine Nut Paste, page 247
Kiwi Chutney, page 151
Lemon, Caper, and Olive Sauce, page 206
Melon and Jalapeño Salsa, page 84
Mock Hoisin Sauce, page 106
Orange and Onion Marmalade, page 192
Papaya or Kiwi Chutney, page 151
Polynesian Mango Sauce, page 207
Red Pepper Pesto, page 43
Red Pepper Sauce, page 258
Rum Plum Sauce, page 164
Spicy Pecan Sauce, page 159
Tomatillo Sauce, page 85
Tomato Salsa, page 82
Tomato Tarragon Sauce, page 175

Roast Pork Loin with Apricot, Lemon Peel, Almond Stuffing, and New Potatoes

Plenty for 6

1 to 2 hours

3 garlic cloves
9 dried apricots
1 tablespoon olive oil
⅓ cup sliced almonds
1½ teaspoons chopped lemon peel
3-pound pork loin roast
Salt
Freshly ground black pepper

24 small new potatoes
2 tablespoons chopped fresh parsley leaves, preferably Italian

Heat the oven to 475°F.

Peel the garlic and cut into thin slivers. Cut the apricots into ¹⁄₁₆-inch dice.

Heat the oil in a medium skillet. Add the almonds and toast, stirring over medium-high heat 2 minutes, until browned. Stir in the garlic, apricots, and lemon peel. Remove from the heat.

If the pork roast is tied, cut the strings. Open the roast; it should come apart into 2 pieces. Spread the apricot mixture in the center. Put the roast back together and tie with kitchen string.

Liberally season the top of the roast with salt and pepper. Place it, fat side up, in a roasting pan large enough to hold the roast and the potatoes.

Place in the oven, and roast 10 minutes.

Reduce the heat to 350°F. Roast 1 hour to 1 hour and 10 minutes, or until a meat thermometer registers 158°F.

Wash the potatoes.

When the roast has cooked 50 minutes, add the potatoes to the roasting pan. Roast 20 minutes.

Turn the potatoes and continue cooking until the roast is done.

When the roast is cooked, remove to a platter, leaving the potatoes in the pan. Turn the potatoes. Increase the oven to 475°F. Finish cooking the potatoes 15 minutes while the roast rests.

Arrange the potatoes around the roast. Sprinkle the parsley over the potatoes. Cut the roast into ⅛-inch-thick slices and serve.

NOTES AND AFTERTHOUGHTS

Most pork loin roasts come already boned, in 2 pieces, one on top of the other, and tied together. If you would like a bone-in pork roast, cut an opening in the roast between the meat and the bones, and stuff the opening.

Perfect Roast Chicken

1 lemon
1 medium onion (about 7 ounces)
2 chickens (about 3½ pounds each)
Salt
Freshly ground black pepper

Heat the oven to 475°F.

Cut the lemon in half and cut each half into 6 wedges. Peel the onion and cut it in half. Cut each half into 8 wedges.

Stuff the cavity of each chicken with half the lemon and onion wedges. Liberally season the chickens with salt and pepper.

Place the chickens, breast side up, in a baking dish or pan. Roast 50 minutes, until the leg easily separates from the thigh, or until a meat thermometer registers 190°F in the thigh.

Remove from the oven. Serve hot or cold.

NOTES AND AFTERTHOUGHTS

The stuffing in the chicken is to keep the bird moist while it roasts. The lemon and onion pieces will be only partially cooked and are not intended for eating. You can also add garlic and herbs to the lemon and onion stuffing for a more complex flavor.

VARIATIONS

TO SPRINKLE ON TOP OF THE CHICKEN: You can vary Perfect Roast Chicken in countless ways by seasoning the skin during or after cooking.

Herbs—sprinkle chopped fresh or dried herbs over the top of the chicken before roasting. Try thyme, tarragon, rosemary, oregano, sage, basil, or marjoram.

Garlic—press peeled or unpeeled garlic cloves over the top of the chicken before roasting.

Lemon or Lime—squeeze lemon or lime juice over the top of the chicken after roasting, just before serving.

Wine—pour ½ cup red or white wine over the chicken 20 minutes before it is done. Baste with the wine-flavored rendered juices 2 or 3 times while it finishes cooking. We don't consider this a sauce because the rendered chicken juices are so fat laden. However, you can make a sauce by pouring off all the juices into a bowl when the chicken is done. Let rest about 10 minutes for the fat to rise to the top. Spoon off the fat.

TO INSERT UNDER THE SKIN: You can richly season the meat of the chicken, not just the skin, by inserting seasonings under the skin. With your fingers,

(continued)

Plenty for 8

40 to 60 minutes

If you've ever thought "a chicken is a chicken, why pay more for poultry store or better brands?", there's a reason. Most modern poultry plants that supply major grocery chains rid chickens of feathers by first scalding the chickens in hot water. This works, but also removes the flavorful outer layer of their skin. Then the chickens are plunged into ice water to chill them quickly. They remain soaking until, waterlogged, they are crated and shipped, often hours later. The skin of such chickens, those common to supermarkets, is whitish and smooth to the touch. Such chickens are further identifiable by rosy colored water in the bottom of their packages.

On the other hand, better chickens are plucked by loosening their feathers in warm, not hot, water. The outer skin remains intact and the plucked birds are chilled in air, not water, so flavor is not soaked out. Kosher chickens have their feathers loosened in completely cold water and are salted for 3 hours before any chilling. Chickens for Chinese markets are also often processed without hot scalding and ice water baths. All the better chickens have skin that is dry, bumpy, slightly oily, and yellow. Their meat has not been waterlogged, and their flavor is far superior.

carefully separate the skin from the breast all the way to the top of the thigh and push in any or all of the following:

Herbs—chop fresh or dry savory herbs and spread them evenly under the skin.

Garlic—peeled and in slivers

Onion—spread minced onion, alone, with herbs, or with garlic and herbs.

TO PUT IN THE PAN WITH THE CHICKEN AS IT ROASTS: While it roasts, surround the chicken with ½-inch-thick rounds of potato, sweet potato, or yams; 1-inch pieces of carrot or celery; 1-inch onion wedges; zucchini or other summer squashes, cut in half the long way; 1-inch slices of acorn squash or pumpkin; quartered parboiled or marinated artichokes.

You can also add about ½ cup red or white wine to the vegetable-surrounded chicken for the last 20 minutes of cooking to flavor the vegetables. If you use red wine and are roasting the chicken with potato rounds, be prepared for the wine to turn the potatoes pink.

OTHER STUFFINGS: Replace the simple lemon and onion moisturizing stuffing with a more elaborate, edible one. Try:

Orange, Kumquat, or Apple—Peel ½ orange per chicken and separate the sections. Or halve 8 kumquats per chicken. Or cut ½ apple per chicken into thin wedges. Mix the orange, kumquat, or apple pieces, or a combination of them, with ½ thinly sliced onion.

Garlic—Boil 30 to 35 garlic cloves per chicken for 15 minutes. Peel them. Pack the cavity of the chicken with the garlic instead of the lemon and onion. By all means, eat the stuffing.

Rice, Currant, and Red Pepper Stuffing for Game Hens (page 245)—This stuffing for game hens is also fabulous for chickens. Make the entire amount, and don't forget to stuff the neck cavity as well as the belly cavity.

SAUCES TO ACCOMPANY PERFECT ROAST CHICKEN

Almost every sauce and salsa in this book, from Spicy Pecan Sauce to Vietnamese-Style Dipping Sauce, can serve as an accompaniment to Perfect Roast Chicken. Try:

Ancho Chili Sauce, page 85
Chive Salsa, page 83
Corn and Red Bell Pepper Salsa, page 84
Corsican Lasagne Sauce, page 255
Curry Yogurt Sauce, page 162
Dill Cream Sauce, page 174
Garlic Horseradish Sauce, page 149
Garlic Pine Nut Paste, page 247
Lemon, Caper, and Olive Sauce, page 206
Melon and Jalapeño Salsa, page 84
Mock Hoisin Sauce, page 106
Orange and Onion Marmalade, page 192
Papaya or Kiwi Chutney, page 151
Polynesian Mango Sauce, page 207
Red Pepper Pesto, page 43
Red Pepper Sauce, page 258
Rum Plum Sauce, page 164
Spicy Pecan Sauce, page 159
Tomatillo Sauce, page 85
Tomato Salsa, page 82
Tomato Tarragon Sauce, page 175
Vietnamese-Style Dipping Sauce, page 107
Zesty Garlic Mayonnaise, page 209

Festive Stuffed Chicken

This stuffing turns an ordinary bird into a festive dish and stretches 1 chicken to serve 4, or 2 chickens for 8. More than its economy, this dish gives us a gracious and subtle flexibility that frees us from complaint. The only-beef-for-me diners—usually the younger members—get their beloved hamburger and the poultry lovers get chicken.

Plenty for 6

1 to 2 hours

FOR THE STUFFING:

1 medium onion (about 7 ounces)
½ pound mushrooms
¾ cup chopped walnuts (about 3 ounces)
2 chicken livers (optional)
½ pound ground beef, preferably chuck
1 tablespoon olive oil
1¼ cups Bread Crumbs (page 136) or fine diced toasted bread
¼ cup chopped fresh parsley leaves, preferably Italian
⅛ teaspoon ground allspice
1 teaspoon salt
¼ teaspoon freshly ground black pepper
¼ cup red wine
2 chickens (about 3½ pounds each)
1 tablespoon olive oil for coating the chickens
Salt
Freshly ground black pepper

Heat the oven to 475°F.

Peel and medium chop the onion. Clean and trim the mushrooms and medium chop them. Medium chop the walnuts.

If using the chicken livers, cut into ¼-inch dice.

Heat the 1 tablespoon oil in a heavy skillet. Add the ground beef, onions, mushrooms, walnuts, and chicken livers. Stir over medium-high heat, breaking up the meat, for 3 minutes, or until the meat is slightly browned. Stir in the bread crumbs, parsley, allspice, salt, pepper, and wine.

Remove from the heat and set aside to cool a few minutes.

Spoon half the stuffing into the neck and belly cavities of each chicken. Fold the flaps over the cavity openings. Rub ½ tablespoon olive oil over each chicken. Season liberally with salt and pepper.

Place the chickens in a baking pan. Roast 55 minutes, or until a meat thermometer registers 190°F in the thigh.

NOTES AND AFTERTHOUGHTS

1. When stuffing chickens, turkeys, game hens, or for that matter, vegetables, the filling should be packed in firmly, but not tightly. It should fill the cavity completely, leaving a little room at the opening for the stuffing to expand while cooking. No trussing is necessary, just close the natural fat flaps at the cavity opening and set in the roasting pan.

2. Remember, whenever stuffing poultry of any sort, do not stuff the bird ahead of time, and always eat the stuffing within a day or two. Once inside the bird, the stuffing is as prone to developing salmonella when it sits around as the bird itself.

Oven Chicken with Lemon, Capers, and Shallots

2 chickens, cut up
3 lemons
15 medium shallots (about ½ pound)
½ teaspoon fresh rosemary leaves or ⅛ teaspoon dried
¼ teaspoon salt
¼ teaspoon freshly ground black pepper
3 tablespoons capers
¼ cup olive oil
1 cup white wine (optional)

3 or 4 fresh rosemary sprigs, for garnish (optional)

Heat the oven to 350°F.

Remove as much skin from the chicken pieces as you can. Arrange the chicken in a single layer in a large, nonreactive baking dish.

Cut the lemons into ¹⁄₁₆-inch-thick rounds. Peel the shallots and cut them into ¹⁄₁₆-inch-thick rounds. Sprinkle the chicken pieces with the rosemary leaves, salt, and pepper. Arrange the lemons, shallots, and capers around and about the chicken. Pour the oil and optional wine over all.

Roast for 25 minutes. Remove the breast pieces and roast the remaining pieces 5 minutes more.

Arrange the chicken on a platter, and decorate with rosemary sprigs. Accompany with a sauceboat of the cooking liquid. Serve accompanied by Saffron Rice (page 218), Armenian Pilaf (page 218), or Herbed Polenta (page 219).

NOTES AND AFTERTHOUGHTS

We usually save the back and wing tip pieces from a whole cut-up chicken for stock. If you like to eat these pieces, include them in the dish. They are virtually impossible to skin, however, so don't bother trying.

Plenty for 6

20 to 40 minutes

Capers are the buds of the flowering caper vine, which in the Mediterranean wanders freely over the rock and limestone terraces dividing the countryside. If you've ever had wild capers, as we have, thanks to Susanna's sojourns in Greece, you know why they are a pantry staple in Mediterranean cooking. Rinsed and squeezed dry, wild capers lend a beautiful floral aroma and piquant flavor to salads or sauces for veal, chicken, fish, and pasta. Wild capers don't have the somewhat medicinal taste most of the tiny, cultivated varieties have. Fortunately you can buy wild capers under the Peloponnese label. They are almost as good as the ones Susanna gathers and brines herself, brings back sealed in basket-covered wine jugs, and lovingly doles out to dear friends.

Sherry-Steeped Chicken in Paprika Mayonnaise Sauce

Plenty for 6

20 to 40 minutes

2 chickens, cut up
2 medium onions (about ¾ pound)
3 tablespoons olive oil
2 cups oloroso (semidry) sherry
2 teaspoons paprika
2 cups Basic Mayonnaise (page 275)
¼ teaspoon salt
2 tablespoons chopped fresh chives

Heat the oven to 400°F.

Remove as much skin from the chicken pieces as you can. Peel the onion and rough chop.

In a large nonreactive pot that can be used on the stovetop and in the oven, heat the oil. Add the chicken pieces and brown them on both sides over medium-high heat for about 5 minutes.

Stir in the onions, sherry, and paprika and turn the pieces to coat, leaving the pieces meaty side down.

Transfer the pot to the oven, and roast for 20 minutes.

While the chicken is baking, make the Basic Mayonnaise. Place in a large bowl.

When the chicken is done, remove the pieces to a platter.

Slowly, ½ cup at a time, whisk the cooking liquid into the mayonnaise.

Pour the sauce over the chicken. Sprinkle with the chopped chives and serve.

NOTES AND AFTERTHOUGHTS

1. If the thought of making mayonnaise sends you to the store to buy take-out food instead of cooking this dish, use a good bottled or delicatessen mayonnaise. Don't miss this dish.

2. The extraordinary and abundant sauce on this dish is perfect for noodles. You might make some fresh ones from the Basic Pasta Dough recipe (page 115).

≡ You can make Sherry-Steeped Chicken on the stovetop or in a pressure cooker. In a pressure cooker cook the chicken pieces, sherry, onions, and paprika under pressure for about 8 minutes. Release the pressure and whisk the broth into the mayonnaise as above.

Game Hens Stuffed with Currants, Red Pepper, and Rice

FOR THE STUFFING:

3 cups rice
1 medium onion (about 7 ounces)
½ large red bell pepper (about 4 ounces)
Livers and gizzards from the game hens (optional)
4 tablespoons butter (½ stick)
½ cup dried currants
Peel of 1½ lemons
6 tablespoons chopped fresh sage leaves
6 tablespoons chopped fresh parsley leaves, preferably Italian
½ teaspoon salt

6 game hens

To make the stuffing, cook the rice according to the instructions on page 218.

While the rice cooks, peel the onion. Remove the core and seeds from the bell pepper. Fine chop the onion and red pepper in a food processor or with a chef's knife.

If using, cut the livers and gizzards from the game hens into ¼-inch dice.

Melt the butter in a frying pan. Add the onion, bell pepper, liver, gizzard, and currants. Cook, stirring, 1 minute.

When the rice is cooked, add the onion mixture to it. Mince the lemon peel and add to the rice, along with the sage, parsley, and salt. Stir to mix well.

Heat the oven to 350°F.

Fill the neck and belly cavities of the game hens with the stuffing, using about 1 heaping cup per bird.

Place the stuffed birds in a baking pan. Bake 40 minutes at 350°F. Increase the temperature to 475°F and bake 10 minutes more.

NOTES AND AFTERTHOUGHTS

Leftover stuffed game hen is delicious as a cold snack, or remove the meat from the bones and shred it. Add the shredded meat to the remaining rice stuffing and dress the mixture with a Basic Vinaigrette Dressing or one of its variations (page 272), Hot Peanut Sesame Sauce (page 127), or Tomato Onion Rémoulade (page 290) for a great salad.

Plenty for 6

1 to 2 hours

While it's really currants in the black and red currant jams and the currant liqueurs, the dried currants we most use in cooking are actually a variety of tiny grape. They were introduced to Greece and Italy by way of France in the sixteenth century. Unlike raisins, dried currants retain some of the tartness of fresh grapes, which makes them a superior cooking ingredient.

Roast Turkey with Garlic Pine Nut Paste and Holiday Cranberry Cumberland Sauce

1¾ cups Garlic Pine Nut Paste (page 247)
1 12- to 14-pound turkey

3 cups Holiday Cranberry Cumberland Sauce (page 248, optional)

Plenty for 6 with leftovers

2 to 2½ hours

A whole turkey is a cornucopia of family meals, starting with the night you roast it and on through the week. Roasting a turkey is not the trauma it used to be. Small ones are commonly available fresh, making it feasible to have turkey on a regular basis. You can cook a small turkey in 2 hours and you don't have to baste it. Save the stuffing for the holidays—for daily fare, don't bother. Just go for the abundance of tender lean meat. When the turkey is coated in Garlic Pine Nut Paste, the stuffing may be superfluous anyway, and the gravy certainly is.

Turkeys don't require as much cooking as you may have been led to believe. They easily dry out, get stringy and tough. Ten minutes per pound is really adequate for an unstuffed bird, and 15 for a stuffed one.

Make the Garlic Pine Nut Paste.

Heat the oven to 450°F.

Pull the giblets and neck out of the turkey cavity. Cut off the skin flap from the neck end and pull out any excess fat from the belly cavity. Wash the turkey. Pat dry with paper towels.

Place the turkey, breast side down, in a roasting pan. Rub the back of the turkey with ¼ cup of the Garlic Pine Nut Paste. Place in the oven and cook 30 minutes.

Reduce the heat to 375°F. Roast 45 minutes more for a 12-pound turkey, or 1 hour for a 14-pounder.

After the turkey has been in the oven 1 hour and 15 to 30 minutes, turn it over, breast side up. Spread ½ cup of the Garlic Pine Nut Paste over the breast and tops of the legs. Increase the oven heat to 475°F. Roast 45 minutes more, or until a meat thermometer registers 185 to 190°F in the thigh. This will amount to 2 hours total cooking time for a 12-pound turkey, or 2 hours and 15 minutes for a 14-pounder.

While the turkey roasts, make the Holiday Cranberry Cumberland Sauce if using.

Remove the turkey from the oven. Let rest 20 minutes to allow the juices to settle.

To carve the turkey, cut off the leg, thigh, and wing from one side, severing them at the joints. Slice the breast meat. Carve the other side as need demands.

To serve, arrange the turkey on a platter and accompany with a bowl of the remaining Garlic Pine Nut Paste and another of Holiday Cranberry Cumberland Sauce.

NOTES AND AFTERTHOUGHTS

1. The timing in the recipe is for an unstuffed, 12- to 14-pound turkey. For a larger bird, calculate 10 minutes per pound for the entire cooking time and turn the bird breast side up 45 minutes before it is done. For a stuffed bird, calculate 15 minutes per pound. With a large bird like turkey, it is particularly important to count on the 20 minutes resting time before serving so the meat is tender and juicy all the way through and easy to carve.

2. We cook the turkey breast side down part of the time so that we don't have to baste it or cover it. Basting is a bother, and covering the turkey breast to keep it from drying out prevents the skin from crisping. Breast side down, it bastes itself with juices and fat dripping from above. Also, cooking it breast side down for part of the time allows the skin and its Garlic Pine Nut Paste coating to brown all the way around.

Garlic Pine Nut Paste

1 medium russet potato (about 8 ounces)
15 medium garlic cloves
1 cup olive oil
⅓ cup pine nuts
1½ tablespoons red wine vinegar
½ teaspoon salt
Pinch cayenne pepper

Peel the potato and cut into about 8 pieces. Place the potato in a small saucepan and add water to cover. Bring to a boil. Cook about 10 minutes, until cooked all the way through. Drain.

While the potato cooks, peel the garlic cloves.

Combine the potato, garlic, oil, pine nuts, vinegar, salt, and cayenne in a blender or food processor. Puree until smooth.

NOTES AND AFTERTHOUGHTS

To make Garlic Pine Nut Paste without a blender or food processor, first puree the pine nuts with a mortar and pestle. Remove the pine nut paste to a bowl. Mash the potato with a fork and add to the pine nuts. Press the garlic. Add the garlic, oil, vinegar, salt, and cayenne and blend well.

(continued)

Makes 2 cups

You can hasten the process of peeling garlic in several ways. If the cloves are to be pressed or chopped anyway, simply smash them with a pestle, mallet, hammer, or knife handle to break open and loosen the skins. You can also bend the two ends of large cloves toward one another, and the skin will pop open. For garlic that is going to be cooked, you can parboil the cloves for 5 minutes to soften and loosen the skins. But easiest of all, you can skip the peeling altogether for many sautéed or roasted dishes. Press or chop the cloves with the skins still on. The skins sauté, broil, or roast up into crisp tidbits.

Holiday Cranberry Cumberland Sauce

Makes 3 cups

The Holiday Cranberry Cumberland Sauce need not be limited to the fall and winter holidays, when cranberries are in season. You can buy several extra packages of cranberries at Thanksgiving time and freeze them whole in their packages. Then you can have Holiday Cranberry Cumberland Sauce on any meat or poultry on any special day of the year—Easter, the Fourth of July, Bastille Day, the vernal equinox.

12 ounces cranberries (about 2½ cups)
2 whole cloves
1 1-inch piece fresh ginger root
1½ cups port wine
2 tablespoons sugar
Grated peel of 2 oranges
Grated peel of 1 lemon
⅔ cup orange juice
1 tablespoon lemon juice
1 teaspoon dry mustard
Pinch cayenne pepper
¼ cup red currant jelly
½ cup dried currants
½ cup slivered almonds

Wash the cranberries. Stick the cloves into the ginger.

In a medium-size nonreactive saucepan, combine the cranberries, ginger, and cloves. Add the port and cover. Bring to a boil. Cook over medium heat 5 minutes, or until the cranberry skins pop.

Add all of the remaining ingredients. Simmer, uncovered, until the liquid thickens, about 10 minutes more. Discard the ginger and cloves. Transfer the sauce to a bowl and chill before serving.

NOTES AND AFTERTHOUGHTS

1. You can substitute half oloroso sherry and half Marsala in place of the port. Also, you can substitute some other fruit jam or jelly, singly or in combination, for the more usual red currant.

2. If the sauce hasn't thickened after 5 minutes, simmer it a little longer, just until it is no longer liquid.

3. This sauce is less sweet than the traditional American cranberry sauce. If you prefer a sweeter version, add sugar to taste.

Duck with Honey Mustard Sesame Rum Glaze on a Bed of Braised Red Cabbage

Plenty for 6

1 to 2 hours

FOR THE GLAZE:

2 tablespoons sesame seed
½ cup Dijon mustard, preferably country-style with seeds
¼ cup aromatic honey
½ cup rum
¼ cup lemon juice

2 ducks (about 4½ pounds each)
Braised Red Cabbage (page 250)

Heat the oven to 450°F.

To make the glaze, place the sesame seed in a small saucepan and stir over medium heat 4 to 5 minutes, until the seeds are browned. Stir in the mustard, honey, rum, and lemon juice. Bring to a boil. Stir and remove from the heat.

Remove the excess fat from the cavity and neck ends of the ducks. With a sharp knife, cut through the fold of skin and fat between the leg and thigh just up to, but not through, the meat. With a fork, poke through the skin to the meat at 1-inch intervals all over the front, back, and sides of each duck to allow fat to escape during cooking. Put the ducks, breast sides down, on a rack in a baking pan. With a pastry brush or spoon, spread half the glaze over the back of each duck.

Place the ducks in the oven. Roast for 45 minutes, pricking each duck every 15 minutes.

Turn the ducks breast side up. Spread remaining glaze over breasts and tops of the legs. Roast 20 minutes more, pricking once after 10 minutes.

Increase the heat to 500°F. Prick the ducks again. Roast 15 minutes more, or until a meat thermometer registers 175 to 180°F in the thigh.

While the duck cooks, prepare the Braised Red Cabbage.

When the duck and cabbage are done, spread the cabbage on a large serving platter. Place the ducks on top and serve, accompanied by Little Toasts (page 38) or Herbed Polenta (page 219).

To carve the ducks, first cut the legs off at the thigh joint. Cut the thighs off the back. Cut off the wings. Finally, carve the breast meat.

NOTES AND AFTERTHOUGHTS

1. In this recipe we make an exception to our usual rule of curing duck before cooking it. The duck doesn't need the cure to tenderize it because of the cooking method.

2. For another semisweet glaze, try Rum Plum Sauce (page 164). Or, if you like a non-sweet glaze for duck, coat it with Garlic Pine Nut Paste (page 247) or Spicy Pecan Sauce (page 159).

3. You can substitute brandy for the rum in this glaze.

Most modern cookery books say to roast duck at a moderate temperature, around 350°F. We think this is misconceived. Duck should be roasted hot and fast and the skin poked often during the cooking, all to aid in the rendering and escape of the duck fat. By poking, we mean all over in 12 to 15 places every 15 minutes during the cooking. This high heat, oft-pierced method of cooking also leaves the duck skin crispy in parts, soft and chewy in parts, and not at all tough. Once you have duck this way, it will become one of your "five easy pieces," those dishes you do repeatedly.

Braised Red Cabbage

3 pounds red cabbage (about 2 medium heads)
2 medium garlic cloves
6 tablespoons duck fat or butter
2 tablespoons red wine vinegar
½ teaspoon salt
¼ teaspoon freshly ground black pepper

Cut the cabbage heads in half, remove the cores, and cut into ⅛-inch-wide shreds. Peel the garlic.

Heat the duck fat or butter in a large nonreactive pot. Add the cabbage and stir over medium heat until the cabbage wilts, about 5 minutes.

Press the garlic and add it, along with the vinegar, salt, and pepper. Stir to mix.

Reduce the heat to medium-low and cook 25 minutes on the stovetop or 15 minutes in the 475°F oven along with the duck.

Basic Baked Fish Steaks or Fillets with Sesame Spinach Garnish

Oven baking fish with butter and white wine keeps the fish succulent and firm. Here we garnish simply baked fish steaks or fillets with sesame and lemony, wilted spinach to provide a taste counterpoint and eliminate the need for a sauce. Instead of the spinach garnish, you could serve a Basic Green Salad (page 272) with a lemon mustard vinaigrette with the fish, or prepare a vegetable to accompany it. To vary baked fish still more, add a sauce.

2 cups Sesame Spinach Garnish (page 251, optional)
1 small onion (about 4 ounces)
6 fish steaks or fillets, cut ½ to 1 inch thick (⅓ to ½ pound each)
2 tablespoons butter
Salt
Freshly ground black pepper
½ cup white wine

1 lemon

Heat the oven to 400°F.

Make the Sesame Spinach Garnish first, if using.

Peel the onion and cut in half. Cut the halves into ⅛-inch-thick slices.

Place the fish in a nonreactive baking pan. Arrange the onion over the fish. Dot the butter over the onions on top of each fillet or steak. Season with salt and pepper. Pour the wine over all.

Place the fish in the oven. Bake about 9 minutes for ½-inch-thick fish, 12 minutes for ¾-inch-thick fish, and 14 minutes for 1-inch-thick fish, or until a soft, white curd forms on the top of the pieces, the fish is slightly resistant to the touch, and a meat thermometer registers 115°F.

When the fish is done, arrange it on a serving platter, leaving room in the center for the Sesame Spinach Garnish. Cut the lemon into 6 wedges. Arrange around the spinach and serve.

NOTES AND AFTERTHOUGHTS

1. Although we usually do this recipe with one of the meatier fishes such as salmon, sea bass, tuna, swordfish, or shark, it will also work with leaner, thin fish fillets such as sole. The cooking time will vary according to the thickness of the fish, taking as little as 6 minutes for sole fillets.

2. Marinating fish that is destined for the oven causes the flesh to become soggy. You don't really need a marinade because the fish turns out plenty tasty from the butter, white wine, and onion flavorings.

≈ Basic Baked Fish Steaks or Fillets is one of those dishes that turns out well with microwave cooking. Check microwave instructions for timing.

VARIATIONS

GARLIC: That divine bulb that adds its savor so well to so many things also gives baked fish an added zest. Use slivered garlic instead of, or in addition to, onion.

OLIVE OIL: Olive oil goes as nicely with fish as butter and has no cholesterol. Use the same amount as butter and pour over the fish before baking.

HERBS: Fish readily takes up the flavor of any herb. Before baking, sprinkle the fish with thyme, dill, oregano, tarragon, bay leaf, or *herbes de Provence.*

Sesame Spinach Garnish

4 bunches fresh spinach (about 3 pounds)
2 tablespoons soy sauce
1½ tablespoons lemon juice
1 tablespoon sesame seed

Makes 2 cups

Cut the spinach leaves crosswise into ¼-inch-wide strips, stopping just before the stems become thick. Wash the spinach in plenty of cold water, swishing it about and then allowing the water to settle and the dirt to sink to the bottom. Repeat with clean water if the spinach is very dirty.

Lift the spinach out of the water into a large nonreactive pot. Add the soy sauce and stir over medium-high heat 3 to 5 minutes, or until the spinach is completely wilted.

Drain the spinach in a colander. With the back of a wooden spoon, press out as much liquid as you can. Toss the spinach with the lemon juice.

Form into a mound or oblong shape with your hands. Top with the sesame seeds and use as a garnish in the center of a fish platter.

NOTES AND AFTERTHOUGHTS

You can prepare the spinach garnish hours in advance and chill if you like. The lemon will cause the spinach to turn a darker green color as it sits.

(continued)

Oven-Steamed Trout Chinese Style

Plenty for 6

20 to 40 minutes

Trout, with the possible competition of salmon, is America's best-liked fish. So popular is it, you can even get it fresh in the grocery store on a daily basis. Though trout is not used in Chinese cooking, oven baking it Chinese style with green onions, soy, and ginger is one of the best ways to prepare it.

When choosing any whole fish, select those with clear eyes and glossy, undamaged skin. If the eyes are cloudy and the skin bruised, the fish is too old and will taste fishy.

1 1-inch piece ginger root
3 medium garlic cloves
2 bunches green onions
1 jalapeño chili pepper (optional)
6 trout (about 10 ounces each)
2 teaspoons salt
3 tablespoons soy sauce
3 tablespoons white wine

¼ cup cilantro leaves
1½ tablespoons peanut oil
1 tablespoon sesame oil

Heat the oven to 425°F.

Peel the ginger and garlic cloves. Trim the root ends and limp green tops off the green onions. Cut the green onions crosswise into 1-inch sections, then cut the sections lengthwise into shreds. Remove the core and seeds from the jalapeño and fine chop it.

Put the trout on a flat rack and set in a nonreactive baking dish. Rub the trout, inside and out, with the salt. Press the ginger and garlic over the top of the trout and rub a little inside the cavities. Sprinkle on the jalapeño, if using. Arrange the green onion shreds over the trout and in the cavities. Pour the soy sauce and wine over all.

Cover the dish with aluminum foil, pinching the edges to seal. Bake 18 minutes. (For smaller trout, about 8 ounces each, bake 16 minutes.)

When the trout is done, arrange the cilantro leaves over the top. Pour the peanut and sesame oils over all and serve.

You can also use a larger fish such as rockfish, snapper, or black sea bass, as the Chinese would. A fish between 2 and 3 pounds takes about 22 minutes to cook.

Lasagne with Chard, Turnips, Pine Nuts, Ricotta, and Fontina

¾ pound lasagne noodles
4 teaspoons olive oil
1¾ pounds chard (about 2 bunches)
5 medium garlic cloves
1¼ teaspoons salt
4 medium turnips (about 1 pound)
½ cup pine nuts (2 to 3 ounces)
5 medium tomatoes (about 1¼ pounds)
8 ounces Italian mascarpone cheese or Montrachet goat cheese
2 pounds ricotta cheese, preferably ricotta pecorino
½ cup grated Parmesan, Romano, or aged Asiago cheese
¼ teaspoon ground nutmeg
8 ounces Fontina cheese

Plenty for 6

1 to 2 hours

It's true lasagne is a bit of an endeavor. It takes precooking several ingredients, including the noodles, then building the pie like a culinary Frank Lloyd Wright or an old Italian fresco artist. But this dish is unique and makes the effort worth your precious moments.

Bring a large pot of water to boil. Cook the lasagne noodles until cooked through but still slightly firm.

Drain the noodles and rinse with cold water. Toss with the 3 teaspoons of the olive oil, and set aside.

Cut the chard crosswise into ¼-inch-wide strips. If the stems are large, chop them up a bit. Wash the chard in plenty of water. Lift into a colander and let drain a minute.

Place the wet chard in a large saute pan or pot over medium heat. Peel and press in the garlic. Add ¼ teaspoon salt. Stir until the chard is completely wilted, 2 to 3 minutes. Remove to a colander and set aside to drain.

Peel the turnips and slice ¼ inch thick. Place the turnips in a medium saucepan and add water to cover. Bring to a boil and cook until easy to pierce with a fork, about 3 minutes. Drain.

Heat the remaining 1 teaspoon oil in a small skillet. Add the pine nuts and stir over medium-high heat until browned, about 3 minutes.

Slice the tomatoes into ⅛-inch-thick rounds.

In a bowl, combine the mascarpone, ricotta, Parmesan, nutmeg, and 1 teaspoon salt. Mix well.

Grate the Fontina through the large holes of a hand grater, or slice ⅛ inch thick.

Heat the oven to 350°F.

To assemble the lasagne, line the bottom of a 4-quart casserole or rectangular baking pan (approximately 8½ by 13½ by 2 inches) with a layer of

(continued)

lasagne noodles, overlapping a bit. Coat with 1 cup of the cheese mixture. Spread ¾ cup chard over the cheese. Arrange turnip slices over the chard; arrange tomato slices over the turnips. Season liberally with salt and pepper. Sprinkle on 1 tablespoon pine nuts. Cover with a layer of Fontina. Continue layering as above until all the ingredients are gone, finishing with a layer of the cheese mixture topped with a layer of Fontina.

Cover the lasagne with foil. Bake, covered, 1 hour. Remove the cover, and bake 30 minutes more.

NOTES AND AFTERTHOUGHTS

1. Mascarpone is an Italian cheese that has the texture of cream cheese and the flavor of the richest farm butter you can imagine. It has become available in containers in supermarkets as well as in delis and cheese shops. If you cannot find mascarpone, use 8 ounces additional ricotta.

2. Fresh noodles from a pasta shop make the lasagne softer and tastier than dry noodles, though dry will do. Best of all, make a 4-egg batch of the Basic Pasta Dough recipe (page 115) and roll the dough into 3-inch-wide strips.

Corsican Lasagne with Corsican Lasagne Sauce

7 to 9 cups Corsican Lasagne Sauce (page 256)
¾ pound lasagne noodles
1 tablespoon olive oil
1 pound mozzarella cheese
1 pound ricotta pecorino, Montrachet goat, or regular ricotta cheese
¾ cup milk
½ cup grated Parmesan, Romano, or aged Asiago cheese

Make the Corsican Lasagne Sauce.

While the sauce simmers, bring a large pot of water to boil. Cook the lasagne noodles until cooked through but still slightly firm.

Drain the noodles in a colander. Rinse briefly with cold water. Toss with the oil and set aside.

Grate the mozzarella or thin slice with a cheese slicer.

Combine the ricotta and milk in a bowl and mix well.

Heat the oven to 375°F.

To assemble the lasagne, line the bottom of a 4-quart casserole or non-reactive baking pan (approximately 8½ by 13½ by 2 inches) with a layer of lasagne noodles, overlapping them slightly. Cover the noodles with a thin layer of the Corsican Lasagne Sauce. Top the sauce with a layer of mozzarella cheese. Spread on some ricotta mixture. Dot with more sauce. Cover with another layer of lasagne noodles and continue layering in the same way until all the ingredients are used, finishing with a layer of lasagne noodles. Sprinkle the grated cheese over the top.

Cover the lasagne with aluminum foil and bake 45 minutes.

Remove the foil. Bake 15 minutes more.

Cut into squares and serve.

NOTES AND AFTERTHOUGHTS

1. If you have an unglazed pottery casserole, such as a Römertopf, you can use it for lasagne. The noodles turn out especially light and airy, the cheese soft and fluffy, and the sauce condensed and rich.

2. The lasagne can be assembled in advance and cooked just before serving. Or you can cook it in advance and reheat it just before serving.

Plenty for 6 with leftovers

1 to 2 hours

Whoever the first Corsican was to stew prunes in a red lasagne sauce and bury them among the flat noodles deserves the Corsican culinary award of the century.

Corsican Lasagne Sauce

Makes 7 cups without meat
9 cups with meat

40 to 60 minutes

Corsican Lasagne Sauce is an aromatic, spicy, sweet, all-purpose sauce for Italian and other dishes. You can make it vegetarian or with meat. Like Red Pizza Sauce, Basic Meat Sauce Bolognese, and Basic Red Zucchini Tomato Sauce, it can be used in many ways. Toss it with spaghetti, or use as a sauce for Desperation Chicken, over rice or pilaf, or as a topping for Corsican (!) hamburgers. The meatless version is an excellent condiment for pork or lamb roast. It is quick and easy, and like other cooked tomato sauces, can be made ahead of time and frozen.

1 medium onion (about 7 ounces)
5 garlic cloves
⅓ cup olive oil
1 pound ground chuck (optional)
6 cups crushed tomatoes in puree (about two 28-ounce cans)
1 teaspoon dried oregano
1 medium bay leaf
⅛ teaspoon ground cinnamon
¼ teaspoon ground nutmeg
¾ teaspoon ground allspice
¼ teaspoon cayenne pepper
1 cup red wine
24 pitted prunes

Peel the onion and garlic. Fine chop them in a food processor or with a chef's knife. Heat the oil in a large nonreactive sauté pan or saucepan. Add the onion and garlic and cook over medium-low heat until wilted but not browned, about 10 minutes.

If you are making the meat version, add the ground chuck to the onions and garlic and, stirring occasionally to break up any chunks, cook 5 minutes to brown the meat.

Stir in the tomatoes, oregano, bay leaf, cinnamon, nutmeg, allspice, cayenne, and red wine. Bring to a boil. Reduce the heat to medium-low and simmer 30 minutes.

Cut the prunes into quarters and add to the tomato sauce. Continue simmering 20 minutes more.

Remove the pot from the heat and use right away, or cool and store in the refrigerator or freezer.

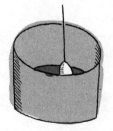

TWO MEATLOAVES

Some of us remember homemade meatloaf from childhood days. Some of us never had it until it appeared to rave reviews in bars and grills touting home cooking. Served with mashed potatoes and a quick sauce, meatloaf is still one of the best and quintessential American home cooking dishes.

Beef and Pork Meatloaf with Red Pepper Sauce

1½ pounds ground chuck
¾ pound ground pork
1 large white potato (about ½ pound)
1 medium onion (about 7 ounces)
1 large garlic clove
2 eggs
3 tablespoons tomato paste
½ cup heavy cream
1½ tablespoons fresh thyme leaves or ½ teaspoon dried
1¼ teaspoons salt
½ teaspoon freshly ground black pepper
1 bay leaf
6 bacon slices (about 6 ounces)

1½ cups Red Pepper Sauce (page 258)

Heat the oven to 350°F.

Combine the ground chuck and ground pork in a large bowl. Peel the potato. Grate it through the large holes of a hand grater and add to the bowl. Peel the onion and garlic and fine chop in a food processor or with a chef's knife. Add the onion, garlic, eggs, tomato paste, cream, thyme, salt, and pepper to the bowl. Mix with your hands, making sure to blend well.

Place the meatloaf in a 2-quart loaf pan, ovenproof bowl, terrine, or other baking dish. Tamp down on the top to make sure the meat is packed well with no air pockets. Place the bay leaf on top. Cover the loaf with the bacon. Bake 1½ hours.

While the meatloaf cooks, make the Red Pepper Sauce.

When the meatloaf is done, remove from the oven. Allow to cool at least 15 minutes before slicing.

To serve, cut the meatloaf into ½-inch-thick slices and top each slice with a dollop of the Red Pepper Sauce.

Plenty for 6

1 to 2 hours

Pork is often included in meatloaf because the rich fat in pork keeps the meatloaf juicy and tender. Without pork, a meatloaf will not be as soft or succulent. Pork also adds a depth and richness to the flavor. To a lesser extent, heavy cream serves the same purpose as ground pork. Meat steeped in milk or cream, an old culinary trick, becomes much softer because the lactic acid in milk or cream breaks down the meat tissue. Also, adding minced vegetables, such as onions or the mushrooms in the Spicy Ground Beef Meatloaf that follows, prevents the meat from compacting into a tough mass.

Red Pepper Sauce

Makes 1½ cups

3 medium red bell peppers (about 1 pound)
2 tablespoons olive oil
1 teaspoon lemon juice
⅛ teaspoon cayenne pepper
¼ teaspoon salt

Roast and peel the bell peppers according to the instructions on page 47.

    Puree the peppers in a food processor, blender, food mill, or in a mortar with a pestle. Stir in the olive oil, lemon juice, cayenne, and salt.

Spicy Ground Beef Meatloaf with Hard-Boiled Eggs, Jalapeño, Sherry, and Cilantro

Plenty for 6

1 to 2 hours

4 large eggs
6 ounces mushrooms, about 1½ cups minced
1 medium onion (about 7 ounces)
1½ jalapeño chili peppers
2¼ pounds ground chuck
¾ cup heavy cream
¼ cup sherry
1¼ teaspoons salt
1½ tablespoons chopped cilantro leaves

FOR THE SAUCE:

Juices from the cooked meatloaf
1 cup crushed tomatoes in puree
1⁄16 teaspoon ground nutmeg
2 tablespoons chopped cilantro leaves

Place 3 of the eggs in a small saucepan. Add water to cover and bring to a boil. As soon as the water boils, cover the pot, turn off the heat, and set aside for 9 minutes. Drain the eggs immediately, rinse with cold water to cool, and peel.

    Heat the oven to 350°F.

    Clean the mushrooms and trim the stem ends. Mince in a food processor or with a chef's knife.

    Peel the onion. Remove the stems from the jalapeño peppers. Mince the onion and peppers in a food processor or with a chef's knife.

    In a large bowl, combine the ground chuck, mushrooms, peppers, and onion. Add the remaining egg, cream, sherry, and salt. Mix with your hands to blend well.

    To assemble the meatloaf, place half of the meat mixture in a 2-quart loaf pan, ovenproof bowl, terrine, or other baking dish. Cut the hard-boiled eggs lengthwise in half. Place 3 of the halves cut side up in a row down the center of the meatloaf. Sprinkle on 1½ tablespoons cilantro. Cover each egg half with one of the remaining egg halves. Spread the remaining meat mixture over the top.

Place the meatloaf in the oven and bake 1 hour and 15 to 20 minutes, or until a meat thermometer registers 145°F. Remove from the oven and allow to cool 15 minutes.

When the meatloaf has cooled, pour the juices into a small saucepan. Bring to a boil. Stir in the tomatoes, nutmeg, and the 2 tablespoons cilantro. Remove the sauce from the heat.

To serve, cut the meatloaf into ½-inch-thick slices. Top each slice with a spoonful of the sauce. Serve the remaining sauce on the side.

NOTES AND AFTERTHOUGHTS

1. If using a round dish, mark the ends with toothpicks so you know which way to cut in order to have a cross section of egg in the middle of the meatloaf slices when you cut it.

2. Because we use the juices rendered from the meatloaf for a sauce base and want to keep the fat content at a minimum, we don't add ground pork to this meatloaf. If you want the softer texture and richer flavor that pork adds, you can use ¾ pound ground pork and 1½ pounds ground chuck for the meatloaf and serve a different sauce with it.

Poor Man's Stuffed Eggplant

FOR THE STUFFING:

2 medium onions (about 1 pound)
12 medium garlic cloves
2 tablespoons olive oil
1½ pounds ground chuck
3 tablespoons tomato paste
1½ tablespoons chopped fresh oregano or 2 teaspoons dried
1 cup red wine
3 medium eggplants (1 to 1¼ pounds each)
4 tablespoons olive oil

½ cup grated Parmesan, Romano, or aged Asiago cheese

Plenty for 6

40 to 60 minutes

Susanna contrived this version of stuffed eggplant, with wilted eggplant shells and water in the baking dish, to avoid the over-sopping of precious olive oil. She pronounced it "Poor Man's Imam." Victoria, upon tasting it, adapted it as her first take-out dinner for Pig-by-the-Tail and renamed it "Aubergine Susanna." On eggplant baking day, it was a sight to see all the deli's enormous baking trays lined with simmering purple eggplant shells.

Make the stuffing first. Peel and medium chop the onion and garlic in a food processor or with a chef's knife.

Place 2 tablespoons olive oil in a large skillet and heat until the oil smokes. Add the onions and garlic and cook over medium heat about 5 minutes, until translucent.

Add the ground chuck and cook, stirring occasionally, about 5 minutes, until the meat is browned and any clumps are broken up.

(continued)

Meanwhile, cut the eggplants lengthwise in half, leaving the stems and green cap on. With a spoon, scoop out most of the pulp, leaving about ⅜ inch of pulp around the eggplant shell. Set the shells aside. Chop the pulp into ½-inch dice.

Add the pulp, tomato paste, oregano, and wine to the meat mixture. Simmer over medium heat for 30 minutes.

While the meat and eggplant mixture simmers, pour 2 tablespoons oil in a large skillet and heat until the oil begins to smoke. Add as many eggplant shells as will fit and brown quickly over high heat, until lightly wilted on all sides. Remove the shells, cut sides up, to a baking dish. Continue with another batch, adding more oil as needed until all the shells are wilted.

Heat the oven to 375°F.

Divide the meat mixture among the eggplant shells, filling evenly. Sprinkle the grated cheese over the tops. Pour in enough water to reach ¼ inch up the sides of the baking dish.

Bake 45 minutes. Remove from the oven and serve hot or cold.

NOTES AND AFTERTHOUGHTS

1. Poor Man's Stuffed Eggplant is one of those dishes in which the longer the ingredients are together, the better they taste. The dish can be baked in 45 minutes, but if you have the time, reduce the oven temperature and cook the dish longer and slower, about 1 hour at 325°F or 1½ hours at 300°F. On the other hand you can rush the dish and cook it at 400°F for 30 minutes, although this sacrifices some depth of flavor. Indeed, partially cooking the stuffed eggplants in advance then finishing later enhances this dish.

2. You can also partially cook the stuffed eggplants in advance and freeze until ready to use. Defrost, then finish cooking 20 to 30 minutes at 375°F.

Quick Upside-Down or Right-Side-Up One-Crust Pot Pies

1 batch Quick Pastry Dough (page 263)
All-purpose flour, for rolling out the dough

Chicken, Mushroom, and Cream Pot Pie Filling (see below), or Beef, Potato, and Saffron Pot Pie Filling (see below)
3 tablespoons grated Parmesan, Romano, or aged Asiago cheese
1 egg yolk mixed with 1 teaspoon water, if making Right-Side-Up Pot Pie

Make the pastry dough, remembering it needs to chill at least 1 hour before rolling out.

To make an Upside-Down Pot Pie:
Heat the oven to 425°F.

Lightly flour a work surface. Shaping the dough to fit the pie pan you are

Plenty for 3

20 to 40 minutes for Upside-Down
40 to 60 minutes for Right-Side-Up

Pot pies remain near and dear to American diners. While everyone loves them, not many want to spend the time making one these days. This quick version of pot pie uses only one crust, and carries the innovation a

using, roll out about ⅛ inch thick and large enough to cover the bottom and sides of the pan, extending ½ inch beyond.

Place the dough in the pie pan. Fold the extra dough under to meet the rim. Pinch the edge of the crust all around. Pierce the bottom of the crust in 3 or 4 places with a fork to keep it from puffing up and the sides from pulling down.

Bake 15 minutes.

While the crust is baking, make the filling.

When the crust is done, spoon in the filling. Sprinkle on the grated cheese. Bake 5 minutes.

Remove from the oven and serve right away.

To make Right-Side-Up Pot Pie:

Heat the oven to 425°F.

Make the filling. Spoon into a small pie pan or baking dish.

Lightly flour a work surface. Shaping the dough to fit the pan you are using, roll out about ⅛ inch thick and large enough to cover the top of the pan, extending ½ inch beyond.

Place the dough on top of the filling, tuck in the extra dough, and pinch the edge of the crust all around. With a knife, make 2 or 3 slits in the crust to allow steam to escape.

Brush the crust with the yolk mixture. Sprinkle on the grated cheese.

Bake 40 minutes.

Remove from the oven and serve right away.

Chicken, Mushroom, and Cream Pot Pie Filling

1½ cups cooked chicken
6 ounces mushrooms (about 2 cups sliced)
2 medium yellow wax chili peppers
1½ ounces Canadian bacon (about 2 thin slices)
1½ tablespoons butter
1½ tablespoons lemon juice
1½ cups heavy cream
1½ tablespoons chopped fresh chervil or 2 teaspoons dried
¼ teaspoon salt
Pinch cayenne pepper

Cut the chicken into ½-inch dice. Clean and trim the stem ends off the mushrooms. Slice ¼ inch thick. Remove the core and seeds of the chili peppers and mince the peppers. Cut the Canadian bacon into fine slivers.

Melt the butter in a nonreactive medium skillet. Add the mushrooms and chilies and stir over medium-high heat 2 minutes. Stir in the lemon juice. Immediately add the chicken, cream, bacon, chervil, salt, and cayenne. Bring to a boil. Cook 1 minute. Remove from the heat.

step further, turning the one-crust pot pie upside down. We still have the pastry we love, but adding the filling after the crust is cooked gives a fresher pie in half the time. A quick return to the oven to heat the cheese topping, and the pie is on the table in 20 minutes. If you want the crust on top, the old-fashioned way, the one-crust Right Side Up version still gives you a sumptuous pot pie in 40 minutes.

Enough for one 8-inch pie crust

Beef, Potato, and Saffron Pot Pie Filling

Enough for one 8-inch pie

1 large red or white potato (about ½ pound)
1 small or ½ large onion (about ¼ pound)
¼ large red bell pepper (about 2 ounces)
1 teaspoon peanut oil
3 tablespoons sliced almonds
1½ cups shredded leftover beef
3 teaspoons unbleached all-purpose flour
1½ cups chicken stock
½ teaspoon ground turmeric
Large pinch saffron
¼ teaspoon ground coriander
Pinch cayenne pepper
¾ teaspoon salt
¼ teaspoon freshly ground black pepper

Wash the potato and cut into ¼-inch dice. Place the potato pieces in a small saucepan. Add water to cover by 1 inch, and bring to a boil. Cook 4 minutes. Drain and rinse to cool.

Peel the onion. Remove the core and seeds from the bell pepper. Medium chop the onion and pepper in a food processor or with a chef's knife.

Heat the oil in a large skillet. Add the onion, bell pepper, and almonds. Stir over medium-high heat 3 to 4 minutes. Add the beef and potatoes. Sprinkle on the flour and stir until incorporated. Stir in the chicken stock. Add the turmeric, saffron, coriander, cayenne, salt, and black pepper. Stir to blend.

NOTES AND AFTERTHOUGHTS

Leftover lamb or chicken can replace the beef in this recipe.

FILLING VARIATIONS

Leftovers from other dishes can make quick fillings for pot pies. Especially good are:

Braised Beef and Rabbit Greek Style, page 230
Dos Equis Oven Beef Stew, page 229
Sherry-Steeped Chicken in Paprika Mayonnaise Sauce, page 244
Stewed Chicken, page 94
Vegetables Stewed with White Wine, page 103

Quick Pastry Dough

½ cup unbleached all-purpose flour
⅛ teaspoon salt
4 tablespoons (½ stick) cold butter
⅛ cup ice water

Place the flour and salt in a food processor. Cut the butter into 8 pieces and place on top of the flour. Pulse 2 or 3 times to cut the butter into the flour, until it looks like pebbles. While pulsing 2 or 3 more times, drizzle in the ice water through the top opening. Stop as soon as you have added the water.

Gather the dough into a ball and wrap in plastic wrap. Press the dough package flat like a fat pancake. Refrigerate at least 1 hour before rolling out the dough.

NOTES AND AFTERTHOUGHTS

1. You can make this dough in the morning, the night before, or even freeze it weeks ahead. In fact it's better if you do, because the dough becomes easier to roll out. If it sits only 1 hour, it will roll out well but is more likely to shrink during baking.

2. If you don't have a food processor, cut the butter into small bits and use your fingers or a fork to work the butter into the flour and salt until the flour resembles coarse, pebbly sand. Add the water all at once, mix it into the flour and gather the dough into a ball.

Enough for one 8-inch pie crust

The quick pastry crust we use for making these pot pies is delicious, but rich in butter, so the sides and edges have a tendency to pull in a bit. We don't worry about this. These are home-style pies. If you want your pie crust to be picture perfect, when you bake the empty crust for the Upside-Down Pot Pie, lay aluminum foil over the crust and fill with a good layer of raw rice or beans to weigh the crust down and keep the sides up. Remove the foil and weights after 10 minutes to allow the bottom to brown well.

OVEN VEGETABLES

When a vegetable takes to roasting, the results are incomparable. The ones that do roast well are by and large the heartier vegetables. They have dense flesh, like potatoes and winter squash, or their own strong flavor, like garlic and tomatoes.

Corn

Leave whole corn ears in their husks with silks intact. Soak the ears in water for 10 to 15 minutes. Place on the oven rack and roast at 375°F to 425°F 15 to 25 minutes, depending on the age and freshness of the corn. Younger corn takes less time, older corn takes longer. Serve with a ¼-inch-thick slab of butter, cut the long way from a whole stick, so that each person can roll their corn on the butter. Pass the peppermill.

≈ Corn cooks very well in the microwave. Leave whole corn ears in their husks with the silks intact. Check microwave instructions for timings.

Eggplant

Slice regular eggplants into ¾-inch-thick rounds, or cut small Oriental eggplants lengthwise in half. Pour ⅛ inch of olive oil into a nonreactive baking dish. Sprinkle the oil with salt and about 1 tablespoon fresh chopped herbs such as thyme, oregano, or *herbes de Provence* or about 1 teaspoon dried herbs. Place the eggplant slices or halves, cut sides down, in the oil. Bake in a 450°F oven 25 minutes for slices, or 20 minutes for halves.

Once cooked, you can jazz up eggplant in many ways. Spread the eggplant with a little pressed garlic just before serving. Or, dress them up with a spicy Oriental-style sauce. Mix half soy sauce and half lemon juice and stir in a little minced chili pepper. Or, place a dollop of sour cream and ½ teaspoon caviar on top of each eggplant piece just before serving.

Often, in a hurry to get dinner on the table, we have tried to make use of our microwave oven for cooking vegetables. We think that while vegetables do cook quickly in the microwave, most are not worth eating. Microwaving does not thoroughly cook the natural sugars in vegetables. Without their sugars cooked, most vegetables come out quite flavorless. The vegetables that we have found cook best in a microwave are corn and some of the winter squashes.

Garlic

Together with a roast or on its own, roasted garlic is a treat for the gods. Peel off the papery outer skin of whole heads of garlic, leaving the cloves intact. Place the garlic in the pan along with a roast and bake in the pan juices. Cook 50 minutes at 350°F, or adjust the timing depending on the roast's baking temperature.

Alternatively, wrap individual whole peeled garlic heads along with a pat of butter and a few fresh mint leaves in foil. Bake the packages in a 350°F oven 50 minutes.

To serve, squeeze out the roasted pulp from each clove onto meat slices, Little Toasts (page 38), oven-roasted potatoes (page 266), or almost any other vegetable.

Onions

The delight of roasting onions is that you don't have to peel them! Roast them whole, unpeeled, brown skins and all. After cooking, strip off the crisp peel to reveal their soft, steamy centers. To cook them this way takes 1 hour at 350°F, so it matches up nicely with cooking a roast or turkey.

For zestier and slightly faster roast onions, cut the onions in half and deglaze them with vinegar as in the recipe for Vinegar-Deglazed Onions (page 235). Omit the vinegar if you want plain baked onions.

Peppers

See the directions for roasting and peeling bell peppers in Mom's Marinated Red and Green Bell Peppers (page 47). After they are roasted and peeled, marinate the peppers as in the same recipe, or simply douse them in olive oil and spread some pressed garlic over the top before serving.

Bell peppers can also be roasted the same way as they are sautéed. Put the strips of red or green pepper, olive oil, and garlic (as in the recipe on page 47), into a baking pan instead of a skillet. Place in a 400°F oven and cook for 20 minutes.

You can also stuff peppers with many and varied fillings and roast them the same way as stuffed tomatoes (see below). Stuffed peppers take 1 hour to bake.

Potatoes

King of all the oven-cooked potatoes is the classic baked potato, and russet potatoes are the king of baking. If your market has Finnish yellows, they also are excellent. White potatoes work in the oven for oven stews and the like, but red potatoes are best saved for the grill or stovetop.

To make perfect baked potatoes, wash the potatoes—1 medium to large russet per person—and place them on the oven rack. Bake at an oven temperature between 400°F and 450°F 1 hour, or until the skins are crisp and the potatoes give completely when squeezed between your thumb and forefinger. The higher the oven temperature, the crisper the skins. If you need to bake the potato at a lower oven temperature because of other foods in the oven, but still want crisp skins, extend the baking time to 1½ hours.

For a yet crispier baked potato, cut the potatoes in half the long way. Rub the halves all around with olive oil. Place them, cut sides down, on a metal baking pan and bake 40 minutes at 450°F. Turn and bake 20 minutes more.

To fulfill your desire for fried potatoes without heating a gallon of oil and double frying, make Oven Fries.

Oven Fries

Plenty for 6

40 to 60 minutes

6 russet or white potatoes (about 3 pounds)
3 tablespoons olive or peanut oil

Heat the oven to 425°F.

Wash the potatoes. Cut into ¼-inch-wide by ¼-inch-long strips.

Place as many potato strips as will fit in a single uncrowded layer in 1 or 2 baking pans. Drizzle the oil over the potatoes and stir to make sure all the potato strips are lightly coated.

Bake 35 minutes.

Turn the strips over, and bake 20 to 25 minutes more, until golden and crispy all around.

Serve immediately.

NOTES AND AFTERTHOUGHTS

If you have nothing else in the oven that's cooking at a lower temperature, you can make oven fries in less time by cooking them at 500°F. They will take about 30 minutes.

Tomatoes

No vegetable roasts in quite the special way a tomato does, making a sauce of their own juices. And no vegetable accepts other flavors quite like tomatoes. You can herb, crust, stuff, sauce, or vinegar them.

Perhaps the simplest, most classic roast tomato is with a bread crumb topping. Follow the recipe for Baked Tomatoes to accompany Provençal-Style Roast Leg of Lamb on page 235 and add whatever herb you'd like.

For stuffed tomatoes, use the Currant, Red Pepper, and Rice Filling for game hens (page 245), the filling for the Festive Stuffed Chicken (page 242) or the Beef with Currants and Pine Nuts taco filling (page 89). Cut the tops off whole tomatoes. Scoop out their centers, reserving them. Place the shells in a baking dish and fill with whatever stuffing you are using. Chop the pulp, then pour the pulp and juices over the tops of the stuffed tomatoes. Place the tops back on the tomatoes like caps. Bake at 400°F 30 minutes.

Winter Squash

Acorn, banana, butternut, spaghetti, little pumpkin, sweet dumpling—all winter squashes roast to sweet perfection, whether plain or with a little butter.

To roast winter squash, cut acorn, butternut, sweet dumpling, spaghetti, or little pumpkin squash in half or quarters and scoop out the seeds. (Banana squash usually comes already cut and seeded.) Dot the squash with butter or oil. Place the squash pieces in a roasting pan along with meats, or bake separately in a pan or directly on the oven rack 40 minutes to 1 hour, depending on the size of the pieces.

With the centers scooped out, acorn or sweet dumpling squash have wells that beg for filling. They bake deliciously with all kinds of tidbits placed inside. Try adding a mixture of minced celery, minced garlic, tiny pieces of bacon, and a pat of butter. Bake at 350°F 1 hour.

≈ Acorn and banana squashes, because they are so naturally sweet, bake particularly well in a microwave oven. Prepare the squash as above. Wrap tightly in plastic wrap and microwave for about 9 minutes. Stuffed squash can be prepared in the microwave, although the bacon bits won't get crisp. Prepare as above and microwave about 9 minutes.

Yams and Sweet Potatoes

Since yams and sweet potatoes are much sweeter than white potatoes, they require more baking time for their sugars to cook completely. Then they become truly sublime. Bake medium yams or sweet potatoes 1½ hours at 350°F. Slit open the skins, slip in a pat of butter and eat immediately. Nothing else is needed.

SIMPLE AND SATISFYING DINNER SALADS

Basic Green Salad
  Variations
  Basic Vinaigrette Dressing
  Variations
  Basic Mayonnaise
  Salad Croutons

Good & Plenty Chef's Salad

Farmer's Vegetable Salad with Any Meat or Fish

Warm Spicy Sautéed Beef Salad with Lettuce, Mint, and Peanuts

Warm Strip Steak Salad with Spinach, Mushrooms, Sprouts, Pine Nuts, Pumpkin Seeds, and Tomato Vinaigrette
  Tomato Vinaigrette

Warm Marinated Pork Salad with Pimientos, Gorgonzola, and Walnuts

Warm Salami, Potato, and Watercress Salad

Lentil Salad with Ham, Belgian Endive, and Feta Cheese

Leftover Lamb Roast Salad with White Beans, Jalapeño Peppers, and Tomatoes

Chicken Salad with Red Cabbage, Snow Peas, Broccoli, and Toasted Almonds

Turkey Salad with Beets, Spinach, Hard-Boiled Egg, and Curried Sour Cream Dressing

Shredded Duck or Chicken Salad with Papaya, Jícama, Mint, and Cashews

Duck Salad with Napa Cabbage, Turnips, and Kumquats

Fish and Avocado Salad with Crispy Hot Potatoes and Tomato Onion Rémoulade
  Tomato Onion Rémoulade

Surf and Turf Salad on a Bed of Grated Zucchini with Green Goddess Dressing
  Green Goddess Dressing

Crab or Lobster Salad with Tarragon and Shallot Poppy Seed Dressing

Salad, when we were young, meant a wedge of iceberg lettuce with a plop of Thousand Island, bottled French, or that white concoction euphemistically called Roquefort dressing. It came in little bowls or on a small plate to the side of the main entree.

Salad has come a long way since then. It has evolved into full-meal fare. Now it *is* the lunch or the dinner as often as it is only a segment of the repast. Sometimes it is even warm, presenting hot meats, or vegetables wilted with a sizzling dressing seconds before serving. A far cry from the chef's or Louis salad familiar to ladies' luncheon rooms of large department stores, modern salads are hearty, hefty, healthful, inventive, intriguing, filling, full-fledged food.

Dressings have departed the past as well. They are lighter, more refreshing. Of all the things that go into a salad, the dressing is the simplest to prepare. You can mix together a homemade dressing in a matter of seconds, and it will have none of the stale or preservative flavors of bottled dressings.

Preparing the rest of the salad ingredients is a little more demanding. They need touching, trimming, washing, and there's no way around it. But you can wash and dry lettuce by the head when you come home from the market and store the leaves, ready to dress. You can cook meat and vegetables hours before. Indeed, you can often use leftovers.

It's worth it. There's nothing like a salad for dinner, when you want to be active again after eating, when you've been too active to eat much, when you crave fresh, raw food or a veritable symphony of flavors.

We've arranged the dinner salads in this chapter in two ways. Some are tossed in a bowl, and some are layered on a platter. We give many of the dressings as separate recipes so you can use a dressing you particularly like on other salads of your own invention. ∎

SALAD GREENS

In the salad recipes, we list the salad greens in cup amounts. Here is a checklist of approximately how many cups various common kinds of greens will yield.

BOSTON, BIBB, OR BUTTER LETTUCE: 1 medium head yields about 5 cups.

CHICORY: 1 head yields about 6 cups.

CRESS: 1 medium bunch equals a little less than 1½ cups.

CURLY ENDIVE: 1 head yields about 6 cups.

ENDIVE: 1 head yields about 6 cups.

ESCAROLE: 1 head, with the spines removed from the leaves, yields about 6 cups.

RED LEAF LETTUCE: 1 medium head yields about 6 cups.

Salad greens must be completely dry for the dressing to adhere to the leaves. Otherwise, you wind up with a soggy salad, the dressing running to the bottom of the bowl, the leaves wet with water but no touches of oil or vinegar. To dry greens completely, the salad dryer basket should be only partially filled. This not only give the leaves room to dry thoroughly, but it prevents the leaves from bruising each other from their own weight when they are spun.

You can shred, wash, and spin dry salad greens up to 5 or 6 days in advance. Loosely pack the dried greens in a plastic bag and refrigerate until ready to serve.

ROMAINE LETTUCE: 1 medium head yields about 5 cups.

SMALL LEAF EXOTIC GARDEN GREENS: such as arugula (rocket), Chinese spinach, curly cress, lambs' tongues, *mâche, mizuna,* and others, yield approximately
1 cup for every 2 ounces of leaves.

SPINACH: a ¾-pound bunch yields about 3 cups salad leaves.

EQUIPMENT

A meal salad for 6 or even 4 takes a considerable quantity of ingredients. To facilitate your salad making, you should have a large salad bowl or platter. If you don't have one, though, you can toss salads in individual bowls or arrange them on individual plates.

Modern plastic salad spinners are wonderful contraptions. They dry salad greens in a jiffy.

If you like garlic in salad dressing, we recommend a garlic press. The press swiftly minces the garlic cloves and softens the pulp so that it blends throughout the dressing. ■

Basic Green Salad

9 cups salad greens, such as romaine, butter, Boston, red leaf, curly leaf, escarole, endive, cress, arugula (rocket), spinach, *mâche,* chicory, *mizuna,* or a mixture of these.
⅓ cup Basic Vinaigrette (page 274)

Plenty for 6 as an accompaniment to the meal

20 minutes or less

Remove and discard the limp or browned outer leaves from the greens. Separate the remaining leaves from the core. Tear leaves into bite-size pieces.

Fill a basin or large bowl with cold water. Place the greens in the water. Swirl the leaves in the water to make sure all are rinsed and the dirt and debris are freed to sink to the bottom.

To dry the leaves, place enough greens in the basket of a salad spinner to fill it one third full. Spin. Remove the basket from the salad spinner, pour out the water from the bottom, and spin once again to dry the leaves completely. Or you can dry the leaves by swinging them in a wire salad drying basket. Half fill the basket, step outside, and swing the basket in full circles with one arm. Or, you can dry salad greens by placing them in a single layer on dish or paper towels. Cover with another layer of towels and gently pat the top layer to dry the leaves. Or, you can roll up the leaves in the towels and place the roll in the freezer for 2 or 3 minutes to dry.

Place the dry leaves in a large salad bowl. Continue cleaning the remaining leaves until all are dried.

Just before serving, toss with the Basic Vinaigrette.

VARIATIONS

You can vary the components of a basic green salad in any of the following ways.

HERBS: For a pungent, herbaceous accent to your salad, add ⅓ to ½ cup whole small leaves of fresh basil, tarragon, chervil, mint, Italian parsley, or cilantro leaves before tossing the greens.

FLOWERS: One cup whole edible flowers or ½ cup edible flower petals add an exotic and colorful touch to a green salad. Especially good are nasturtiums, pansies, violets, rose, chrysanthemum, marigold, or geranium petals, lavender flowers, or the flowers of any herb.

CROUTONS: One cup croutons tossed with the greens provides a pleasing crunch to a salad. To make croutons, see page 275.

CHEESES: One-third cup grated or crumbled cheese—Parmesan, Romano, or aged Asiago or crumbled Roquefort, Bavarian Blue, Gorgonzola, or Feta—is always a welcome addition to salad greens and makes a more substantial dish.

Tossed salads taste
superior, and turn out
better dressed, when the
oil and vinegar are not
mixed together before
tossing. Instead, add
the oil and vinegar
separately. One of the
best ways to accomplish
this is to mix the vinegar,
lemon, and aromatics in
the bottom of the bowl,
put the salad greens over
the lemon and vinegar,
then pour the oil over the
greens and toss. Another
way is to mix the vinegar
and aromatics in a large
spoon or bowl, pour them
over the salad, then pour
on the oil and toss. Either
way, the vinegar and
aromatic elements end
up in dots and dashes
over the oil-coated
leaves, providing a lacy
taste texture rather than
a homogenized smear.

One reason to mix a
dressing in advance is to
keep a batch ready as a
timesaving device. If you
do mix one in advance,
whether for a layered or
a tossed salad, remember
two things: Mix the
ingredients with a few
gentle stirs or a few
gentle shakes. Don't
overblend. Also, don't
add any garlic or onion
until just before using.
Neither keeps well. This
is why you should avoid
garlic or onion powders
or flakes and pressed
garlic packed in jars.

Basic Vinaigrette Dressing

½ tablespoon balsamic, red wine, or sherry vinegar
½ tablespoon lemon juice
⅛ teaspoon salt
⅛ teaspoon freshly ground black pepper
3 tablespoons olive oil

In the salad bowl, mix together the vinegar, lemon juice, salt, and pepper. Pour on the oil after adding the greens to the bowl.

VARIATIONS

As well as the greens, you can change the character of the Basic Vinaigrette Dressing in numerous ways.

MUSTARD: Mix ½ teaspoon dry mustard or 1 teaspoon prepared mustard into the Basic Vinaigrette. We prefer Coleman's dry mustard for salad dressings because it is pure powdered mustard and has no other flavors to interfere with the balance between vinegar and oil. Another good choice is an imported smooth Dijon mustard made with only white wine and no vinegar.

GARLIC: Press 1 to 3 garlic cloves, depending on how deep your affection for garlic, into the Basic Vinaigrette.

SOY: Mix ½ tablespoon soy sauce into the Basic Vinaigrette. The wheaty, earthy taste of soy makes an interesting addition. Because soy has a high sodium content, it also serves as another way of adding salt to the dressing, so when using soy omit the salt in the basic recipe.

HERBS: Almost any herb, fresh or dried, can be added to the Basic Vinaigrette. Mix in 1 teaspoon chopped fresh or ¼ teaspoon dried herb, depending on what else you are serving and the whim of the moment.

OTHER VINEGARS: Many vinegars besides the basic balsamic, red wine, or sherry vinegar can be the base of a vinaigrette. Each lends its own distinctive taste to a salad dressing. Experiment with malt vinegar, the berry vinegars, and white wine, champagne, or flavored wine vinegars.

OTHER OILS: If you want a change from the fruity flavor of olive oil, try peanut, walnut, or hazelnut oil for differing nutty flavors. Walnut oil is particularly good with raspberry vinegar. For those who want a bland, unassertive oil, safflower, avocado, or corn oils are good and healthful. Palm and coconut oils should be avoided because they are heavily saturated.

Mayonnaise is not a salad dressing by itself. But we include a recipe for Basic Mayonnaise here because it is the base for many salad dressings. Stirred into other salad dressings, as in the Tomato Onion Rémoulade, it provides thickening and enrichment.

Basic Mayonnaise

2 egg yolks
1 teaspoon Dijon mustard or ¼ teaspoon dry mustard
1 teaspoon lemon juice
⅛ teaspoon salt
1¼ cups olive or peanut oil
½ tablespoon very hot water

With a wire whisk, electric beater, blender, or food processor, beat the egg yolks until thickened.

Stir in the mustard, lemon juice, and salt. Then, starting with droplets and working up to tablespoon amounts and finally to a slow steady stream, beat in the oil until the mayonnaise is quite thick. Stir in the hot water.

NOTES AND AFTERTHOUGHTS

1. We prefer a light, non-virgin olive oil or peanut oil for mayonnaise. Extra-virgin olive oil is too assertive for this delicate sauce.

2. When using a food processor to make mayonnaise, use a light touch. Overprocessing makes the mayonnaise bitter.

3. Practically no bottled mayonnaise is a worthy substitute for the real thing. In a time bind, Best Foods, Hellman's, or a good one from your specialty grocer or deli will do.

Salad Croutons

2 medium garlic cloves
⅓ cup olive oil
6 ounces French or Italian bread, cut ¾ inch thick

Peel the garlic and press into the olive oil.

Cut the bread into ¾-inch cubes

Heat the olive oil and garlic in large skillet until the oil begins to smoke. Remove the garlic with a slotted spoon. Add the bread cubes and stir constantly over medium-high heat 1 minute, or until the bread is golden. Remove the croutons and drain on paper towels.

NOTES AND AFTERTHOUGHTS

Croutons may be made in advance and stored in an airtight container.

Makes about 1½ cups

With a food processor, homemade mayonnaise is a snap to make. It will keep 3 or 4 days in the refrigerator, but not much longer. Even in an oil emulsion, fresh eggs spoil easily. So never use homemade mayonnaise on kids' lunch sandwiches left in hot cloakrooms for hours.

The reason we stir in a little hot water at the end of making mayonnaise is to thin it to a smoother consistency and to set the egg yolks. When the egg yolks are set in this fashion, homemade mayonnaise doesn't separate.

Makes 2½ cups

The Good and Plenty Chef's dinner salad reveals an entire evolution in meal salads. In the fifties what we called a chef's salad had canned beets and asparagus. Mushrooms were never to be seen. In the sixties, the canned vegetables turned fresh and mushrooms became essential, followed shortly by sprouts and seeds. In the new vegetable consciousness, the meat disappeared. In the seventies, enter gourmet and esoteric edibles. In the eighties, turkey came back and the greens became escarole and red leaf lettuce. Meanwhile, it's moved from luncheonettes through funky cult cafés and fancy bistros into our homes, and become dinner.

Good & Plenty Chef's Salad

4 cups escarole (about ¾ head)
4 cups red leaf lettuce (about ¾ head)
4½ cups red cabbage (about ¾ pound or ½ medium head)
3 cups alfalfa sprouts (about 6 ounces)
1 large or 2 small carrots (about ¼ pound)
¼ pound mushrooms, preferably shiitake
6 green onions
½ pound cooked ham (about 2 cups)
½ pound cooked turkey (about 3 cups)
12 ounces good Swiss type cheese, preferably Gruyère, Emmentaler, or Jarlsberg
4 tablespoons sunflower seeds

FOR THE DRESSING:

5 tablespoons red wine or sherry vinegar
¼ teaspoon salt
¼ teaspoon freshly ground black pepper
8 tablespoons olive oil

Remove the limp and browned outer leaves from the escarole and lettuce head. Separate the remaining leaves and tear into bite-size pieces. Wash the leaves and spin dry. Place them in a large salad bowl.

Remove the core from the red cabbage. Slice crosswise into thin-as-possible shreds. Arrange the cabbage over the lettuces.

Separate the alfalfa sprouts and sprinkle over the cabbage.

Peel and trim the carrots. Grate them over the sprouts.

Clean and trim the mushrooms. Slice the mushrooms ⅛ inch thick and add to the bowl.

Trim off the root ends and limp green tops from the green onions. Slice into ⅛-inch-thick rounds. Add to the bowl.

Cut the ham and turkey into ½-inch-thick shreds. Mound separately in the center of the salad.

Cut the cheese into strips the same size as the turkey and ham. Mound on one side of the turkey and ham.

Place the sunflower seeds in a small ungreased frying pan. Stir over medium heat until browned, about 3 minutes. Sprinkle over the salad.

To dress the salad, mix together the vinegar, salt, and black pepper. Pour over the salad, then pour on the oil. Toss just before serving.

Farmer's Vegetable Salad with Any Meat or Fish

½ medium cauliflower (about 1 pound)

12 ounces cold cuts such as salami, capocollo, or mortadella, or 3 cups leftover beef, pork, chicken, fish, shrimp, or scallops

12 ounces Swiss type cheese such as Gruyère, Emmentaler, Jarlsberg, or Greek Kasseri, Mexican Cotija, or Italian Provolone, about 3 cups julienned

6 medium bell peppers, preferably a mixture of green, red, and yellow (about 2 pounds)

1 medium red onion (about ½ pound)

¾ cup black olives, preferably Kalamata or Niçoise

1 cup chopped fresh parsley leaves

FOR THE DRESSING:

2 tablespoons Dijon mustard

½ teaspoon salt

½ teaspoon freshly ground black pepper

1 tablespoon chopped fresh oregano leaves or 1 teaspoon dried

½ cup red wine vinegar

½ cup olive oil

24 Little Toasts (page 38)

Bring a pot of water to a boil. Mix together the mustard, salt, pepper, oregano, and vinegar in the bottom of a large salad bowl.

Remove the core from the cauliflower. Cut into bite-size pieces. When the water boils, drop in the cauliflower and cook 1 minute. Drain, and rinse with cold water to cool completely. Pat dry. Place the cauliflower in a large bowl.

Cut whatever cold cuts, meat, or fish you are using into thin strips and add to the bowl.

Cut the cheese into strips the same size as the cold cuts, meat, or fish, and add to the bowl.

Remove the core and seeds from the bell peppers. Cut the peppers lengthwise into ⅛-inch-wide strips. Add to the bowl.

Peel the onion and cut it into ⅛-inch-thick quarter rounds. Add to the bowl.

Add the olives and parsley to the bowl.

Sprinkle on the olive oil and toss.

To serve the salad, arrange it on a large platter or individual plates. Place the Little Toasts around the edges and serve.

NOTES AND AFTERTHOUGHTS

Most people remove and discard cauliflower and broccoli leaves. There is no need to. They are quite tender and tasty.

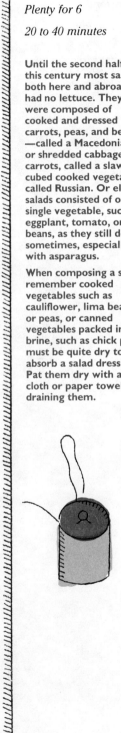

Plenty for 6

20 to 40 minutes

Until the second half of this century most salads, both here and abroad, had no lettuce. They were composed of cooked and dressed carrots, peas, and beans —called a Macedonian— or shredded cabbage and carrots, called a slaw, or cubed cooked vegetables, called Russian. Or else salads consisted of only a single vegetable, such as eggplant, tomato, or beans, as they still do sometimes, especially with asparagus.

When composing a salad, remember cooked vegetables such as cauliflower, lima beans, or peas, or canned vegetables packed in brine, such as chick peas, must be quite dry to absorb a salad dressing. Pat them dry with a dish cloth or paper towel after draining them.

There are three ways to make a warm salad: by dressing just-cooked meats or vegetables while they are still warm; by heating the dressing just before pouring it over and tossing the salad; and by the way we've created here, heating pan juices combined with wine and ladling the hot mixture over the already dressed greens to infuse them with a tangy, meaty flavor.

For warm salads, select the more hearty greens, such as escarole, romaine, curly endive, and spinach, because they stand up under heat. Tender greens, such as butter or red leaf lettuce and cress, wilt into nothingness. Also, hearty lettuces with their sharper taste are a better vehicle for the pungency of hot dressings.

Warm Spicy Sautéed Beef Salad with Lettuce, Mint, and Peanuts

1½ medium onions (about 10 ounces)
2 tablespoons peanut oil
3 garlic cloves
1½ pounds lean beefsteak
¾ cup white wine
1 cup shelled peanuts
3 cups escarole strips (about ½ head)
3 cups romaine strips (about ½ medium head)
3 cups curly endive strips (about ½ head)
3 cups whole mint leaves

FOR THE DRESSING:

4 large garlic cloves
1 teaspoon dry mustard
2 tablespoons lemon juice
¼ teaspoon cayenne pepper
½ teaspoon salt
4 tablespoons red wine vinegar
1 tablespoon chili oil
4 tablespoons peanut oil

Make the dressing first so the onions can marinate in it. Peel the 4 garlic cloves. Press into a large bowl. Add the dry mustard, lemon juice, cayenne, salt, vinegar, chili oil, and the 4 tablespoons peanut oil and mix together.

Peel the onions and cut into ⅛-inch-thick half rounds. Add to the dressing and toss together. Set aside.

Heat the 2 tablespoons peanut oil in a large nonreactive skillet. Peel the 3 garlic cloves and press into the peanut oil.

Place the steak in the skillet and cook until medium rare, 3 to 6 minutes per side, depending on the thickness (see page 188).

Remove the steak to a plate and set aside for the juices to settle.

Add the white wine to the skillet. Bring to a boil and cook 1 minute over high heat. Set the skillet aside.

While the onions marinate and the steak rests, place the peanuts in a small frying pan. Stir over medium heat 2 to 3 minutes, until browned. Medium chop the toasted peanuts. Set aside.

Remove the limp and browned outer leaves from the greens. Cut the remaining leaves crosswise into ¼-inch-wide strips.

Wash and spin dry the greens and mint. Add to the onion mixture.

Cut the steak crosswise into ⅛-inch-thick strips. If the steak was more than ½ inch thick, cut the strips in half the long way to make thinner strips. Add the steak strips and any meat juices to the reserved skillet.

To assemble the salad, toss together the greens, mint leaves, onions, and dressing. Spread the mixture on a large platter.

Heat the white wine, steak juices, and steak strips in the skillet just until the liquid boils.

Arrange the meat over the salad. Pour the liquid over all. Sprinkle the peanuts on top and serve.

NOTES AND AFTERTHOUGHTS
If you don't like too much spice, reduce the amount of cayenne and/or chili oil.

Warm Strip Steak Salad with Spinach, Mushrooms, Sprouts, Pine Nuts, Pumpkin Seeds, and Tomato Vinaigrette

1½ pounds fresh strip steak, or 3 cups leftover steak
3 tablespoons pine nuts
3 tablespoons pumpkin seeds
2 bunches spinach (about 1½ pounds)
¾ pound mushrooms, preferably shiitake
3 cups alfalfa, clover, or radish sprouts, or a mixture (about 6 ounces)

2 cups Tomato Vinaigrette (page 280)

Plenty for 6

20 minutes or less

If using fresh strip steak, cook in a skillet over rock salt until barely medium-rare, 5 to 7 minutes, depending on the thickness (see page 188). Remove the steak to a plate and set aside for the juices to settle while preparing the rest of the salad.

If using leftover steak, take it out of the refrigerator to come to room temperature.

Place the pine nuts and pumpkin seeds in an ungreased frying pan. Stir over low heat about 3 minutes, until browned.

Remove the spinach leaves from the stems, setting aside the larger, tough ones for another dish. Wash the smaller, tender leaves in 2 or 3 changes of cold water. Spin dry.

Clean the mushrooms and trim off the stem ends. Slice the mushrooms ⅛ inch thick.

Cut the steak crosswise into ⅛-inch-thick slices.

To assemble the salad, spread the spinach leaves and sprouts on a large platter. Place the mushrooms on top, and arrange the steak strips over the mushrooms.

Make the Tomato Vinaigrette. Place in a nonreactive saucepan and bring to a boil. Pour the hot dressing over all. Sprinkle the pine nuts and pumpkins seeds over the top and serve.

NOTES AND AFTERTHOUGHTS
This salad is also delicious cold. If using fresh steak for a cold version, cook the steak, and then chill in the refrigerator for at least 1 hour before assembling the salad. Do not heat the dressing.

(continued)

Tomato Vinaigrette

½ **cup onion juice**
½ **cup canned crushed tomatoes in puree**
¼ **teaspoon salt**
¼ **teaspoon freshly ground black pepper**
½ **cup balsamic or red wine vinegar**
¾ **cup olive oil**

Mix together the onion juice, tomatoes, salt, pepper, vinegar, and oil.

NOTES AND AFTERTHOUGHTS

To avoid pureeing the tomatoes or homogenizing the oil, this dressing should not be made in a food processor or mixed with a wire whisk. Gently and briefly stir the ingredients together with a fork.

Warm Marinated Pork Salad with Pimientos, Gorgonzola, and Walnuts

FOR THE MARINADE:

3 tablespoons soy sauce
3 tablespoons walnut oil
3 tablespoons dry white wine
1 teaspoon fresh rosemary leaves or ⅓ teaspoon dried
1 garlic clove

1½ pounds boneless pork, tenderloin, chops, or loin roast, or 6 cups leftover pork roast

¾ pound green beans
12 cups butter or Boston lettuce (about 2 large heads)
2 jars (4 ounces each) sliced pimientos
1 cup walnuts (about 6 ounces)
2 tablespoons peanut oil, for frying
3½ tablespoons balsamic or red wine vinegar
¼ teaspoon salt
¼ teaspoon freshly ground black pepper
1 medium garlic clove
6 ounces Gorgonzola, Bavarian Blue, or Roquefort cheese
½ cup walnut oil

In a small bowl, mix together the soy sauce, the 3 tablespoons walnut oil, wine, and rosemary. Peel the garlic cloves and press into the soy sauce mixture.

Slice the pork into 2-inch-long strips about ¼ inch thick and ½ inch wide. Add the pork to the soy sauce mixture and toss to coat. Set aside to marinate 30 minutes to 1 hour at room temperature.

While the pork marinates, bring a medium pot of water to boil. If the green beans are small and tender, leave them whole. Otherwise, halve them

---

Plenty for 6

30 minutes or so to marinate the pork; 20 minutes or less to assemble the salad

Dressing greens with the hot liquid of a marinade is another innovative way of warming a salad. If the meat is pork or poultry, though, be sure to cook the marinade a few minutes so that the meat juices are not raw.

lengthwise. When the water boils, cook the beans 4 to 6 minutes, until just cooked through but still crunchy. Drain and pat dry on paper towels.

Remove and discard the limp or browned outer leaves from the lettuce. Separate the remaining leaves from the core. Tear into bite-size pieces. Wash the lettuce and spin dry.

Drain the pimientos.

Heat a small ungreased skillet. Add the walnuts and stir over medium heat 2 to 3 minutes, until browned. Remove to a cutting board and medium chop.

To cook the pork, heat the peanut oil in a heavy skillet until the oil smokes. Lift the pork strips out of the marinade, reserving the marinade. Add the pork to the skillet and stir over high heat, 4 minutes for fresh pork, 2 minutes for cooked pork. Remove the skillet from the heat.

Place the reserved marinade in a small saucepan. Bring to a boil. Simmer 5 minutes.

To assemble the salad, place the vinegar, salt, and pepper in the bottom of a large salad bowl. Peel the garlic clove and press it into the vinegar. Mix together with a fork.

Place the lettuce in the salad bowl around the edges of the vinegar mixture. Arrange the green beans and pimientos over the lettuce. Crumble the Gorgonzola into the salad bowl. Arrange the pork strips over the vegetables. Sprinkle the walnuts over the pork. Drizzle the ½ cup walnut oil and the reserved marinade evenly over all. Toss just before serving.

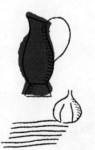

Plenty for 6

20 minutes or less

This "all-season sports salad" is terrific for skiing in New Hampshire, boating near Houston, fishing in Wisconsin, four-wheeling in Colorado, and camping and picnicking anywhere. Salami and potatoes are always available and always satisfying. What's more, it's simple.

Warm Salami, Potato, and Watercress Salad

5 medium red or white potatoes (about 2 pounds)
3 medium green bell peppers (about 1 pound)
3 large bunches watercress (a bit more than 1 pound)
6 ounces sliced Italian dry salami (about 1½ cups julienned)
¼ cup black olives, preferably *Niçoise*
6 tablespoons grated Parmesan, Romano, or aged Asiago cheese

FOR THE DRESSING:

3 tablespoons Dijon mustard
¾ cup balsamic or red wine vinegar
1 cup olive oil

Bring a large pot of water to a boil.

Cut the potatoes into quarters. Cut the quarters crosswise into ¼-inch-thick quarter rounds. When the water boils, cook the potatoes 6 minutes.

While the potatoes cook, remove the seeds and cores from the bell peppers. Cut the peppers into ⅛-inch-wide strips.

In a small container, mix together the mustard, vinegar, and oil for the dressing. Remove half to a bowl large enough to hold the potatoes and pepper strips.

When the potatoes are done, drain. Immediately add them to the bowl with the dressing. Add the bell pepper slices and toss.

Pluck the leaves off the watercress stems. Wash and spin dry.

Cut the salami into ¼-inch-wide strips.

To assemble the salad, spread the watercress leaves across a large platter. Arrange the warm potatoes and green peppers down the center of the watercress, pouring the remaining dressing all around. Arrange the salami strips over the potatoes. Strew the olives around the edges. Sprinkle the grated cheese over all. Serve right away, while the potatoes are still warm.

Lentil Salad with Ham, Belgian Endive, and Feta Cheese

2 cups lentils
8 cups water
¾ pound Belgian endive (about 3 medium heads)
3 tablespoons walnut oil
Salt
2 bunches green onions
1 pound thin-sliced cooked ham (about 4 cups)
8 ounces Feta cheese, preferably Bulgarian or Corsican

FOR THE DRESSING:

6 tablespoons lemon juice
½ teaspoon salt
½ teaspoon freshly ground black pepper
⅔ cup walnut oil
⅔ cup chopped fresh parsley leaves, preferably Italian

Place the lentils and water in a medium saucepan. Bring to a boil and simmer for 10 minutes. Drain into a colander and set aside to drip dry.

While the lentils drain, cut the bottoms off the Belgian endive and separate the leaves down to the core. Reserve the core for a tossed salad. Cut the leaves lengthwise into strips about ¼ inch wide. Place them in a small bowl and toss with the 3 tablespoons walnut oil.

Trim the root ends and limp green tops off the green onions. Slice the onions into thin-as-possible rounds.

Cut the ham into ¼-inch-wide strips.

To make the dressing, mix together the lemon juice, salt, pepper, and ⅔ cup walnut oil.

When the lentils are almost dry, place them in a bowl. Add the green onions, parsley, and dressing. Toss.

To assemble the salad, arrange the endive around the edges of a large platter. Mound the dressed lentils in the center and over the endive. Arrange the ham between the lentils and endive. Crumble the Feta over the top and serve.

NOTES AND AFTERTHOUGHTS

1. For salad, lentils should be cooked only until they are done through but still retain their shape without bursting through their skins. Ten minutes is about right.

2. French lentils, small, spherical, and nutty tasting, are the best. They come in 1-pound boxes or cellophane packages and are available in many specialty food shops. They take a little longer to cook, about 17 minutes after the water boils.

Plenty for 6

20 minutes or less

Pig-by-the-Tail sold so many quarts of lentil salad that Victoria had to keep it in stock daily for 10 years. One day when she arrived to fire up the ovens at 7:30 A.M., there was a man at the door crying, "Lentils, lentils." Deciding that humor was the better part of valor, she one day devised a lentil contest. Whoever could most closely guess the number of lentils in a quart container won. The prize was a whole day in the kitchen helping make the lentil salad, mellowed by champagne, of course. A dapper middle-aged professor won the contest, and showed up on the appointed morning with his own clean apron and chef's hat. He was a devoted amateur chef, and he, Victoria, and her staff ate —you guessed it— excellent lentil salad all day long.

We think of Abraham, Isaac, and the lamb; mares eat oats and does eat oats but little lambs eat ivy; lambs on spits; and Mary had a little one. But we rarely think of lamb for salad. Yet it's divine, a natural with almost any vegetable, herb, or dressing. This salad is also the answer to a hard question: what to do with leftover lamb.

To make the final preparation of this lamb salad with beans speedier, you can cook the beans the day before or in the morning and have them ready for the dressing and the lamb.

Leftover Lamb Roast Salad with White Beans, Jalapeño Peppers, and Tomatoes

2 cups small white navy beans
Water
1 teaspoon salt
4 medium jalapeño peppers
1 small tomato (about ¼ pound)
2 medium garlic cloves
1½ pounds leftover lamb roast (about 6 cups)
12 whole butter or Boston lettuce leaves
⅔ cup chopped fresh parsley leaves, preferably Italian
2 teaspoons thinly shredded fresh sage leaves, or ½ teaspoon dried rubbed sage
¼ teaspoon salt
¼ teaspoon freshly ground black pepper
¾ cup olive oil

Place the beans in a large pot. Add water to cover by 2 inches and bring to a boil. Remove the pot from the heat and set aside 1 hour to soak the beans.

Drain the soaked beans and rinse well. Return the beans to the pot and add 3 quarts of water and the 1 teaspoon salt. Bring to a boil. Reduce the heat to low, and simmer 55 minutes, or until the beans are cooked through but still retain their shape with the skins intact.

Drain the beans in a colander and set aside to drip dry.

Cut the stems off the jalapeño peppers. Mince the peppers. Cut the tomato into ¼-inch dice. Peel the garlic cloves.

Cut the lamb into strips of any length and about ⅛ inch thick and ¼ inch wide.

Wash and spin dry the lettuce leaves.

Place the beans in a large bowl. Press the garlic and add to the bowl. Add the tomato, parsley, sage, the ¼ teaspoon salt, black pepper, half of the jalapeños, and ½ cup of the olive oil. Toss.

Place the lamb in another mixing bowl. Add the remaining jalapeños and the remaining ¼ cup olive oil.

To assemble the salad, arrange the lettuce leaves around the edge of a large platter. Spread the lamb strips over the lettuce. Mound the beans in the center of the platter and serve.

NOTES AND AFTERTHOUGHTS

White beans take a while to prepare. But the advantage is, as long as you're at it, you can make enough to have for soup, a side dish, or more bean salad.

Chicken Salad with Red Cabbage, Snow Peas, Broccoli, and Toasted Almonds

2 pounds fresh chicken, preferably thighs and legs, or 2¾ cups leftover chicken
2 tablespoons Dijon mustard, if using fresh chicken
Salt
Freshly ground black pepper
½ pound snow or Chinese peas
2 cups broccoli florets (from about 10 ounces broccoli)
½ medium red cabbage (about ½ pound)
1 teaspoon sesame oil
⅔ cup sliced almonds (about 2½ ounces)

FOR THE DRESSING:

3 tablespoons Dijon mustard
3 tablespoons Basic Mayonnaise (page 275)
3 tablespoons soy sauce
4 tablespoons red wine vinegar
6 tablespoons peanut oil

Plenty for 6

Less than 20 minutes with leftovers; 40 to 60 minutes with fresh chicken

If using fresh chicken, heat the oven to 425° F. Place the chicken pieces in a baking pan and brush the tops with 1 tablespoon of the mustard. Lightly season with salt and pepper. Roast 15 minutes.

Turn the chicken pieces and coat the other side with the remaining 1 tablespoon mustard. Roast 20 minutes more.

Remove to a plate. Chill in the refrigerator at least 30 minutes or as long as overnight.

Remove the skin from the chicken. Pull the meat off the bones and cut into bite-size pieces.

Bring a large pot of water to a boil. Trim the snow peas. Cut the broccoli florets into bite-size pieces.

When the water boils, drop in the peas and broccoli. Cook 1 minute. Drain in a colander and rinse under cold water to cool completely. Spread on paper towels and pat dry.

Remove the core from the red cabbage. Cut the cabbage into thin-as-possible shreds.

Heat the sesame oil in a small skillet. Add the almonds and stir constantly over medium-high heat until browned, 1 minute or less.

To make the dressing, place the mustard and mayonnaise in a small bowl. Stir together with a whisk until smooth. Very slowly stir in the soy sauce. Whisk in the vinegar and peanut oil.

To assemble the salad, spread the cabbage over a large platter. Arrange the broccoli and peas over the red cabbage. Mound the chicken in the center. Pour the dressing over all. Sprinkle on the toasted almonds and serve.

Turkey Salad with Beets, Spinach, Hard-Boiled Egg, and Curried Sour Cream Dressing

Plenty for 6

40 to 60 minutes

If you're going to peel hard-boiled eggs and you want them smooth and pretty, they should not be too fresh. The fresher an egg is, the harder it is to peel; the older it is, the easier.

1 pound fresh turkey, tenderloin or thigh, or 3 cups leftover cooked turkey
Salt, freshly ground black pepper, and 1 teaspoon curry powder, if using
   fresh turkey
2 bunches beets
4 eggs
1 medium red or white onion (about 7 ounces)
2 bunches spinach (about 1½ pounds)

FOR THE DRESSING:

1½ cups sour cream
¾ cup heavy cream
3 tablespoons lemon juice
1 tablespoon curry powder
½ teaspoon salt

If using fresh turkey, heat the oven to 425°F. Lightly sprinkle the turkey with salt, pepper, and 1 teaspoon curry powder. Place the turkey in a baking pan. Roast 20 minutes for tenderloins, or 45 minutes for thighs.

Remove and let rest for 30 minutes for the juices to settle.

Trim the green tops off the beets, cutting them 1 inch above the root. Place the beets in a pot and add water to cover. Bring to a boil. Reduce the heat and simmer 40 minutes to 1 hour, depending on the size of the beets, or until tender when pierced with a fork.

Drain, cool, and peel the beets. Cut the beets in half if they are small, or into quarters if they are large. Cut the halves or quarters crosswise into ⅛-inch-thick slices.

Place the eggs in a small saucepan and add water to cover. Bring to a boil. Cover the pot, turn off the heat, and let sit 7 minutes if the eggs are large or 9 minutes if they are extra large. Immediately drain the eggs. Rinse under cold water and peel them.

Cut the turkey into strips about 1 inch long and ¼ inch wide.

Peel the onion and cut into ⅛-inch-thick quarter rounds.

Remove the spinach leaves from the stems, setting aside the larger, tough leaves for another dish. Wash the smaller, tender leaves in 2 or 3 changes of cold water. Spin dry.

To make the dressing, place the sour cream in a bowl and stir with a whisk until smooth. Slowly whisk in the heavy cream. Whisk in the lemon juice, curry powder, and salt.

To assemble the salad, spread the spinach leaves over a large platter. Arrange the beet and onion slices over the spinach. Mound the turkey in the center. Quarter the eggs, and arrange around the turkey. Drizzle the dressing over all and serve.

Shredded Duck or Chicken Salad with Papaya, Jícama, Mint, and Cashews

6 ounces snow or Chinese peas
1 cooked duck or large chicken
2 large ripe papayas
1½ pounds jícama
2 tablespoons thinly shredded fresh mint leaves
3 tablespoons cashew nuts (about 2 ounces)

FOR THE DRESSING:

½ cup lime juice
1 cup peanut oil

Bring a pot of water to boil. Snap off the stem ends of the peas. When the water boils, drop in the peas and cook 1 minute. Drain and rinse under cold water to cool completely. Pat dry.

Remove the skin from the duck or chicken and separate the meat from the bones. Cut the meat into pieces about 1 inch long and ¼ inch wide.

Peel the papayas. Cut them in half lengthwise and remove the seeds. Cut the halves crosswise into thin half rounds.

Peel the jícama. Grate through the large holes of a hand grater or with the grating blade of a food processor. Place the jícama in a bowl and toss with the mint leaves.

Place the cashews in a small ungreased frying pan and stir over medium-high heat until the cashews are browned, about 3 minutes. Rough chop the cashews.

To make the dressing, mix together the lime juice and peanut oil in a small bowl.

To assemble the salad, arrange the papaya slices down the center of a large platter. Mound the jícama on one side and the shredded duck or chicken on the other. Arrange the peas around the jícama and duck or chicken. Pour the dressing over all. Top with the toasted cashews.

NOTES AND AFTERTHOUGHTS

1. When purchasing a cooked duck or chicken, buy one that is smoked or plain roasted, not barbecued.

2. If cooking your own bird, roast it according to the instructions on page 239 for chicken or page 248 for duck (omitting the glaze). Or, sauté cut-up pieces according to the instructions on page 166. Chill in the refrigerator at least 1 hour or up to 2 days.

Plenty for 6

20 to 40 minutes

The family story of jícama shows you can be fooled by appearances. It looks like a rutabaga, a potato, or a turnip. In fact it is not an *umbelliferae* at all, but a legume, related to peas, beans, and lentils. As its botanical name, *Pachyrhizus erosus*, implies, it is an irregular, thick-skinned root, meaning you must peel its tough skin to get to the prize. Its taste most closely resembles water chestnut, only sweeter, and it is especially good grated or sliced raw. Mint and lime juice particularly enhance its flavor.

Plenty for 6

20 minutes or less

One day we were shopping for inspiration in an open-air market. What to put on the table for our families that night without really having to cook? We spied a bin of ripe yellow-orange kumquats situated not too far from a display of baby vegetables that included the tiniest turnips we had ever seen. What would go with both? Luckily, across the street was a deli that carried smoked duck. The Napa cabbage looked fresh, and the sesame seeds in the pantry at home were a natural. We tied it all together with a walnut-oil-based dressing, reinforcing the combination's Oriental quality with a touch of soy. And no cooking!

Duck Salad with Napa Cabbage, Turnips, and Kumquats

1 smoked or Peking style duck

2 small or 1 large head Napa (Chinese) cabbage (about 3 pounds)
2 medium turnips (about ½ pound)
18 kumquats (about ½ pound)
4 green onions
2 tablespoons sesame seed

FOR THE DRESSING:

6 tablespoons red wine vinegar
4 tablespoons soy sauce
¼ teaspoon salt
¼ teaspoon freshly ground black pepper
1 cup walnut oil

Remove the skin from the duck, cut the meat off the bones, then slice the meat into shreds.

Cut the Napa cabbage lengthwise in half. Cut the halves crosswise into ¼-inch-wide strips.

Peel the turnips. Cut into thin strips.

Cut the kumquats into ⅛-inch-thick rounds.

Trim the root ends and limp green tops off the green onions. Cut the onions lengthwise into thin shreds.

Place the sesame seed in a small ungreased frying pan over medium heat. Stir constantly until browned, about 3 minutes.

To make the dressing, mix together the vinegar, soy sauce, salt, pepper, and walnut oil.

To assemble the salad, spread the Napa cabbage over a large platter. Arrange the turnip strips over the cabbage. Mound the duck in the center. Strew the kumquats and green onions over the top. Pour the dressing over all, sprinkle on the sesame seeds, and serve.

NOTES AND AFTERTHOUGHTS

Gourmet delicatessens and Chinese markets are the best bets for finding cooked duck.

Fish and Avocado Salad with Crispy Hot Potatoes and Tomato Onion Rémoulade

1½ pounds fresh sea bass, swordfish, or halibut steaks or fillets, or 6 cups leftover
    cooked fish
2 tablespoons butter or olive oil, salt and pepper, and ½ cup dry white wine, if using
    fresh fish

3 medium white or russet potatoes (about 1¼ pounds)
1 tablespoon olive oil
8 cups curly endive (about 1⅓ heads)
2 large or 3 small avocados
2 medium red bell peppers (about ¾ pound)

Tomato Onion Rémoulade (page 290)

Plenty for 6

20 to 40 minutes

Heat the oven to 500°F.

If using fresh fish, place it in a baking pan. Dot the fish with the butter, pour on the white wine, and sprinkle with salt and pepper. Cover the dish with aluminum foil, pinching the edges to seal.

Cook fish steaks or ½-inch-thick fillets 12 minutes, or ¾-inch-thick steaks or fillets 16 minutes. Remove the baked fish from the oven and let rest to allow the juices to settle while preparing the other ingredients.

If using leftover cooked fish, remove from the refrigerator to come to room temperature.

While the fish cooks and cools, prepare the potatoes. Cut the potatoes into ¼-inch-thick strips. Pour the olive oil onto a baking sheet or baking pan large enough to hold the potatoes in a single uncrowded layer. Spread the potatoes across the pan. Place in the oven and bake 10 minutes. Turn with a spatula and bake 15 minutes more, stirring every 5 minutes.

Meanwhile, tear the curly endive into bite-size pieces. Wash and spin dry.

Quarter the avocados and discard the seeds. Peel each quarter and cut into thin slices.

Remove the seeds and cores from the bell peppers. Cut the peppers into ⅛-inch thick strips.

Make the Tomato Onion Rémoulade.

To assemble the salad, spread the curly endive across a large platter. Arrange the hot potatoes over the greens. Pile the avocado slices in the 4 corners. Break the fish into large chunks. Mound the chucks in the center. Strew the red pepper slices on top. Pour the rémoulade over all, and serve.

(continued)

Makes about 1 cup

Tomato Onion Rémoulade

½ medium onion (about 4 ounces)
2 tablespoons canned crushed tomatoes in puree
2 tablespoons Dijon mustard
2 tablespoons Basic Mayonnaise (page 275)
2 tablespoons red wine vinegar
6 tablespoons olive oil
2 tablespoons chopped cilantro or fresh chervil leaves

Peel the onion and grate through the small holes of a hand grater held over a bowl until you have 1 tablespoon onion juice.

Add the tomatoes, mustard, mayonnaise, vinegar, and oil to the bowl. Blend until smooth. Stir in the cilantro.

NOTES AND AFTERTHOUGHTS

If you are not inclined to make a whole batch of homemade mayonnaise, the amount in this dressing is small enough that bottled mayonnaise will do just fine.

Surf and Turf Salad on a Bed of Grated Zucchini with Green Goddess Dressing

1 pound fresh steak, or 2 cups leftover cooked steak
1 bay leaf
1 teaspoon chili flakes
½ cup white wine
3 cups water
1 pound medium-size raw shrimp
2 cups shelled peas (from about 2 pounds in their shells)
6 medium zucchini (about 1½ pounds)

2 cups Green Goddess Dressing (page 292)

Plenty for 6

20 to 40 minutes

For anyone who has ever been disappointed by the taste of a raw zucchini, the trick is to grate it! Grated raw zucchini is subtle and full of flavors that usually only come out when you sauté it, and it makes a fanciful and beautiful bed for a salad.

If you are using fresh steak, cook it according to the instructions on page 188. Remove the steak to a plate and let rest at least 15 minutes to allow the juices to settle.

If using leftover cooked steak, remove it from the refrigerator to come to room temperature.

To cook the shrimp, combine the bay leaf, chili flakes, white wine, and water in a large nonreactive saucepan. Bring to a boil. When the liquid boils, drop in the shrimp and cook 3 minutes. Drain the shrimp and let cool. When cool enough to handle, peel. If they have a sand vein, remove with a sharp paring knife.

Bring a small pot of water to boil. When the water boils, drop in the peas. Cook 1 minute and drain right away. Rinse under cold water to cool. Pat dry with paper towels.

Trim off the ends from the zucchini. Grate the zucchini through the large holes of a hand grater.

Make the Green Goddess Dressing.

To assemble the salad, slice the steak crosswise into thin strips. Spread the zucchini across a large platter. Sprinkle on the peas. Arrange the shrimp in the middle and the steak slices around the shrimp. Pour the dressing over all and serve.

NOTES AND AFTERTHOUGHTS
Classic "Surf and Turf" means lobster—from the sea—and steak—from the land. That would be good, too, but fresh shrimp is somewhat less costly and considerably more available than fresh lobster.

(continued)

Green Goddess Dressing

Makes 2 cups

In the home cooking of our youth, both our mothers commonly took pickle relish and ketchup and added them to mayonnaise to produce Thousand Island dressing. For special occasions Victoria's mother also made Green Goddess Dressing. Green Goddess Dressing is a rarity nowadays. But for a recent special occasion we decided to try it on a shrimp and beef combination, although it traditionally dresses a green salad. The result was divine. Green Goddess should return to the Pantheon.

12 anchovy fillets, preferably salt-packed
3 green onions
1 tablespoon chopped fresh tarragon leaves or 1 teaspoon dried
1 cup chopped fresh parsley leaves
2 egg yolks
4 tablespoons tarragon vinegar
½ teaspoon salt
2 cups olive oil
½ cup heavy cream

Chop the anchovy fillets.

Trim off the root ends and limp green tops from the green onions. Rough chop the onions.

To make the dressing with a food processor, combine the anchovies, green onions, tarragon, parsley, egg yolks, vinegar, and salt. Process until well chopped. With the machine running, slowly add the olive oil and process until well blended. Stir in the heavy cream.

To make the dressing by hand, mince the anchovies, green onions, parsley, and tarragon with a chef's knife. Place in a bowl, add the egg yolks, vinegar, and salt. Beat with a wire whisk or electric mixer until well blended. Slowly add the olive oil. Stir in the heavy cream.

Crab or Lobster Salad with Tarragon and Shallot Poppy Seed Dressing

2 pounds crabmeat, or 6 small or 3 large live lobsters (1¼ to 2½ pounds each)
12 cups mixed tender young salad greens, including some arugula, if possible
1 cup whole fresh tarragon leaves
12 tender celery ribs, from the centers of 2 bunches

FOR THE DRESSING:

2 medium shallots
½ cup lemon juice
2 tablespoons poppy seed
⅔ cup olive oil

24 Little Toasts (page 38)

Plenty for 6

20 to 40 minutes

■f using lobsters, cook and clean them according to the instructions on page 99. Cut the lobster tails and claw meat crosswise into ¼-inch-thick chunks. Place the green liver, pink roe, and white marrow in a small bowl and set aside.

Wash the salad greens and spin dry. Place the greens and tarragon in a large salad bowl.

Cut the celery ribs lengthwise in half. Then cut crosswise into ⅛-inch-wide slivers. Sprinkle the celery over the greens.

Mound the crab or lobster in the center of the bowl.

To make the dressing, peel the shallots and then mince. In a small bowl, mix together the shallots, lemon juice, poppy seed, and oil

Pour the dressing over the salad and toss. Arrange the Little Toasts around the salad. Serve with the reserved liver, roe, and marrow on the side.

DELIGHTFUL
DO-ABLE
DESSERTS

Melon Fruit Bowl with Peach Sherbet

Papaya Filled with Raspberry Sherbet, Mint, and Lime

Fresh Fruit Pie in Quick Cookie Crust
  Apple Pie
  Cherry Pie
  Cherry Berry Pie
  Peach Pie
  Variations
  Quick Cookie Crust

Fresh Fruit Crisp

Fresh Grape Parfait

Poached Pears in Blush and Berry Sauce

Orange Slices Poached in White Wine, Cardamom, and Bay with Toasted Coconut

Sweet Sesame and Brown Sugar-Crusted Figs with Mascarpone Cheese

Alice Olson's Swedish Wedding Cookies

Lace Cookies with Oatmeal, Garlic, and Pine Nuts

Quick Cornmeal Shortcake with Fresh Berries and Cream

Quick Sponge Cake with Kahlúa Cream
  Variations
  Scotch Syrup

Burnt Sugar and Blue Cornmeal Cake with Thickened Cream Topping
  Thickened Cream Topping

Icebox Whipped Cream Cookie Roll

Chocolate Obsession

Mascarpone Cheese Pie in a Chocolate Cookie Crust

Sweet Dessert Taco

Ice Cream Toppings
  Bourbon Pecan Caramel Cream
  Burgundy Wine and Thyme Sauce
  Chocolate Kahlúa Macadamia Sauce
  Strawberry Orange Sauce
  Other Toppings and Sauces for Ice Cream

The end of the meal. It's been a yeoman's day, now work is over, our hunger satisfied. Time to have something a touch special. Time for dessert.

But who wants to work for that last savor? For dessert, we want a delight, a surprise, but without much effort. Easy and do-able are the dictates. And with our minds turned to light and refreshing these days, we want a sweet taste that does not cloy with sugary heaviness.

The solutions are pies with no crust to fret over, fruit you lightly poach, ice cream made extra special with a dollop of decadently different homemade topping. Or there are tortillas to toss and turn into a sweet taco, grapes spun into a parfait, figs crusted in sesame and brown sugar and proffered warm with a bowl of the freshest cream cheese.

As with appetizers, for desserts we take full advantage of many of the superior packaged products available today. We employ cookies—Pepperidge Farm or bakery ones with no preservatives—to make crusts, crisps, and cakes. (Though for cookies alone we whip up a quick batch of our own, homemade.) We use store-bought ice creams—there are so many good ones—and top them with a quickly executed concoction of fruit, chocolate, or caramel.

We are firm advocates of fresh fruit. What could be better to crown the day than an offering from the bounty of our orchards? We might embellish the berries with cream, the apples with nuts, the oranges with bay leaf and coconut, but fruit remains the core of most of our desserts.

EQUIPMENT

It is helpful to have a food processor and electric mixer for dessert making. The food processor makes quick work of cookie and pie dough mixing, and is almost indispensable for chopping nuts. It is not the tool to use, however, for whipping cream, because it turns the cream into butter almost instantaneously. For whipping cream, an electric mixer is handy unless you enjoy the zen of beating the cream to peaks with a wire whisk.

A *cake rack* is necessary for the important step of cooling a cake. If you cool a cake on a plate, the bottom steams and becomes soggy.

A *rubber spatula* is helpful for scooping batter, parfaits, or toppings out of their mixing bowls or saucepans.

Last but not least, one or two *baking sheets* makes cookie baking easy. The best kind of baking sheet is the Cushion-aire. It is constructed with two sheets of metal that allow for an insulating layer of warm air between. This eliminates hot spots and ensures even browning. ■

Melon Fruit Bowl with Peach Sherbet

Plenty for 6

20 minutes or less

1 medium to large honeydew melon (about 4 pounds)
3 cups (about 2 baskets) raspberries
3 to 4 cups blueberries (about 2 baskets), or 6 to 7 cups mixed berries
¼ cup rum or tequila
1 pint peach sherbet

Chill the honeydew melon and all the berries.

Just before serving, halve the honeydew, and remove the seeds. With a round soup spoon, scoop the melon pulp into bite size pieces, leaving the pieces in the half melon shells.

Divide the berries and rum between the melon halves. Spoon bite-size scoops of sherbet over the fruit. Toss the ingredients together.

Place a half honeydew at each end of the table. Bring spoons and bowls for serving.

NOTES AND AFTERTHOUGHTS

If the melon and berries turn out to be disappointingly unsweet, puree 1 cup of the berries with 2 tablespoons powdered sugar. Add half the puree to each melon bowl. Or, if you happen to have a fruit syrup or leftover plum syrup from canned plums, add ¼ cup to each melon half.

Papaya Filled with Raspberry Sherbet, Mint, and Lime

Plenty for 6

20 minutes or less

Papayas are ready to eat when they are deep yellow or orange all over with no green spots and they give easily to a gentle press. With luck you can pick up ripe papayas the day you want to serve the dessert. If the papayas in the store are underripe, just leave them out of the refrigerator for 2 to 5 days until they are ready.

3 ripe papayas
1 large or 2 small limes
2 pints raspberry sherbet
6 small mint sprigs

Halve the papayas lengthwise and scoop out the seeds.

Cut the lime into 6 wedges.

Fill each papaya half with raspberry sherbet. Decorate with a wedge of lime and a mint sprig. Serve immediately.

NOTES AND AFTERTHOUGHTS

1. We used to make this dessert with boysenberry sherbet, which not only tastes wonderful, but with its purple color against the papaya looks terrific. Mysteriously, ready-made boysenberry sherbet seems to have disappeared, so now we use raspberry.

2. Lime is best with papaya, but if limes are not in season when you serve this dessert, lemons will do.

FRESH FRUIT PIE IN QUICK COOKIE CRUST

You could probably divide the nation by who likes apple pie better and who likes cherry pie better. How about rhubarb, peach, or berry? Trouble is, who has time to make a pie nowadays, for one thing, what about that crust? . . . unless someone could invent a way to do it quick and easy. Now here it is. The three-minute crust. We make it with packaged cookies, and they turn into an irresistible golden-edged, flaky pie shell. The fillings hardly take more preparation than washing and slicing the fruit, and they bubble up with an inticing aroma in 40 minutes, just enough time to serve, eat, and clear away the main meal.

Apple Pie

4 medium Pippin, Granny Smith, McIntosh, or other good pie apple (about 1½ pounds or 5 cups when sliced)
1 tablespoon brandy
1 tablespoon lemon juice
2 tablespoons granulated sugar
4 tablespoons (½ stick) butter

One 9-inch Quick Cookie Crust (page 301)

Heat the oven to 400°F.

Wash the apples. Cut into quarters and remove the cores. Cut the quarters crosswise into ⅛-inch-thick slices. Place the apple slices in a bowl. Add the brandy, lemon juice, and sugar and toss together.

Fill the Quick Cookie Crust with the apple mixture. Cut the butter into small pieces and dot over the top of the apples. Cover the pie with foil.

Bake 25 minutes. Remove the foil and bake to 10 to 15 minutes more, until the apples are soft and the crust is browned around the edges.

Serve warm or at room temperature.

(continued)

For thickening pie fillings or sauces we use arrowroot. Unlike flour and cornstarch, arrowroot imparts no flavor of its own to whatever you are cooking, nor does it leave a cloudy color. Arrowroot is a pure root starch, not a grain derivative, and therefore does the job of thickening in small quantity and without any simmering.

Should you not have any arrowroot on hand at the moment, you can use flour or cornstarch to thicken the fruit pies. Use 1 tablespoon of either per 1 teaspoon of arrowroot. The fillings will have a somewhat muddier taste and color.

If you prefer a traditional pastry crust, use the recipe for Quick Pastry Dough on page 263, adding 1 tablespoon granulated sugar if you like the crust sweet.

For one 9-inch pie

20 minutes or less to prepare
40 minutes to cook

We don't like using lots of sugar on fresh fruit. We rely on a touch of sugar complemented by the punch of a distinctive liquor. For apples we use brandy. Brandies from different grapes and regions have different tastes. The most famous are Cognac and Armagnac, from the districts of the same names in France. Greek, Italian, and California brandies also have distinct flavors. Each brandy adds its own spark and aroma to your apple pie.

There's no need to peel the apples for pie (or much else for that matter). Unpeeled apple slices retain their integrity and don't turn into applesauce.

Cherry Pie

4 cups pitted cherries
2 tablespoons white zinfandel or Marsala wine, or kirsch
2 tablespoons granulated sugar
2 teaspoons arrowroot

One 9-inch Quick Cookie Crust (page 301)

Heat the oven to 400°F.

Combine the cherries, wine, sugar, and arrowroot in a bowl and toss together.

Fill the Quick Cookie Crust with the cherry mixture.

Bake 40 minutes, until the juices are bubbling up and the edges of the crust are browned.

Serve warm or at room temperature.

Cherry Berry Pie

2 cups pitted cherries
2 cups boysenberries, blackberries, or olallieberries
2 tablespoons tawny or ruby port
2 tablespoons granulated sugar
2 teaspoons arrowroot

One 9-inch Quick Cookie Crust (page 301)

Heat the oven to 400°F.

Combine the cherries, berries, port, sugar, and arrowroot in a bowl. Toss together to mix well.

Fill the Quick Cookie Crust with the fruit mixture. Bake 40 minutes.

Serve warm or at room temperature.

Peach Pie

4 medium peaches (about 1½ pounds or 5 cups when sliced)
2 tablespoons Curaçao or rum
2 tablespoons granulated sugar
2 teaspoons arrowroot

One 9-inch Quick Cookie Crust (page 301)

For one 9-inch pie

20 minutes or less to prepare
40 minutes to cook

Kirsch is a type of brandy made from cherries. White Marsala is a blended dessert wine with a base of white wine and baked grape must. It originated in Sicily and is particularly beloved by Italian cooks for adding a sweet accent to dishes. Both work nicely to that effect with cherries.

For one 9-inch pie

20 minutes or less to prepare
40 minutes to cook

Port is a heady, rich dessert wine made by fortifying wine grapes with brandy so that fermentation, which converts sugar into alcohol, is stopped and the wine stays sweet. Ruby port is a young wine, fruity and sweet. Tawny port, through aging, becomes a golden, tawny color with a more refined sweetness.

For one 9-inch pie

20 minutes or less to prepare
40 minutes to cook

Heat the oven to 400°F.

Peel the peaches. Cut in half and remove the pits. Cut each half in half again, then cut the quarters crosswise into ¼-inch-thick slices.

In a bowl, combine the peaches, liquor, sugar, and arrowroot and toss together.

Fill the Quick Cookie Crust with the peach mixture. Bake 35 to 40 minutes, until the liquid is bubbling and the edges of the crust are browned.

Serve warm or at room temperature.

VARIATIONS

ALL BERRY: Use the Cherry Berry Pie recipe using all one type or a mixture of berries (except strawberries or raspberries, which do not bake well) instead of half cherries.

RHUBARB: Use 4 cups thin-sliced rhubarb. Follow the Cherry Berry Pie recipe.

RHUBARB AND CHERRIES OR BERRIES: Mix 2 cups sliced rhubarb with 2 cups cherries or berries. Follow the Cherry Berry Pie recipe.

RHUBARB AND APPLE: Use 2 cups sliced rhubarb and mix with 3 cups sliced apples. Use the Apple Pie recipe.

PEACH AND APRICOT: Use 2 cups sliced apricots mixed with 2 cups sliced peaches. Follow the Peach Pie recipe.

Quick Cookie Crust

**1 package Pepperidge Farm Almond Supreme or Lemon Nut Crunch cookies, or
about 8 ounces other good almond or lemon butter cookies**
6 tablespoons butter

Place the cookies and butter in a food processor and process until the cookies are crumbled and the mixture is well blended. Or, crumble the cookies with a rolling pin, place the cookie crumbs in a bowl, and work in the butter with your fingers.

Press the mixture into a 9-inch pie plate, taking care to cover the bottom and sides.

Chill the cookie crust while preparing the filling.

NOTES AND AFTERTHOUGHTS

Check the crust after the pie has been in the oven 25 minutes. If the edge of the crust is getting too browned before the pie is finished baking, cover with a strip of aluminum foil.

Both Curacao and rum are spirits from the West Indies. Rum is produced from one of the major crops, sugar cane, which was probably brought to the islands by Columbus on his second voyage to the New World. Curaçao is made from another major crop, oranges. The Curaçao oranges are a derivative of Seville oranges, brought to the island via the Spanish even though the island was Dutch. Grand Marnier and Cointreau, two French made versions of Curaçao, and the generic Triple Sec, are equally good orange liqueurs. Curaçao and rum separately or mixed together are delicious with peaches.

When grandmother used to make an apple crisp, she blended flour, butter, and sugar for the topping. It was good, but it wasn't Amaretti. Crunchy, toothsome Italian Amaretti make an incredibly fast crisp topping, better than you ever tasted.

The reason to drive south and west out of London or ferry over to Ireland isn't just to see the great stone circles or the great cathedrals or to wander Dublin's cobbled roads and misty parks. It's the cream!

As you wind out from Kent and Surrey, the cream gets thicker and thicker. By the time you reach the Devon coast, the people make no bones about it. They call it "clotted cream" and slather it over scones. At Penzance in obstinate Cornwall, you wonder why the pirates ever sailed off when at home they could sate themselves on buttery cream as rich as doubloons.

In Ireland, a friend was given a pot of cream "for pudding" as a welcoming gift on her first day of field work in a small village. She thanked the people, but remarked that in her present itinerant state she had no mixer or whisk with which to whip it. The villagers looked at her as if she were as naive as a lass, and she with three children. Just a fork, they told her. In four turns of her fork, the cream was whipped stiff and the children ate it like lollipops.

2 pounds apples, peaches, pears, or rhubarb (about 6 to 7 cups when sliced)
1 tablespoon sugar
1 tablespoon lemon juice
1 small box (4.4 ounces or 125 grams) Amaretti cookies (about 2 cups crumbled)
8 tablespoons (1 stick) butter, at room temperature

1½ cups heavy cream

Heat the oven to 375°F.

Cut the fruit into quarters. Remove the cores or pits. Cut the quarters crosswise into ⅛-inch-thick slices. If using rhubarb, trim the stalks and cut crosswise into ⅛-inch-thick slices.

Place the fruit in a 2-quart baking dish. Add the sugar and lemon juice to the fruit and toss.

Crush the cookies in a food processor or with a rolling pin until about the size of popcorn kernels. Add the butter and mix in.

Spread the cookie crumb mixture over the fruit.

Bake 45 minutes.

To serve, spoon into bowls. Pour some heavy cream over each portion.

NOTES AND AFTERTHOUGHTS

≈ If you haven't remembered to take the butter out of the refrigerator in time for it to be room temperature, you can use a microwave oven to soften it. It takes about 30 seconds.

Fresh Grape Parfait

1½ pounds seedless red grapes (about 3¾ cups)
⅔ cup pecan halves or pieces
⅓ cup red currant jelly
¼ cup white zinfandel or rosé wine
3 teaspoons arrowroot
1½ cups heavy cream

Wash the grapes and fine chop in a food processor or puree through a food mill. Fine chop ⅓ cup pecans in a food processor or by hand.

Combine the pecans and grapes in a small nonreactive saucepan. Add the jelly and wine and bring to a boil. Stir in the arrowroot and cook over medium heat 2 minutes, or until slightly thickened.

Remove the mixture to a bowl. Cover with plastic wrap and chill at least 2 hours or overnight.

When ready to serve, place the remaining ⅓ cup pecans in a small ungreased frying pan. Stir over medium-high heat about 3 minutes, until browned. Fine chop the toasted pecans in a food processor or with a chef's knife.

Whip the cream until soft peaks form. Place about 2 tablespoons of the whipped cream in the bottom of a glass. Spoon a generous ½ cup of the grape mixture over the cream. Top with another dollop of whipped cream. Sprinkle some of the toasted pecans over the top of each parfait and serve.

Plenty for 6

20 minutes or less plus 2 hours chilling time

Almost everywhere people grow grapes they make a quick grape pudding with the overflow from their crops, particularly with the grapes left long on the vine and made even sweeter by languishing in the sun. They tramp the dusty vineyards, big leaves now dry and crumbly, pick the last bunches, seed them, and cook them with sugar. With grapes from the market, anyone, not just those in vineyard farmhouses, can make a fresh grape pudding. The advent of seedless table grapes, such as the delicious Red Flame, make this derivative parfait still quicker. A few scoops of cream between the purple or green layers and you will have another super-fast dessert.

Pears of every type should be picked from the tree or market bin while still firm and ripened at home at an even temperature. They are ready to eat when they give to a light press around the stem, but are not at all soft to the touch. Our first choice for poaching are Comice pears, which are available from October to May. Their complex winy taste imparts a particularly fruity essence to the sauce. They have less "sand grain" in them than many other pears— they are smooth as satin on the tongue. And they don't surrender their shape while simmering in the blush and berries.

The white zinfandels— most of which are actually pink—are slightly too sweet for dinner but make wonderful light dessert drinking and dessert making wines. Sometimes called "blush," they are available now from most of the major California wine growers. They are inexpensive enough that even the good ones are affordable both for cooking and sipping.

Poached Pears in Blush and Berry Sauce

1 bottle white zinfandel ("blush") or rosé wine
¾ cup granulated sugar
6 whole allspice berries
6 ripe but still firm pears
1½ cups fresh or frozen boysenberries
1 tablespoon lemon juice
3 tablespoons sliced almonds

Combine the wine and sugar in a nonreactive medium saucepan. Smash the allspice berries with a hammer or mallet and add to the wine. Bring the mixture to a boil. Cook 2 minutes to dissolve the sugar.

Peel the pears. Drop them into the boiling wine sauce. Poach over medium heat 15 minutes, turning 2 or 3 times to cook all around, or until the pears give a little when pressed. Remove the pears to a bowl and set aside while finishing the sauce.

While the pears cook, puree the boysenberries in a blender or food processor or through a food mill. After removing the pears, add the boysenberries and lemon juice to the wine sauce and cook 7 to 10 minutes over medium heat, until slightly thickened. Pour the sauce over the pears.

Just before serving, toast the almond slices in an ungreased frying pan, stirring over medium heat until browned.

Sprinkle the toasted almonds over the pears. Serve the pears chilled or warm.

NOTES AND AFTERTHOUGHTS

There's no need to halve and core the pears. It's extra work, and when you core them, they break apart during handling and cooking.

Orange Slices Poached in White Wine, Cardamom, and Bay with Toasted Coconut

6 medium Valencia, navel, or blood oranges
4 cups white wine
1 cup granulated sugar
1 large bay leaf
12 cardamom seeds
1½ cup unsweetened dry coconut strips

Peel the oranges. Cut into ½-inch-thick rounds.

Combine the wine, sugar, and bay leaf in a nonreactive medium saucepan. Smash the cardamom seeds with a hammer or mallet. Add to the saucepan. Bring to a boil and cook 2 minutes until the sugar is dissolved.

Add the orange slices to the wine and cook 2 minutes, or until the slices are barely soft.

Remove the orange slices to a bowl. Discard the bay leaf.

Boil the wine sauce 5 minutes, until slightly thickened. Pour the wine sauce over the orange slices and chill.

Just before serving, place the coconut strips in an ungreased frying pan and stir over medium heat for 3 to 4 minutes, until the strips are golden around the edges.

Sprinkle over the orange slices and serve.

NOTES AND AFTERTHOUGHTS

Dry coconut strips are different from the moist shredded sweet coconut in airtight packages found in grocery stores. Unsweetened and unprocessed, the strips still taste like coconut. They are available in produce markets and health food stores.

Plenty for 6

20 minutes or less plus 2 hours chilling time

The exotic combination of white wine, cardamom, and toasted coconut with bay makes a spectacular sauce for oranges. It is a fabulous fresh finisher for almost any dinner, or spoon it over rice pudding for a meal in itself.

To say that figs are a fruit of mythological proportion, redolent with erotic overtones, is to put it mildly. They appear in tales from Adam and Eve to Sinbad to the Thousand and One Arabian Nights. Nude statuary with discreet leafy coverings populates the planet. Their name, or a derivative, plus a gesture to boot, constitutes a good, solid obscenity in many languages. Figs are certainly seductive, what with their Biblical implications and the three-petal shape they so easily fall into. Crusted in sesame and coated in sugar, they are doubly provocative. Perhaps they shouldn't be dessert, but rather a late, *late*, night snack.

Sweet Sesame and Brown Sugar-Crusted Figs with Mascarpone Cheese

8 tablespoons (1 stick) butter
12 to 18 large fresh figs, or 18 to 24 large golden sun-dried figs
5 tablespoons sesame seed
¼ cup brown sugar, if using fresh figs

8 ounces mascarpone cheese

Heat the oven to 475°F. In a small saucepan, melt the butter.

Holding a fig in your hands, carefully press open the bottom round part, and gently tear it into 3 petals, keeping the petals attached at the stem. Gently press the petals flat. Open all of the figs this way.

Place the sesame seed in a small dry skillet over low heat. Toast about 4 minutes, until browned.

Arrange the open figs in a single layer in a baking dish. Sprinkle each fig with about 1 teaspoon of the toasted sesame seeds. If using fresh figs, sprinkle on about ½ teaspoon of the brown sugar. Drizzle the melted butter over all the figs.

Bake 10 minutes.

To serve, place the mascarpone cheese in the middle of a platter and surround with the figs. Pour the juices from the baking dish over the figs. Spread a little cheese on each fig petal as you eat it.

NOTES AND AFTERTHOUGHTS

1. A number of varieties of figs, both fresh and dried, are available. Their sizes vary considerably. If the figs you choose are small, add another per person. If using dry figs, the golden ones in string-tied rounds, not the small, black ones in packages, are the ones to choose.

2. Don't worry if the first few figs you open don't fall into nice, even petals. You will get the hang of it shortly and the torn edges are part of their charm.

3. Good cream cheese is an adequate substitute for mascarpone when the latter is hard to find. Mascarpone tastes like cheesecake ice cream. To simulate its texture with cream cheese, whip 2 teaspoons of cream into it.

Alice Olson's Swedish Wedding Cookies

1¼ cups pecan halves and pieces (about ¼ pound)
½ pound (2 sticks) butter, at room temperature
5 tablespoons powdered sugar
2¼ cups unbleached all-purpose flour
2 teaspoons vanilla
1½ cups powdered sugar

Makes about 6 dozen cookies

2 hours

Alice Olson was Susanna's mother's best friend in nursing school in Moline, Illinois. Though hemlines had already lifted by the twenties, the nursing students at Augustana Hospital were required to wear long starched skirts to the ground and high laced boots to mid-calf. Swedish coffee klatches served as their only entertainment, for their activities were as well supervised as their clothes. The klatches overflowed with sharing, gossip, giggles, and above all, Alice Olson's Swedish Wedding Cookies.

To make the cookies in a food processor, fine-chop the pecans. Add the butter and process until smooth. Add the 5 tablespoons powdered sugar and blend well. Add the flour in three rounds, blending well after each addition. Add the vanilla and blend well.

To make the cookies with an electric mixer or by hand, fine chop the pecans and set aside. In a large bowl, cream the butter until smooth. Add the 5 tablespoons powdered sugar and blend well. Add the flour in three rounds, blending well after each addition. Stir in the vanilla and the chopped pecans. Blend well.

Divide the cookie dough in half. On a floured surface, roll out each half into a log 1½ to 2 inches in diameter. Pat the ends flat, and wrap each log in plastic wrap. Refrigerate about 1½ hours, until quite firm but not hard.

When ready to bake the cookies, heat the oven to 400°F.

Cut the logs crosswise into ¼-inch slices. Place the cookies flat on a cookie sheet.

Bake 10 to 12 minutes, until the edges are just beginning to brown.

While the cookies bake, sift the 1½ cups powdered sugar onto a plate.

When the cookies are done, immediately remove the cookies to the plate with the powdered sugar. Turn each cookie to coat both sides. Remove to a plate and let cool.

To serve, pass the cookie plate around and accompany with coffee or tea if you wish.

NOTES AND AFTERTHOUGHTS

You can make the cookie dough in advance, chill it overnight, and bake the cookies the next day. In this case, remove the dough logs from the refrigerator 20 minutes before baking, so the dough won't crack when you cut it.

Lace Cookies with Oatmeal, Garlic, and Pine Nuts

4 large garlic cloves
½ cup pine nuts
½ cup dry coconut strips
1 egg
½ cup sugar
1 teaspoon melted butter
½ cup oatmeal
½ teaspoon vanilla extract
¼ teaspoon salt

Heat the oven to 400°F. Grease a baking sheet.

Place the garlic in a small saucepan. Add water to cover and bring to a boil. Cook 15 minutes, drain, and peel.

Place the pine nuts and coconut strips in a small dry skillet. Toast until browned, 3 to 4 minutes.

Medium chop the garlic, pine nuts, and coconut in a food processor or with a chef's knife.

In a bowl, beat the egg. Gradually add the sugar and the melted butter. Mix in the oats, garlic, nuts, coconut, vanilla, and salt. Blend well.

Drop the cookie dough by teaspoon amounts onto the baking sheet. Press down with the side of a teaspoon.

Bake 10 to 12 minutes, until golden.

Remove from the baking sheet right away, while still warm. Continue with another round until all the cookes are baked.

Serve warm or at room temperature.

NOTES AND AFTERTHOUGHTS

1. The garlic in these cookies is cooked until it is sweet and adds an extra nuttiness that accents the pine nuts and coconut.

2. Lace cookies will stick to the cookie sheet unless they are removed as soon as they are out of the oven.

3. To melt a small amount of butter, place the butter on a saucer. Set the saucer on the stove to melt the butter.

Quick Cornmeal Shortcake with Fresh Berries and Cream

¾ cup unbleached all-purpose flour
¼ cup cornmeal
⅛ teaspoon salt
½ tablespoon baking powder
4 tablespoons (½ stick) butter, at room temperature
⅓ cup half-and-half, or a mixture heavy cream and milk
2 tablespoons flour, for rolling out the dough

3 baskets strawberries, raspberries, blackberries, olallieberries, boysenberries, or
   other berries
1½ cups heavy cream
2 to 4 tablespoons powdered sugar, depending on taste

Heat the oven to 450°F.

Place the flour, cornmeal, salt, and baking powder in a bowl and mix together. Cut the butter into bits and add to the bowl. With your fingers, work the butter into the dry ingredients until the mixture is pebbly. Add the half-and-half, and mix briefly with your hands. Form the dough into a ball.

Sprinkle a work surface with the 2 tablespoons of flour. Place the dough on top. Knead the dough for half a minute, about 10 turns. Roll out the dough ½ inch thick.

With a round cutter or the lip of a drinking glass, cut the dough into circles about 2½ inches across. Gather the trimmings, roll, and cut the dough again to make a total of 6 or 7 circles.

Place the rounds on an ungreased baking sheet.

Bake 10 to 12 minutes, until the tops are just beginning to turn golden.

While the shortcakes are baking, wash and drain the berries. If using strawberries, cut them into slices or halves as you like.

Whip the cream until slightly thickened. Add the powdered sugar and mix until just blended.

To serve, cut the shortcakes into 2 thin disks. Place the bottom half on a plate. Spread ½ cup or so of berries over the shortcake bottom. Place the top of the shortcake over the berries. Spoon a dollop of cream on top of the shortcake. Garnish with a few more berries on top of the cream.

NOTES AND AFTERTHOUGHTS

Quick Cornmeal Shortcake should be stored out of the refrigerator if you are making it a day or two in advance. Or make the shortcakes even further in advance and freeze them. When ready to serve, defrost and freshen briefly in the oven. Don't use a microwave to defrost or heat the shortcakes, though —it makes them tough.

Plenty for 6

20 to 40 minutes

What spring, summer, and fall is complete without at least one baseball game, some fireworks, and a helping of fresh berry shortcake? As the seasons roll on, the berries change from strawberries to boysenberries to raspberries and back to strawberries. It's hard to choose a favorite berry, though strawberry shortcake reigns as the all-time American classic.

You can even fill your yearning for shortcake and berries in winter. With the exception of strawberries, berries freeze surprisingly well. Sadly, strawberries acquire an altered flavor and strange consistency in the freezer chest. But blackberries, blueberries, boysenberries, and raspberries bag and ice quite nicely.

Serviceable as a silver platter, elegant as a Tiffany glass, sponge cake *always* makes a great dessert. It serves as a shortcake—just add fresh fruit or whipped cream. It shines as a fancy cake, just add Kahlúa Cream, berries, or chocolate sauce. It even serves you. You can store it out of the refrigerator for several days. You can freeze it and revivify it with Scotch Syrup 10 minutes before presenting it, perhaps with a touch of whipped cream peaked on top.

Quick Sponge Cake with Kahlúa Cream

5 eggs
½ cup granulated sugar
⅛ teaspoon salt
1 cup unbleached all-purpose flour
2 tablespoons lemon juice

1½ cups heavy cream
2 teaspoons Kahlúa

Heat the oven to 375°F. Butter and flour the bottom and sides of an 8-inch-square baking pan.

In a large bowl beat the eggs, sugar, and salt until the mixture is very pale yellow, about 15 minutes.

One-third at a time, sift the flour over the egg mixture. Fold in after each addition. Mix in the lemon juice.

Pour the batter into the prepared cake pan. Bake 30 to 35 minutes, until the top is golden and a knife inserted in the center comes out clean.

Unmold the cake onto a rack and let cool.

Just before serving, whip the cream until soft peaks form. Stir in the Kahlúa.

Cut the cake into portions and spoon the Kahlúa cream over the top of each piece.

NOTES AND AFTERTHOUGHTS

The eggs really must be beaten for 15 minutes, or until pale as described. The cake won't be properly spongy if you rush this step.

VARIATIONS

SLICED FRESH FRUIT: Top sponge cake portions with some sliced fresh fruit such as berries, peaches, pears, nectarines. Serve as is, or with plain whipped cream, Kahlúa cream, or Scotch Syrup (see below).

POACHED PEARS IN BLUSH AND BERRY SAUCE (page 304): Serve alongside a slice of sponge cake and pour the syrup over the top.

ORANGE SLICES POACHED IN WHITE WINE, CARDAMOM, AND BAY (page 305): Serve the orange slices and some of their syrup heaped over the sponge cake. Include the toasted coconut or not, as you wish.

FRUIT COMPOTES OR PUREES: Pour cooked fresh fruit, whole or pureed, and its syrup over the sponge cake slices.

ICE CREAM TOPPINGS: Pour warm Chocolate Kahlúa Macadamia Sauce (page 318), cold Strawberry Orange Sauce (page 319), or warm or chilled Burgundy Wine and Thyme Sauce (page 319) over the cake.

Scotch syrup makes a particularly good variation on the theme of sponge cake toppings, especially if you have made the Quick Sponge Cake in advance and frozen it. After defrosting, a syrup bath plumps and refreshes the cake.

Scotch Syrup

¾ cup granulated sugar
1 cup water
½ cup Scotch whiskey

Combine the sugar and water in a saucepan. Bring to a boil over medium heat, then simmer 5 minutes. Turn off the heat and stir in the Scotch.

Pour over the Quick Sponge Cake and set aside to soak for 10 minutes before serving.

NOTES AND AFTERTHOUGHTS

1. Beware. This syrup is ecstasy, but tipples toward intoxicating because the alcohol is not burned off. You can cook it longer to burn off the alcohol, but it turns into more of a sugar syrup and becomes less aromatic.

2. In place of Scotch, you can use any other good whiskey or rum.

3. Scotch syrup also makes an excellent ice cream topping.

Makes 1½ cups

Burnt Sugar and Blue Cornmeal Cake with Thickened Cream Topping

½ cup granulated sugar
½ cup boiling water
¾ cup (1½ sticks) butter, at room temperature
1¼ cups granulated sugar
2 egg yolks
1 cup water
1¼ cups Blue Cornmeal Pancake Mix (see Note 1 below)
1 cup unbleached all-purpose flour
1½ teaspoons baking powder
1 teaspoon vanilla extract
2 egg whites

3 cups Thickened Cream Topping (page 312)

Heat the oven to 400°F. Butter and flour the bottom and sides of a 9-inch cake or bundt pan.

Place the ½ cup granulated sugar in a small skillet. Stir over medium-high heat until the sugar melts and turns brown, about 5 minutes. Carefully, to avoid splashing, add the boiling water. Cook a few seconds until the mixture is well blended. Set aside.

(continued)

For one 9-inch cake or bundt pan
Enough for 12 servings

1 to 2 hours

Burning sugar intensifies its flavor and modifies its form from refined granules closer to molasses. Though they may have known about it from the Spanish, the Pueblo Indians probably never added such a contrivance to their native staple, blue corn. Nor did they leaven blue corn flour to make it into a risen cake. But blue corn, so nutty in flavor, seems a perfect partner for an American sugar classic, burnt sugar cake.

In a large bowl, cream the butter with the 1¼ cups granulated sugar until blended and pale, about 3 minutes. Beat in the egg yolks and 1 cup water. The batter will be watery with lumps of butter at this point.

Gradually add the pancake mix, the flour, and the baking powder, blending well after each addition. Mix in the burnt sugar mixture and the vanilla.

In another bowl, beat the egg whites until stiff peaks form. With a rubber spatula, fold the egg whites into the batter.

Pour the batter into the prepared pan. Bake 1 hour, or until the top is well browned and the edges are very crisp and pull away from the sides of the pan.

Cool the cake in the pan for 10 minutes. Run a sharp knife around the inside edge of the cake pan and invert onto a rack.

To serve, place the cake on a plate. Cut into slices and top each slice with some Thickened Cream Topping just before eating.

NOTES AND AFTERTHOUGHTS

1. Blue Cornmeal Pancake Mix is available in health food and better grocery stores. Or, if you can't find the mix, use blue cornmeal in its place and add an extra 1 teaspoon baking powder to the recipe. If you don't have any blue cornmeal at all, use all unbleached white flour and an extra 1 teaspoon baking powder.

2. This cake should be quite crispy on the top and edges to get the full benefit of the burnt sugar flavor and texture. Even if a knife inserted in the middle comes out clean, the cake is not quite done until the top and edges are crunchy.

3. Burnt sugar cake grows richer overnight and keeps well out of the refrigerator wrapped in plastic wrap for a good 2 weeks.

Thickened Cream Topping

1½ cups sour cream
1½ cups heavy cream

Place the sour cream in a bowl and stir with a whisk until smooth. Mix in the heavy cream.

NOTES AND AFTERTHOUGHTS

If you would like a thicker topping, whip the heavy cream before mixing it with the sour cream.

Makes 3 cups

Thickened Cream Topping is essentially a mock crème fraîche, that famous French be-all-and-end-all mildly cultured cream that is used in everything from soups to sauces to desserts. If you would like to make the real thing, stir 1 tablespoon buttermilk into 3 cups heavy cream. Place in a bowl, cover tightly with a lid or plastic wrap, and let sit at room temperature for 24 to 36 hours, until thickened and mildly tart.

Icebox Whipped Cream Cookie Roll

1½ cups heavy cream
1½ tablespoons powdered sugar
¾ teaspoon rum
24 to 30 Pepperidge Farm Brussels or Cappuccino cookies, or 1 package of each, or
    24 to 30 good bakery crisp chocolate or coffee cookies

2 ounces bittersweet or semisweet chocolate bar

Plenty for 6

*20 minutes or less
plus several hours or
overnight chilling time*

Pour the cream into a bowl and whip it until soft peaks form. Add the powdered sugar and rum and continue whipping until stiff peaks form.

With a rubber spatula, spread about 1 tablespoon whipped cream on one side of a cookie. Place a second cookie on top of the first, spread the second cookie with whipped cream and place it on the stack. Continue in the same way until you have a stack about 6 high. Place the stack on its side on a platter. Build another stack, turn it over, and attach it to the first stack until you have all the cookies in one long roll. Spread the remaining whipped cream over the top and sides of the roll until it is completely covered. Chill, preferably overnight, until the cookies are soft and saturated with the whipped cream.

Just before serving, shave the chocolate over the top of the roll with a hand grater. Bring to the table and cut into portions.

NOTES AND AFTERTHOUGHTS
Icebox Whipped Cream Cookie Roll is best when chilled overnight. You can rush the dessert with 3 to 4 hours chilling, but the cookies will not yet be soft and creamy. With longer chilling the whole dish blends into a whipped cream cake. Wrapped in plastic, it will keep in the refrigerator up to 3 days.

Plenty for 12 to 18

20 to 40 minutes
plus all day or
overnight chilling time

Chocolate Obsession and the Chocolate Kahlúa Macadamia Sauce (page 318), along with many other chocolate delights, call for melted chocolate. There are four ways to melt chocolate. You can put it in a double boiler or in a pan over some boiling water. You can place it in a bowl and stick it in the oven. Or you can microwave it. If you microwave it, wrap tightly and make sure the chocolate doesn't touch the wrapping. If it does, it will burn a hole through the wrap and some of the chocolate below will crisp into a piece of modern art. Finally, if your recipe includes adding liquid to the chocolate, you can melt the chocolate with the liquid in the saucepan over low heat.

Chocolate Obsession

1 package Pepperidge Farm Chessmen cookies, or about 8 ounces other good butter cookies
1 cup shelled pistachios (about 4 ounces, or about 10 ounces in the shell)
¾ cup golden raisins
⅔ cup granulated sugar
4 tablespoons water
6 ounces bittersweet chocolate bar

¾ cup butter (1½ sticks), at room temperature
1 cup unsweetened cocoa powder
1 whole egg
2 egg yolks
Chopped peel of 1 orange
1 tablespoon orange juice
½ tablespoon brandy

Butter the bottom and sides of a 5- by 8-inch loaf pan.

Break the cookies into ¼- to ½-inch bits and place them in a bowl. Add ½ cup of the shelled pistachios and the raisins. Toss together and set aside.

Combine the sugar and water in a small saucepan. Bring to a boil over medium, not high, heat. When the sugar is dissolved, add the chocolate and stir over low heat until the chocolate melts.

In a medium bowl, cream together the butter and cocoa powder until well mixed. Add the melted chocolate and mix to blend.

Lightly beat together the whole egg and the egg yolks. Add to the chocolate mixture and mix to blend. Stir in orange peel, orange juice, and brandy. Mix to blend. Finally, stir in cookie, pistachio, and raisin mixture.

Fill the loaf pan with the chocolate mixture and pat down well to make sure there are no air pockets. Cover with plastic wrap. Refrigerate at least 8 hours or overnight, until the loaf hardens enough to slice.

When ready to serve, mince the remaining ½ cup pistachios in a food processor or with a chef's knife. Run a sharp knife around the inside edge of the loaf pan. Place the loaf pan in a bowl of hot water to loosen. Invert the loaf pan over a plate and pry out the loaf with the knife. Repeat the hot water bath if the loaf does not fall out right away.

Sprinkle the pistachios over the top of the loaf. Cut the loaf into ½-inch slices and serve.

NOTES AND AFTERTHOUGHTS

1. Pistachios are hard to find unsalted, but if you can, they are the best for this recipe.

2. The beauty of this dessert is that it requires no cooking or baking except for dissolving the sugar and melting the chocolate.

Mascarpone Cheese Pie in a Chocolate Cookie Crust

1 package Pepperidge Farm Brussels cookies, or about 8 ounces other good bakery
   cookies with a hard chocolate filling or icing
5 tablespoons butter, at room temperature

1½ cups mascarpone cheese (about 12 ounces)
2 medium or 1 jumbo eggs
2 teaspoons lemon juice
1 teaspoon grated lemon peel
½ cup granulated sugar

FOR THE TOPPING:

1½ cups sour cream
1½ teaspoons vanilla extract
3 tablespoons granulated sugar

Heat the oven to 375° F.

Break up the cookies and crush in a blender or food processor or with a rolling pin. Add the butter and process or mix with your fingers until blended. Press the cookie mixture evenly into the bottom and sides of a 9-inch pie plate.

In a food processor, with an electric mixer, or with a wire whisk, mix together the mascarpone cheese, eggs, lemon juice, lemon peel, and the ½ cup sugar until smooth and well blended.

Pour the filling into the pie crust. Bake 25 minutes.

While the pie bakes, mix together the sour cream, vanilla, and the 3 tablespoons sugar to make the topping.

When the pie is done, let cool 5 minutes. Leave the oven on.

Gently spread the topping over the pie.

Return the pie to the oven and bake 10 minutes more.

Remove the pie and let cool completely. Refrigerate 5 hours or overnight before serving.

NOTES AND AFTERTHOUGHTS

Before spreading the topping over the pie, be sure to let it cool 5 minutes for the cheese filling to set up a little so the topping doesn't sink into the pie. Also, use a gentle stroke spreading on the topping or you will wind up with the topping mixed into the filling.

Plenty for 12 or more

40 to 60 minutes plus several hours chilling time

This is our fast, unusual variation on cheesecake. New York is the capital of cheesecake. You can find them there made with cheddar cheese and beer; cottage cheese and graham crackers; crusted with almonds, zwieback, or matzoh; topped with strawberry, pineapple, or rum. Numerous delis, restaurants, and whole establishments devoted only to cheesecake have what they claim is the best, and their loyal fans rave about the cheesecake, pay for the recipe, and send off whole cakes by overnight refrigerated mail to offspring in college who just failed an exam, broke up with a fiancé, or broke out in bumps.

Sweet Dessert Taco

Tortillas aren't just a platter for the hot and spicy. Slathered in butter and brown sugar, filled with any fruit from the common to the exotic, dashed with toasted nuts, and splashed with cream, they become something wildly different, dessert tacos.

1 cup sour cream
½ cup heavy cream
1 tablespoon powdered sugar
8 tablespoons (1 stick) butter
2 tablespoons brown sugar
6 flour tortillas
3 cups diced fresh pineapple, bananas, papayas, mango, or a mixture

6 tablespoons pine nuts
1 teaspoon butter, for toasting the pine nuts

In a bowl, beat the sour cream until smooth. Slowly stir in the heavy cream. Add the powdered sugar and blend well.

Combine the 8 tablespoons butter and brown sugar in a large skillet. Heat gently until the butter melts and the sugar dissolves, 3 or 4 minutes. Place a tortilla in the butter and sugar mixture and heat 1 minute. Remove the tortilla to a plate. Fill each with ½ cup of the sliced fruit. Spoon on 2 tablespoons of the sour cream mixture. Continue dipping and filling the remaining tortillas.

Melt the 1 teaspoon butter in a small skillet. Add the pine nuts and toast until browned, 3 to 4 minutes. Top each taco with toasted pine nuts. Fold and serve.

NOTES AND AFTERTHOUGHTS

For an alternative method of serving these tacos, bring the dipped tortillas, fruit filling, cream, and pine nut toppings to the table and let everyone assemble according to personal whim.

ICE CREAM TOPPINGS

The French have their *gâteau,* the Austrians their Sacher torte, the English their pudding, but America has her ice cream. Nobody makes ice cream like we do. Every flavor, every style, every topping imaginable. There's practically no meal that can't be brought to a crescendo of oohs and aahs with ice cream. Make your own or simply buy one of the excellent ice cream brands available, and add a breathtaking topping of your own.

Bourbon Pecan Caramel Cream

2 cups brown sugar
1 cup heavy cream
2 tablespoons bourbon whiskey
2 teaspoons butter
⅔ cup pecan halves or pieces

Makes 1½ cups

20 minutes or less

Combine the brown sugar, cream, and bourbon in a small saucepan. Bring to a boil. Cook over medium-high heat, until the mixture drops off a spoon leaving strings behind or holds the shape of a soft ball when dribbled into cool water, about 10 minutes. Remove from the heat.

Melt the butter in a small frying pan. Add the pecans and stir over medium-high heat until browned, about 2 minutes.

Add the pecans to the brown sugar mixture. Set aside to thicken and cool.

Spoon the sauce over vanilla, chocolate, or nut ice cream.

NOTES AND AFTERTHOUGHTS

Bourbon Pecan Caramel Cream sauce is best when it is freshly made and hasn't been chilled. But if you have some left over, store in the refrigerator. To reheat, place in a saucepan and add 2 or 3 teaspoons water. It will be a little more grainy than when freshly made.

≈ You can also reheat this sauce in a microwave oven.

Burgundy Wine and Thyme Sauce

Makes 1¼ cups

1 bottle or 3½ cups burgundy or hearty red wine
1¼ cups granulated sugar
½ teaspoon fresh thyme leaves or ¼ teaspoon dried

Combine the wine, sugar, and thyme in a large nonreactive saucepan. Bring to a boil over medium heat. Cook 25 minutes until thickened. Remove from the heat.

Serve the sauce warm, at room temperature, or chilled. It is especially good spooned over vanilla or nut ice cream or almost any sherbet.

NOTES AND AFTERTHOUGHTS

Burgundy Wine and Thyme Sauce keeps well in the refrigerator and lasts for months. Reheat or serve cold.

Chocolate Kahlúa Macadamia Sauce

Makes 1¾ cups

8 ounces bittersweet chocolate
1 cup water
6 tablespoons Kahlúa
½ cup macadamia nuts (about 2 ounces)

Combine the chocolate, water, and Kahlúa in a small saucepan. Bring to a boil, stirring often, over medium heat. When the liquid boils, continue stirring and cook 2 minutes.

Rough chop the macadamias in a food processor or with a chef's knife. Stir the nuts into the chocolate sauce.

Serve warm or at room temperature.

NOTES AND AFTERTHOUGHTS

Chocolate Kahlúa Macadamia Sauce can be stored in the refrigerator as long as you like. It will harden somewhat. If you like it as a dollop of fudge, spoon it cold over the ice cream. If you like it runny, reheat it in a pan set over a little boiling water just before serving.

≈ You can also reheat this sauce in a microwave oven.

Strawberry Orange Sauce

3 heaping cups fresh strawberries (about 2 baskets)
½ cup orange juice
Grated peel of 2 oranges
¼ cup granulated sugar
1 tablespoon tequila (optional)

Makes 1¾ cups

Remove the stems and caps from the strawberries. Cut ½ cup of the strawberries lengthwise into ⅛-inch-thick slices and set aside.

Puree the remaining strawberries with the orange juice in a blender or food processor. Or puree the strawberries through a food mill, then stir in the orange juice.

Pour the puree into a small nonreactive saucepan. Add the orange peel and sugar. Bring to a boil over medium heat and cook 2 minutes, until slightly thickened.

Remove the puree to a bowl. Stir in the sliced strawberries and tequila.

Chill thoroughly before serving.

NOTES AND AFTERTHOUGHTS
It is best to use Strawberry Orange Sauce within 3 days because it loses its flavor and aroma when stored longer.

OTHER TOPPINGS AND SAUCES FOR ICE CREAM

Ice cream is like a canvas on which you can paint anything for your palate. You can color it with fruit and nuts, cocoas and creams, liquors of every exotic variety, sprinkles and candies, crusts and pastries. Other sweets in this book that make scrumptious ice cream toppings are:

Orange Slices Poached in White Wine, Cardamom, and Bay with Toasted Coconut, page 305.
Poached Pears in Blush and Berry Sauce, page 304.
Fresh Grape Parfait, page 303, with or without the whipped cream.
Scotch Syrup, page 311.

There's hardly a town or city anywhere—Copenhagen, Hong Kong, Nairobi, Rio, Fort Worth, or Fairbanks—that isn't filled with ice cream vendors. They push their carts along cluttered, noisy shopping streets, selling their thawing supply. They ply their trade ensconced in cool parlors, surrounded by frosty display cases. They stand in booths hawking their wares to carnival crowds. It seems not to matter whether the climate is hot or cold, the days long or short, the moment early or late, ice cream appeals anytime and everywhere.

Chili peppers, 17–18, 24, 78–79, 101–2
grilled, 179
with Pasta and Cheese Alfredo, 121
tacos, pork tenderloin, with, 93
Tex-Mex Pizza with, 65
Chili powder, 79
Chili sauce, from leftover salsas, 82
Chimichangas, 81
Chinese markets, 239, 288
Chinese parsley, fresh, 23
Chinese peas, sautéed, 213
Chinese spinach, 272
Chinese style oven-steamed trout, 252–53
Chives:
fresh, 23, 138, 216
salsa, 83
uses, 39, 91, 101, 102, 104, 169, 182,
227, 233, 237, 241, 252
Chocolate, to melt, 314
Chocolate Cookie Crust, for pie, 315
Chocolate Kahlùa Macadamia Sauce, 310,
318
Chocolate Obsession, 314
Choice quality beef, 227
Chops:
grilled, 148, 150–51
pan-fried, 188, 189, 190
Chuck roast, beef, 227
Chutneys, fresh fruit, 27, 151
Cilantro, 23, 27–28, 103, 195
in Basic Green Salad, 273
grilled fish marinated with, 172
meatloaf with, 258–59
in salsas, 83
Cinnamon, 21, 230
Clams in Garlic Mayonnaise Sauce with
Linguine and Black Pepper, 135
Cleaning of cutting boards, 30
Clotted cream, 302
Cloves, 21, 230
Coconut, orange slices poached with, 305
Coconut milk, canned, 53
Coconut oil, 274
Coconut strips, dried, 53
Cognac, 299
Cointreau, 301
Colanders, 30, 114
Cold cuts, 23, 64
with Pasta and Cheese Alfredo, 120
Cold Noodles, Crispy Fried Pork, and Bean
Sprouts with Hot Peanut Sesame
Sauce, 126–27
Coleman's dry mustard, 19
Colorado chilies, 79
Comice pears, 304
Compotes, fruit, with sponge cake, 310
Confectioners' sugar, 22
Contadina brand pizza sauce, 62
Cookies, 27
Alice Olson's Swedish Wedding, 307
Icebox Whipped Cream Cookie Roll, 313
lace, with oatmeal and garlic, 308
packaged, 297

Cooking oils, 19
Cooking times:
bacon, 67
beef roast, 226
duck roast, 249
fish, 251, 252, 253
grilled chops, 150–51
grilled steaks, 148–49
lamb roast, 231, 234
pan-fried meats, 189
pork roast, 236
potatoes, baked, 266
turkey, 246
Coriander, fresh, 23
Corn, 177, 264
and Red Bell Pepper Salsa, 27, 84
uses, 101, 103, 104, 169, 182, 227, 233,
237, 241, 252
Corn oil, 19, 274
Corn tortillas, 79–80, 104
Cornmeal, 18
cake, 311–12
crust, halibut in, 206–7
Herbed Polenta, 219
mush, 219
in pizza dough, 60
Cornstarch, thickening with, 299
Corsala, 197
Corsican feta cheese, 23, 42
Corsican Lasagne, 255–56
Corsican Lasagne Sauce, 25, 27, 139, 256
uses, 197, 233, 237, 241
Covered grilling, 147
Crab:
cakes with Sage Butter Sauce, 51, 139
salad, 293
tacos, 99–100
Crackers, 18
spreads, 39, 40
Cranberries, 24
Cumberland Sauce, 197, 248
Cream, 23, 88–89, 114, 196, 302
chicken pot pie filling, 261
Icebox Whipped Cream Cookie Roll, 313
in meatloaf, 257
sauces, 122, 128, 129
storage hints, 27
topping for cake, 311–12
to whip, 297
Cream cheese, 40
Creamers (potatoes), grilled, 179
Crème fraîche, 312
Cress, 271
Crisping of tortillas, 80
Crookneck squash, 214, 216
Cross rib, for roasts, 227
Croutons, 273, 275
Crushed red pepper flakes, 17
Crushed tomatoes, 22
Crust, Quick Cookie, 301
Cucumbers, Wilted Salad, 108
Cumberland Sauce, 248

Lizard and Snake found themselves together on a sunny rock.
They fried an egg and shared it.